BIGGER!
BETTER!
BADDER!

BIGGER!
BETTER!
BADDER!

WRESTLEMANIA III
AND THE YEAR IT ALL CHANGED

KEITH ELLIOT GREENBERG

Copyright © Keith Elliot Greenberg, 2025

Published by ECW Press
665 Gerrard Street East
Toronto, Ontario, Canada M4M 1Y2
416-694-3348 / info@ecwpress.com

Editor for the Press: Michael Holmes
Copy editor: Jen Knoch
Cover design: David A. Gee

LIBRARY AND ARCHIVES CANADA CATALOGUING
IN PUBLICATION

Title: Bigger! better! badder! : WrestleMania III and the year it
all changed / Keith Elliot Greenberg.

Other titles: WrestleMania III and the year it all changed

Names: Greenberg, Keith Elliot, 1959- author

Identifiers: Canadiana (print) 2024049587X | Canadiana
(ebook) 20240495888

ISBN 978-1-77041-785-4 (softcover)
ISBN 978-1-77852-371-7 (ePub)
ISBN 978-1-77852-372-4 (PDF)

Subjects: LCSH: WrestleMania (3rd : 1987 : Pontiac, Mich.)
| LCSH: World Wrestling Entertainment, Inc. | LCSH:
Wrestling—United States—History—20th century.

Classification: LCC GV1196.25 .G74 2025 | DDC
796.8120973—dc23

PRINTED AND BOUND IN CANADA

PRINTING: FRIESENS   5   4   3   2   1

In memory of these friends who meant much to the
wrestling business and even more to me:

"The Genius" Lanny Poffo
1954–2023

Wayne "Superstar Billy Graham" Coleman Jr.
1943–2023

Khosrow "The Iron Sheik" Vaziri
1942–2023

"Bring me men to match my mountains,
Bring me men to match my plains,
Men with empires in their purpose and new eras in their brains."

— SAM WALTER FOSS, AMERICAN POET

"The whipping you're gonna get is gonna be shameful."

— "THE AMERICAN DREAM" DUSTY RHODES

CHAPTER 1

"I never thought it could be done, Gorilla Monsoon."

With screams pouring down the canyons of the Pontiac Silverdome, Jesse "The Body" Ventura's words lanced the speakers of television sets around the pay-per-view universe. The villainous color commentator seemed to truly be in awe of the feat that just occurred.

His voice rose above the strains of Hulk Hogan's theme music, "Real American," and the roar of the announced 93,173 in attendance — a number that would take on a mythology all its own. He was referencing the Hulkster retaining his World Wrestling Federation (WWF) World Heavyweight Championship after body-slamming and dropping a big leg on André the Giant. But, in truth, Ventura's sense of wonder was directed less at what had transpired in the ring than the overall spectacle he'd witnessed.

Anyone who'd been around the wrestling business understood that the "Eighth Wonder of the World," as the French leviathan was known, had been hoisted up and driven into the mat before. Yet, according to the rhetoric fans had been hearing on TV in the weeks leading up to *WrestleMania III*, the act was unprecedented — not unlike a wrestling extravaganza selling out an NFL stadium, major licensees and sponsors aligning themselves with the grunt 'n' groan circuit and, 11 years later, Ventura — a man who made his name wearing feather boas and flexing his brawny arms while declaring, "Win if you can, lose if you must, but always cheat" — being elected the 38th governor of the great state of Minnesota.

"André the Giant and Hulk Hogan in the main event — that's all you really needed," explained Jim "J.R." Ross, an Oklahoma-bred announcer, then six years away from launching the most memorable portion of his Hall of Fame career with the WWF, the company that would later be called — and periodically referred to in this book — as World Wrestling Entertainment, or WWE.

"Hogan was the ultimate hero. André had an amazing legacy, and everybody knew the end was getting closer for him. And you had [manager] Bobby 'The Brain' Heenan cutting the promos, or doing all the talking, for André, and that sealed the deal. You couldn't get a more intriguing main event than Hogan and André."

For a few years before the event, Vincent Kennedy McMahon had been hiring away the most gifted talent from the dozen-plus "territories," or carefully delineated wrestling outfits, around North America, ignoring time-honored agreements to confine activities to a specific region.

"Every promoter had their own part of the country," said Jerry Brisco, who'd held dozens of regional championships and owned portions of the Florida and Georgia territories before switching to the WWF and becoming a talent scout for the organization. "When an outlaw came in and tried to run your city, all the other promoters would share their best wrestlers with you, so the other guy couldn't really compete."

The proceedings in Michigan changed the dynamic. After all, who were you going to import to shift interest away from Hogan and André?

"That was the big one that separated everything," Brisco continued, "and kind of put an end to the territories."

With a few notable exceptions, in their place would be Vince McMahon in his tailor-made suit and collared vest, his fist raised defiantly in the air.

He hadn't gotten to this point simply by swiping wrestlers, arenas and TV slots from the other promoters. In the 1980s, McMahon began bringing in A-list celebrities to supplement cards and attract a new audience. Competitors howled, screaming that the sometimes-cartoonish presentations would expose and ultimately kill the business. At the same time, elitists viewed the phenomenon with haughty disdain. "Can you imagine the level of a mind that watches wrestling?" Max von Sydow's character asked in Woody Allen's *Hannah and Her Sisters* in 1986.

Surely, this whole thing was a fad and would soon go the way of the mood ring and CB radio.

WrestleMania III, held on an overcast afternoon in early spring 1987, obliterated the cynicism.

"We get to the big, empty stadium, and I'm thinking, 'Wow, what's this place going to look like?'" said B. Brian Blair, whose tag team, the Killer Bees, wrestled the Iron Sheik and Nikolai Volkoff just prior to the main event. "And they had a section high up for the spouses to sit. So, before the fans get there, I went up to see my wife and make sure everything's okay. And I'm looking down and the ring seems so far away. I know all the guys on the ring crew, and I couldn't make out their faces. And I'm thinking to myself, 'Who wants to sit all the way up here?'

"And then, just before our match, they open the curtain, and the music starts and they announce the Killer Bees. And we go out there, and I look at the crowd. It was just a swarm, more people than I can even glance at, and they were cheering so loud. And I finally saw what pandemonium really is. That's when I understood why somebody would be up in the nosebleeds — just to be part of the whole thing. It just all came together as I was looking around. That was an amazing rush."

It didn't matter if pro wrestling was predetermined, nor if certain story-lines or characters were childish and silly. The people wanted to suspend their disbelief. In years to come, fans would make the annual pilgrimage to *WrestleMania* from Antwerp to Auckland, Nice to Nagasaki, Taipei to Tegucigalpa. But it was *WrestleMania III* that enshrined the event as an institution that could not be missed, and anyone who dared to call the spectacle "fake" had fallen behind.

"When you can't make them see the light, make them feel the heat."

The words had been uttered by President Ronald Reagan, but the term embodied the attitude of American exceptionalism in the go-go '80s. And they might as well have been used by McMahon himself to humble critics of the WWF.

"He was just a master at telling people what they wanted to see," remembered "Cowboy" Bob Orton Jr., an exceptional hand whose match would open *WrestleMania III*.

Although decades later, McMahon's achievements would be viewed through the prism of the scandal that drove him from the industry, the people who were in his orbit in 1987 felt as if they were in the presence of a corporate mystic.

"Vince never asked, 'Is this possible?'" said Dick Glover, the WWF's vice president of business affairs from 1986 to 1992. "He knew it was possible. There were no doubts. It was, 'Okay, let's do this.'"

At the time of *WrestleMania III*, Basil Devito Jr.'s official title was director of promotions. But his organizational skills — and ability to connect with powerful people outside the wrestling subculture — had many crediting his role in the event as almost as significant as the wrestlers.

"What Vince clearly knew — and I had no clue about — was that he was going to teach me what I needed to do to take the company to places we'd never been before, accomplishing more than I ever dreamed of."

In time, Devito would end up on the WWE board of directors, become the CEO and even play a small role in sports history as the inaugural president of the XFL, the alternative football league McMahon initially started in 2001. "But to this day, I would have a hard time saying that *WrestleMania III* was not the best thing I was ever involved with."

To Bruce Prichard, who'd go from portraying an evil televangelist named Brother Love to becoming executive director of WWE's flagship television shows, *Monday Night Raw* and *SmackDown*, the event represented the moment rasslin' became wrestling.

"It was a stamp of certification that said, 'This is not your grandfather's wrestling in the VFW Hall. This is something your mother can enjoy, this is something your little sister can enjoy. This is real.'"

Jacques Rougeau, who teamed with his brother Ray against Greg "The Hammer" Valentine and Brutus Beefcake, compared his participation to "being in the first spaceship on the moon. It was a moment people will always think of as being the first, the most important, a page-turner in history."

By the time the three-hour show ended, the entire wrestling industry was altered. And the reverberations are still felt today.

"How can you compete against this, the vastness, the quality?" said Robbie Brookside, who was establishing himself as a name in the United Kingdom at the time, unaware that the WWF would eventually swallow up much of the British wrestling scene and recruit him to teach the beginners class at the company's Performance Center. "It's like comparing a river to the Atlantic Ocean. It's a nice river. It's got lovely fishing. But look how deep the ocean is. Look how wide it is. Look at the shark, the octopus, the variety of life.

"It goes on forever."

CHAPTER 2

The story of *WrestleMania III* cannot be told in a vacuum. To fully understand it, one must ponder the entrenched regional system that existed before the global product McMahon created came to be. And to do that, it's necessary to go back to 1982, the year Vince and his wife, Linda, bought the WWF from his father and began taking that network apart, territory by territory.

Actually, you have to go back a little further than that.

While Vince's father, Vincent James McMahon (although many refer to the elder McMahon as "Vince Sr.," his middle name was distinct from his son's), was building the largest wrestling territory in North America, his son was being raised by his mother, Vicky, reportedly in a trailer park in North Carolina.

He described a stepfather, an electrician named Leo Lupton, as particularly abusive. "It's unfortunate that he died before I could kill him," McMahon told *Playboy* in 2001. "I would have enjoyed that."

No one knows whether those unpleasant experiences contributed to some of the alleged behavior that would ultimately lead to his stepping away from WWE in 2024. In Vince's telling, he refused to allow the hostility in his household to define him. "There are no excuses for anything," he said in a 1998 interview with *New York Magazine*. "I read about some guy who has excuses for his behavior because he comes from a broken home or he was beaten or was sexually abused . . . all of which occurred in my lifetime. But those are no excuses."

Regardless, the adversity almost certainly instilled a drive in McMahon to humble his enemies or perhaps get the jump on them before they could inflict harm.

In 1956, his father married a second time, and his wife, Juanita, encouraged him to connect with his child. "I didn't meet him until I was 12 years old, and I fell in love with him the moment I met him," McMahon told *Esquire* in 2005.

At the time, the senior McMahon and his partner, Joseph "Toots" Mondt — a retired wrestler who'd played a backstage role in the business for decades — ran the Capitol Wrestling Corporation, which would eventually promote shows from Bangor, Maine, all the way down to Washington, DC. Of all the groups affiliated with the National Wrestling Alliance (NWA), the organization overseeing the various regional promotions, Capitol's influence was commensurate to its size. McMahon and Mondt were said to have had an impact on 70 percent of the NWA's booking decisions, including the selection of the NWA World Heavyweight Champion. Once anointed, the titlist would tour, going from territory to territory, defending the strap and elevating the status of opponents simply by sharing the ring with them.

No promoter could wield the senior McMahon's clout, especially in an industry as dubious as the wrestling trade, without making a few questionable deals and burning a former ally or two. But, while Mondt had a reputation in his younger years for physically torturing uncooperative performers behind the scenes, Vincent James was soft-spoken and dignified, often described as a "gentleman."

"He was always 'Mr. McMahon,'" recalled photographer Steve Taylor, who'd join the WWF in 1983, a year before Vincent James McMahon's death. "You would never call him 'Vince.'"

The younger McMahon would see his father in the summer and on holidays. While engaging in conversation, Vincent James would absentmindedly dangle change in his pockets, speaking in a tone that implied familiarity, his eyes looking directly at the listener and sparkling. Vincent Kennedy was so grateful to his stepmother for bringing this man into his life that, until she was too infirm to attend, Juanita regularly occupied an honored seat at events in New York's Madison Square Garden.

As he developed a bond with the successful promoter, Vince found himself also falling in love with the wrestling business. To the great consternation of the senior McMahon, the boy began hanging out with Dr. Jerry Graham, a rotund, bleached-blond headliner whose flamboyance was at least partially fueled by legitimate mental illness. When Graham's mother died, for instance, he stormed the hospital and slung her corpse over his shoulder, engaging in an armed standoff with police in Phoenix, Arizona.

Among the responding officers was Captain Vance Bingaman — whose real-life sibling Wayne Coleman would become the Good Doctor's gimmick brother, "Superstar" Billy Graham.

Smitten with the brash main-eventer, a 14-year-old Vince apparently convinced Juanita to dye his hair blond.

Vincent James was supposedly aghast. But in his own subdued way, he could be just as bold. In 1963, he and Mondt broke away from the NWA and crowned Buddy "Nature Boy" Rogers the inaugural champion of their World Wide Wrestling Federation (WWWF). On television, fans were told that Rogers had won a tournament in Rio de Janeiro, the same fictitious location where the first WWF Intercontinental title would allegedly be acquired under similar circumstances in 1979.

It was a heady time, but the elder McMahon did not want his son getting too excited. The wrestling business was unstable, he said, and the young man should try to do better. He counseled Vince to maybe find a nice government job that included a pension.

To prepare him for the wider world, the promoter sent the boy to the Fishburne Military School in Waynesboro, Virginia. Vince said that he suffered from dyslexia. But it hadn't been diagnosed and he struggled in class. He also hated the discipline — or, more accurately, being told what to do — and was openly defiant.

Still, he was smart and resourceful and wasn't about to let some rigid instructor in a uniform break him. He overcame each obstacle, managed to graduate and gained acceptance to East Carolina University, majoring in business administration.

He was still in college when he married Linda Edwards. He'd been 16 years old when they'd met. She was three years younger, raised by parents who both worked at the Marine Corps air station based in Cherry Point, North Carolina. On an academic level, at least, she was worlds ahead of her boyfriend. But he apparently liked that. When he wasn't away at school or with his father, he camped out in the Edwards home.

"I had no idea what family was until I met Linda," he told *Cigar Aficionado* in 1999. "There wasn't screaming and beating. 'You see,' I thought, 'there's something else.' I wanted some of that stability and love."

It would be Linda who'd negotiate with vendors and establish the WWF's first line of action figures in 1984. Far later, she'd be appointed administrator of the US Small Business Administration — a cabinet position — by WWE Hall of Famer Donald Trump.

To keep up with her husband, Linda breezed through school, graduating college in three years. After receiving his degree in 1968, Vince tried following his father's edict to avoid wrestling. It was like putting a drag queen in conversion therapy. For a while, he worked as a traveling salesman, hawking disposable cups and cones for ice cream. It suited Vince worse than military school, and his father knew it.

In 1971, Vincent James let his son in, delegating to him responsibility for the northernmost outpost of the WWWF, Bangor, Maine, where the previous promoter was accused of skimming money from the gates.

By the next year, Vince was regularly seen on WWWF television, conducting interviews with the talent; his towering height required André the Giant to stand on a crate during these exchanges to maintain his colossal aura. Each set of interviews was customized for a particular market and edited into the company's syndicated programs to hype upcoming live events in the various regions.

From there, he also became the WWWF's principal play-by-play man — a role he was still playing when *WrestleMania III* took place.

During this period, the company quietly rejoined the NWA, swapping talent with the other territories while still portraying the WWWF Championship as the most important title in the world. With each incarnation of the promotion, Vince's responsibilities continued to expand.

"I have a voracious appetite for life and everything in it," he told *Forbes* in 2014. "To a certain extent, I will die a very frustrated man because I didn't do this or accomplish that."

The quote may explain why, even after fulfilling his goal of finally working alongside his father, he pursued opportunities outside the wrestling business. According to one tale, the elder McMahon once received a phone call from a private investigator laundry-listing the many debts Vince had incurred promoting oldies concerts. If Vincent James lectured his son about this, the younger McMahon did not change his ways. He'd already acquiesced to his father's wishes by selling cups and ice cream cones, and that hadn't really benefited anybody. So even though Vincent James McMahon had the final word on all WWWF business, when it came to everything else, Vincent Kennedy McMahon was going to carve his own unconventional path.

Which brings us to Evel Knievel. Like Dr. Jerry Graham, the motorcycle stuntman seemed more suited to the carnival midway than the legitimate sports world. Yet, as McMahon would later on, Knievel — whose given name was Robert, by the way — managed to burst out of his prescribed surroundings — in his case, rural county fairs — by taking something fringe and selling it to the normies.

Even when he injured himself — which he did all the time — or failed to land where he'd planned, Evel seemed to become more famous with each jump. After attempting to leap 141 feet over the fountains at Caesars Palace in Las Vegas, he landed short, the handlebars coming off in his hands as he hurtled forward, skidding across the parking lot of the Dunes next door. No one doubted that he'd suffered a crushed pelvis and femur. But his tale about being in a coma for 29 days was almost certainly a work — the wrestling term for a con.

In 1974, he proclaimed that he intended to board a rocket-like contraption called the Skycycle X-2 and cross the mile-long gap between the peaks atop Idaho's Snake River Canyon. And this time, he had a tag team partner of sorts. Vincent Kennedy McMahon would handle all closed-circuit chores, telecasting the feat in movie theaters and arenas everywhere.

Vincent James agreed to support his son's efforts, putting up a share of the money. But just to moderate Vince's impulses, his father assigned boxing impresario Bob Arum to keep an eye on the kid.

There was a lot of hype leading up to the event, but the jump itself sputtered out quickly. Knievel's parachute malfunctioned and opened during takeoff. Instead of seeing Evel soar through the heavens, closed-circuit audiences watched his craft float lazily down to the Snake River. What was billed as "The Most Exciting Two-Hour Telecast Ever" turned out to be a dud.

Even with his father's help, Vince had invested heavily in the endeavor and lost money. Within two years, he and Linda filed for bankruptcy.

Still, his craving for risk did not abate. He'd carefully monitored his father's business dealings and wanted to present a different type of product. In 1979, he successfully lobbied Vincent James to drop a "W" from the promotion's name, streamlining it to "World Wrestling Federation." Three years later, Vince and Linda bought the company from his father and partners Gorilla Monsoon, "Golden Boy" Arnold Skaaland and Philadelphia promoter Phil Zacko.

Nothing noticeable happened at first. But change was on the way.

"We were all in a meeting and Vince asked, 'How do you feel about changing wrestling into entertainment?'" the late Nikolai Volkoff told me in 2013 for a story I wrote for *Bleacher Report*. "The older guys like Chief Jay Strongbow said no. That was funny because Strongbow wasn't really an American Indian. He was Italian . . . But that's what guys like him had in their blood. I had a different mentality because I grew up in a communist country and I knew how to adjust to a new system."

Those who couldn't, though, would not be given a choice. "Even if some of the wrestlers didn't like it," Volkoff continued, "Vince was going to take the business to a new level."

Nelson Sweglar would become the WWF's vice president of television production, working closely with the younger McMahon. "His dad had very modest goals for the TV product," Sweglar said. "He never imagined extending the coverage from coast to coast and then going international. He was content with just having the largest territory in North America."

Vince obviously wanted more and was willing to implement his plan in phases. But people like Steve Lombardi noticed some subtle hints of what was ahead.

The New York native began working for the company in 1982, primarily as a jobber, a wrestler paid to enhance interest in more established talent by "doing the job," or losing. "For a long time, all my trips were driving trips," recalled Lombardi, who'd be rebranded the Brooklyn Brawler and receive a mild "push," or chain of wins, in 1989. "Boston, Providence, New Haven, Binghampton, Philly, Baltimore, Washington. Then, I started flying. It was so different that I still remember the first time the company sent me a plane ticket. They wanted me to go to Pittsburgh."

Independent of McMahon, the Hollywood Wrestling office, whose Friday night cards at the Olympic Auditorium in East LA were selling out a decade or so earlier, folded in late '82. By the next year, the WWF was running the Olympic, assisted by longtime local promoter Mike LeBell. At one card, fans sighted Vince and LeBell in the audience, taking in the atmosphere. "This place is a dump," McMahon was heard to gripe, "and I can't have families coming to a place like this."

The entrepreneur was also conscious of how his brand of pro wrestling was being presented to the public. Before WWF television shows began, a logo was shown, as an announcer intoned that the company was the definitive leader in "sports entertainment."

The name irked the rest of an industry where many veterans were uncomfortable with referring to an event as a "show." While Vince had issues with other types of wrestling terminology, this wasn't on his list of banned words. "Promoters tried to tell the audience that this was 100 percent sport," he told *Esquire*. "Professional wrestling has always been a show. When Abraham Lincoln wrestled, it was a show."

Embracing that heritage, McMahon had backstage agents — primarily ex-wrestlers well-versed in the storytelling arcs essential for a compelling physical narrative — go over the bouts with the combatants, sometimes in the ring before the fans trickled in. "I didn't think a wrestling promotion could be run this way," remembered Jimmy "The Mouth of the South" Hart, a wiry manager who'd arrive in the WWF from the Memphis territory in 1985. "We never had agents in Memphis, maybe someone the promoter picked to come over and say, 'Jimmy, your guy is going over [winning] after you use your gimmick,'" or weapon of choice. "If we did go to the ring to rehearse the match, we would have been fired. Holy shit! What if the popcorn people were in the building, or the people who cleaned up? You stayed completely in the back."

Jacques and Raymond Rougeau joined the WWF in 1986, the third generation of a family that included great-uncle Eddie Auger, who participated in a match mere days before succumbing to pancreatic cancer, and their father Jacques Rougeau Sr., who'd formed a popular tag team in Quebec with his brother, Johnny. "When you're brought up in this business, it's like the Cosa Nostra," Raymond said. "And kayfabe"— the term wrestlers used to describe keeping the inner workings of the trade between themselves — "was our omertà," the Mafia code of silence. "The secrets of the trade are sacred. And all of a sudden, you're sports entertainment.

"There's a heck of a transition to be made. It made me uneasy. But I went with it. We were part of a revolution."

Outside of the WWF, the talent was universally resistant. "People would make fun of WWE," said Bruce Prichard, who'd been around the industry since age ten, when he began selling posters at the Sam Houston Coliseum. "'They're exposing the business. They're killing the business.' They neglected to realize the number of eyeballs that were now being exposed to what we do."

Indeed, in a 1985 *Sports Illustrated* article, Prichard's close friend Joel Watts, the stepson of Cowboy Bill Watts, owner of the Oklahoma-based Mid-South territory, characterized McMahon this way: "He plays on the personalities of the wrestlers, making them out to be freaks or something. I think he's generating a fad that will pass away."

Yet, when Vince first bought the company, no one was asking for quotes about him for *Sports Illustrated*. He was still a chapter or two away from gaining that type of notoriety. Before he could fully capture it, he needed a lightning rod to bring everybody to the party.

And he knew exactly where to find him, *brother*.

CHAPTER 3

S teve Taylor betrayed no emotion as he loaded his camera and strapped it around his neck. Just a few months earlier, he'd been a newspaper photographer in upstate New York, worrying about shadows and natural lighting and whether his pictures would develop properly. Now, he'd been dispatched to Chicago on a special operation for Vince McMahon.

Ostensibly, the WWF's young chief photographer had arrived at the American Wrestling Association (AWA) show on a mission of goodwill. McMahon had started a national wrestling magazine and, in the spirit of fraternity between the various promotions, was going to highlight the AWA's stars. That's what the Midwestern company had been told, and they'd been gracious about making sure that someone met Taylor before the event, issued him a pass and escorted him backstage. But it was clear to Taylor that "everyone was suspicious," he said. "They were watching me everywhere I went. Technically, we had a working relationship, but not really."

A few weeks after Taylor was hired, McMahon had traveled to the AWA's home base in Minneapolis to meet owner Verne Gagne, a two-time National Collegiate Athletic Association (NCAA) wrestling champion and alternate for the US freestyle team at the 1948 Olympics, and his son, Greg, a former co-holder of the AWA World Tag Team Championship. "He said he wanted to buy my dad out," Greg said, "and asked, 'What's the number?' And my dad said, 'I have a little problem. I'm not like these other territories where you have only one guy to deal with. I've got partners.'"

According to Greg, Vince was unmoved by the complications and made an offer anyway: $6 million and a job for life for Verne's son.

In Greg's telling, Gagne still wouldn't commit. But everyone was cordial, and the Gagnes even drove McMahon back to the airport.

"As he got out of the car," Greg said, "he turns to us and yells, 'I don't negotiate.' And Verne was hard to hear and he said, 'What did he say?' But Vince was gone by then."

Now, here was a representative from Vince's new magazine, offering to provide the AWA with free publicity. Was Vince simply motivated by kindness and respect for the history that the two companies shared, or was something else going on?

Similar concerns would be raised when McMahon began presenting a show called *WWF All American Wrestling* on the USA network. In addition to WWF talent, the program would feature matches from different territories. Promoters willingly shipped tapes over to the WWF. But why was Vince being so collegial? Maybe he needed extra material for his show. Or, more ominously, perhaps his real motive was poaching some of the featured performers and booking them on WWF cards.

In Chicago, Taylor did his best to ignore the tension and go through the motions of his job. Stashing his gear bag under the ring, he shot the first few matches until, after a while, his minders began to view him as no different than Bill Apter, George Napolitano or the other wrestling magazine photographers who regularly covered the AWA. When he took a break backstage, no one was really watching him that closely anymore. Very quickly, his eyes scanned the talent. And that's when he saw him: bronzed, blond and brawny, his gleaming aura obscuring everyone else.

Taylor stepped forward, introduced himself and shook Hulk Hogan's hand.

"Vince wants you to call him," he whispered, slipping the AWA's most popular attraction a small piece of paper with the promoter's phone number.

When 1983 began, a job in the wrestling business was the furthest thing from Steve Taylor's mind. As a staff photographer for the *Auburn Citizen*, a newspaper serving Cayuga County along the Finger Lakes in central New York State, his responsibilities included creating content for the popular "Picture Page" each Sunday. It was his editor, Ed Helinski, who first suggested attending a WWF show after learning that the promotion was staging an event at Auburn Community College.

Taylor was indifferent; although he'd been an accomplished wrestler in high school, he had no interest in McMahon's product. But Helinski really wanted to cover the show. He'd grown up watching pro wrestling on television stations beamed to his town from Buffalo and Toronto and still followed the week-to-week storylines. Since the *Citizen* generally concerned itself with occurrences like parades, fundraisers and Rotary Club functions, he was looking forward to writing about the WWF instead.

He phoned the WWF office in South Yarmouth, Massachusetts — where Vince was running the Cape Cod Coliseum, presenting concerts, boxing and minor league hockey, in addition to WWF events — and was connected to Ed Cohen. Cohen's primary job was booking arenas. Since the company was so small, though, his responsibilities fluctuated and, on that particular day, his assignments included dealing with the press. "He basically said, 'We don't take kindly to the mainstream media coming to events,'" Helinski said. "I'm pretty certain he didn't want a newspaper coming in and poking around and trying to expose the business. They were very, very particular about keeping outsiders out. But I told him I was a wrestling fan and wanted to do something respectful. And we would devote our Sunday Picture Page to it."

Cohen agreed on one condition: Helinski would send over a copy of whatever the *Citizen* published.

So Helinski headed to the card with Taylor. Despite the photographer's lack of intrigue about the pastime, he immediately saw the entertainment value. "A lot of the WWF's main stars were there," recalled Taylor, who'd eventually become WWE's vice president of event operations, "Ivan Putski,

Sergeant Slaughter. They were all great characters, and it was one of the best Picture Pages we'd ever done."

Vince thought so, too. Days after receiving a copy of the *Citizen*'s coverage, Cohen was on the phone with Helinski again, asking if he and Taylor would be interested in flying to Cape Cod and having lunch with the boss.

At the meeting, McMahon told them that he was starting a new magazine and needed people like them on his staff. "He was talking about taking this thing nationwide and all these other big plans," Taylor said. "And I thought, 'This guy is frickin' nuts.'"

By the time they boarded the plane home, though, both had agreed to work for the WWF. Yet, each had misgivings. "When we getting off, I looked at Steve and said, 'What did we just do?'" Helinski recounted.

Taylor headed to a newsstand and picked up a few wrestling magazines, his eyes fixating on the bloody covers. "I wasn't too impressed," he said. "But then, I spoke to a bunch of people who told me, 'This guy has good credentials. If he pulls it off, you're going to be on the ground floor of this thing. It's worth a chance.' And that made sense to me. You don't want to be remembered as the guy who said no to Bill Gates."

The publication was bi-monthly at first, marketed as *Victory Magazine*. After two issues, the decision was made to call it what it actually was: the official *WWF Magazine*.

By this point, Vince was in the process of divesting from his interests at the Cape Cod Coliseum and moving his operation to an office space in Greenwich, Connecticut. When Helinski asked McMahon about his strategy, the boss explained that, even though he was entirely capable of conducting business from a pay phone, the WWF would expand quicker if its headquarters were within an hour of Madison Avenue.

"I was employee number ten," Taylor said. "We were a very close group, and Vince was very close to us. We'd spend a lot of time talking and joking with him. It wasn't 100 percent business in those days."

In fact, when McMahon would drive to the promotion's television tapings in Allentown and Hamburg, Pennsylvania, he'd frequently invite employees to share the ride with him.

It was at those tapings that Taylor realized that he was becoming a fan. "I spent so much time watching these guys do their promos. They'd do one for wherever the TV show was syndicated. 'I'm coming to Syracuse to do this. I'm coming to Albany to do that.' One after another, one take, boom, boom, boom. And they'd just come up with stuff on the spot. And I'd stand there and go, 'Wow, these guys are good.'"

Three weeks of the company's hour-long shows would be taped at a time. But Taylor noticed a pattern that changed from one taping to the next. "Every three weeks, we were doing tapings for new markets. So you're not just doing 25 interviews, you're doing 35. And then, you're not doing 40, you're doing 63."

But for all the progress, there were forces within the promotion hostile to the interlopers Vince was bringing in. "It's a very complicated business, and it was even more complicated because you had to maintain kayfabe," Helinski said.

"There were certain rules you were just supposed to know. Like, if someone was cutting a promo for TV and you were standing there, you were not supposed to laugh, even if it was funny. I don't know the reasoning behind that. Maybe it was distracting to the wrestlers, maybe the wrestlers thought you were laughing at them. So what you'd do is put your hand in front of your face and turn your back. But when you did that, they knew you were laughing."

Backstage agent Chief Jay Strongbow begrudged the fact that Taylor was sometimes aware of information only wrestlers were supposed to know. "He did not want me in the locker room. And he'd ask me, 'How do you know this? How do you know that?' I mean, I knew about long-term planning because Vince wanted me to be at certain events where things were going to happen.

"I tried to explain this to him one day, and he said, 'Tell Vince he can go fuck himself.' Vince saw us talking and came over to me with this smile on his face. 'What did Strongbow say?' 'Strongbow said you can go fuck yourself.'"

Helinski ended up becoming social friends with future WWE Hall of Famer Howard Finkel, who, in addition to ring announcing, helped the WWF recruit talent. "We played racquetball and Howard would never,

never utter any type of inside information. He wouldn't think of saying, 'I'll tell you this, but you can't repeat it.' He was the perfect soldier. If I ever asked him about what was really going on, he changed the subject."

In time, manager "Classy" Freddie Blassie took the young writer into his confidence, explaining backstage etiquette as well as how babyfaces and heels — fan favorites and villains — each played to the crowd. "I learned the best thing for me was keeping my mouth shut," Helinski said, "and by listening and paying attention, things would click into place."

The lessons would help him ascend quickly, combining his job as magazine editor with public relations, then becoming operations manager of the burgeoning merchandising division.

As he fortified his trust with the talent, Helinski was delegated duties that had little to do with his various job descriptions. "I remember Vince calling Steve Taylor and I into his office and telling us, 'I think our promoter in Buffalo has been skimming.' That's the wrestling mentality. Everyone always thinks there's more money than what's being reported. He said, 'I want you guys to go up there and count the house.'

"I mean, how do you count the house? I didn't say that to him, of course. We just went up to Buffalo to the old Memorial Auditorium. They wouldn't let us in the business office, but they knew they were being watched. So I just observed things and came up with some calculations — 10,000 people in the building, maybe 750 people on the floor. And we added up approximately what the house should have been."

When Taylor was sent to the AWA show in Chicago, Helinski was the one tasked with making the initial request to Verne Gagne. As he discussed the matter with Taylor and McMahon, the promoter suddenly shot a hard look at the editor and asked him to leave the office and close the door.

When Taylor exited a few minutes later, he walked by his friend and said nothing. Helinski didn't ask for an explanation. He understood that Taylor was engaging in "preventive maintenance." The fewer who knew about the situation, the fewer there were to talk.

The truth was that, after just a few months in the wrestling business, Helinski didn't need a description of the scheme about to unfold. He kind of had a feeling.

CHAPTER 4

The real-life Terry Bollea's first, short-lived gimmick was the masked Super Destroyer — a name later adopted by Scott "Hogg" Irwin, beginning in Bill Watts's Mid-South territory in 1980. It was the summer of '77 and Bollea, who'd grown up attending the matches at the Tampa Sportatorium, had recently been trained by Florida promoter Eddie Graham's chief enforcer, Hiro Matsuda, a noted "shooter," or wrestler with legitimate grappling skills capable of stretching and hurting rivals. The territory was trying the kid out, having him win sometimes and lose others, to see if he was really meant for the business.

Although Bollea had long fantasized about performing in Florida, his version of the Super Destroyer was too green to receive any type of push. If he wanted to main-event in St. Pete or Lauderdale one day, he'd have to pick up experience elsewhere.

By 1979, he was in Memphis as Terry Boulder — sometimes called Terry "The Hulk" Boulder — and Southeastern Championship Wrestling, based in Mobile, Alabama. He was still learning how to work, but his deep tan, muscular physique and bleached blond locks qualified him as enough of a personality to receive title matches against NWA World Heavyweight Champion Harley Race in both territories. In Memphis, he also formed a "brother" tag team with a guy named Eddie Boulder — Ed Leslie, the future Brutus Beefcake.

The good friends would later work as brothers again, this time as Hulk and Dizzy Hogan.

In those days, one of the ideal ways of learning the business was by switching territories and adapting to different styles. So Bollea stayed on the move, wrestling in Georgia as Sterling Golden, then returning to Southeastern Championship Wrestling to beat Dick Slater for the group's heavyweight title on December 1 before dropping it to "Bullet" Bob Armstrong on Christmas Day.

In between, he'd debuted in the WWF as Hulk Hogan. Vincent James enjoyed creating ethnic characters, so Hogan was supposed to be an Irish American heel. Bollea was fine with the name but reportedly balked at McMahon's request to dye his hair red. There were no repercussions for the newcomer's intransigence, and, in his Madison Square Garden debut, he was given a win against athletic babyface Ted DiBiase.

Entering the ring in a purple cape, accompanied by sequin-clad manager "Classy" Freddie Blassie, Hogan seemed built for the Big Apple, where, despite his villainous persona, he often received cheers. McMahon gave him a nice push, allowing him to beat WWF Heavyweight Champion Bob Backlund in a few places via countout — the rules stipulated that titles could only change through pinfall or submission — setting up rematches in which the champion triumphed.

In those years before email and texting, photographer Bill Apter — a figure so ubiquitous in the various territories that the magazines in which his photos appeared were collectively known as the "Apter mags" — would generally contact Hogan through his mother, Ruth. Apter said that when Sylvester Stallone's office reached out to him one day, looking to cast someone to battle Rocky in the boxer vs. wrestler scene in *Rocky III*, the photographer offered two recommendations: the Hulkster and the man who'd inspired his entire persona, former WWWF Heavyweight Champion "Superstar" Billy Graham. In the interim, Apter said, he told Ruth to have her son get a hold of Stallone right away.

The link to one of filmdom's biggest names not only changed Hogan's life, it altered professional wrestling — which, for all its ostentation, had been considered a marginal entertainment option at best.

But Vincent James had little taste for Hollywood, subscribing to the logic that outside attention would only hurt the business. Reportedly, he also had his rising star fully booked, leaving no time for Hogan to fly west and make a movie. So the aging promoter is alleged to have pushed back when he learned about the offer, forbidding Hogan from participating in the production.

Remarkably, at this early stage, Hogan was enough of a self-promoter to understand that this was one instance when even a powerful figure like the senior McMahon needed to be defied. By appearing as the character Thunderlips in *Rocky III*, the Hulkster was about to have his first dalliance with pop culture. With his emerging fame, his lack of amateur wrestling credentials or seniority in the business mattered little. Once the blockbuster movie was released, Hogan was positioned to work anywhere he wished.

He chose the AWA.

Despite owner Verne Gagne's relatively conservative worldview — as a top amateur, he tended to favor performers with authentic athletic backgrounds — the AWA was a good place to work. From its base in Minneapolis, Gagne flew his talent to such far-flung locations as Winnipeg, Denver, Omaha, Las Vegas and Salt Lake City, cutting down the grueling road trips common in most other territories.

The promotion was founded when Gagne, a former NWA Junior Heavyweight Champion, realized that the large organization was never going to make him their heavyweight kingpin. So in 1960, he started his own league and quickly awarded himself the belt. Like the WWF, though, he cooperated with the other major companies and even appeared on WWWF shows in Madison Square Garden.

Hogan joined a gifted roster featuring names like Nick Bockwinkel, Ray Stevens, Mad Dog Vachon, Larry "The Ax" Hennig and Baron von Raschke. Manager Bobby "The Brain" Heenan "was, by far, our greatest all-around talent," remembered Greg Gagne's AWA tag team partner "Jumping" Jim Brunzell. "He could talk and he could bump [take falls]. His timing was incredible." By simply walking to ring, Brunzell said, Heenan could generate instant "heat," or fury. "He just knew what the people wanted and gave it to them consistently night after night after night."

The plan was to bring Hogan in as a heel, pairing him up with manager Johnny Valiant. "We went to Milwaukee the first night he was there," Greg Gagne said. "When I came back, of course, my dad asked me, 'How did Hogan do?' And I told him that the people cheered him. It felt so natural. Even with Valiant as his manager, the fans refused to hate him. So we had to make him a babyface."

Although he'd been a fan favorite in places like Knoxville and Dothan, Alabama, Hogan didn't fully understand the psychology of working this way. "The heels we had were really good," Gagne said, "and they could lead him in the ring, showing him how to make a comeback and taking big bumps for him."

Cutting promos was another matter. "I'd really watched him develop," the late "Mean" Gene Okerlund told me in 2013. "Because, boy, some of those early interviews we did, they were a struggle. But eventually, he developed that 'let me tell you, brother' style and never looked back."

While he'd rarely receive credit for it in North America, his in-ring intelligence was also maturing, particularly during his regular tours to Japan. Based on looks alone, Hogan would have been a novelty in Asia. But, perhaps more than the AWA, New Japan Pro-Wrestling, one of the top two wrestling leagues in the country at the time, was a brand that required performers to be both athletic and believable. That meant, rather than simply relying on strongman moves, Hogan would get down on the mat in Japan and wrestle, amateur style.

In the wake of the *Rocky III* release in 1982, the Japanese regarded the mesmeric American as so much of a celebrity that the bass-playing Hogan released an album, perhaps inspiring Vincent Kennedy McMahon — who had his own talent-exchanging deal with New Japan — to see the viability of fusing wrestling and rock 'n' roll.

Back in the AWA, fans clamored for Hogan to win the title. The problem was that, as in the WWF, championship changes were a rarity. Between 1968 and 1982, only two men had worn the belt: Gagne and Nick Bockwinkel, an articulate, technically gifted heel who'd learned the industry from his father, Warren. But he was 47 years old, and the popular consensus was that the Hulkster's time had arrived.

On one card, the AWA presented a battle royal, with the winner guaranteed a shot at the championship in the future. Gagne made a deal with Vincent James McMahon, who controlled André the Giant's bookings, to bring in the big man as a special attraction. Hogan and André were supposed to be allies, but at one point in the match, the pair inadvertently backed into each other, turning around and engaging in a dramatic staredown.

In the end, Hogan won the elimination match and was slated to wrestle the champ at the St. Paul Civic Center on April 18, 1982.

The encounter was highly anticipated, with many fans expecting a title switch. Seemingly overmatched, Bockwinkel resorted to using a foreign object. This prompted Hogan to retaliate with a weapon of his own. But the referee failed to see any of the chicanery and, when Hogan covered the champ for the pin, the official brought his hand down on the mat three times.

Hogan was handed the belt, electrifying the audience.

On the next AWA television broadcast, though, figurehead president Stanley Blackburn announced that, after reviewing the footage, he'd concluded that the championship had switched hands under dubious circumstances. Bockwinkel had been the first to introduce a foreign object and was disqualified. As a result, he maintained ownership of the title.

This was a common pro wrestling device. Although Hogan had been thwarted, fans cried out for a rematch. These were held in all of the AWA's major cities, with Bockwinkel generally exploiting some type of technicality to hold on to his crown.

The saga continued for a full year until, on April 24, 1983, the two squared off again in St. Paul — on a show that would feature Brutus Beefcake, still wrestling as Eddie Boulder, doing the job for Wahoo McDaniel. "We'd sold out the arena," Greg said. "We sold out the building next door with the match on closed circuit."

Somewhere in the course of the night, Hogan tossed Bockwinkel over the top rope. But Bockwinkel got back in the ring, only to be overwhelmed by the challenger and pinned. Once again, Hogan was awarded the belt. And, as before, Stanley Blackburn returned the championship, this time because AWA rules prohibited a competitor from hurling a rival over the cables onto the arena floor.

The ruse would later be labeled the Dusty finish, because of Dusty Rhodes's overreliance on it when he was the booker (the person charged with developing characters and storylines) in the NWA, and would erode the goodwill that existed between the AWA and its fans.

It also obliterated whatever positive feelings the Hulkster had for the AWA.

On December 21, 1983, Verne Gagne received a telegram from Tampa informing him that Hogan was leaving the company. Since the star was booked around the horn — or wrestling circuit — Gagne initially believed the message to be a prank from Tampa-based promoter Eddie Graham. "He just threw it in the basket," Greg said.

There was one indicator, though, that something wasn't right. In his recent interactions with the Gagnes, "André was really mean to us. He'd never been that way before. He wouldn't talk to us and was acting like he just wanted us to get away from him. We couldn't figure it out. We thought he was just drinking too much. But I think he knew what was going to happen."

It seemed that there were many things the Gagnes didn't realize: that Steve Taylor had slipped over Vince's number when the AWA allowed him to roam its locker room and that the subsequent conversations between Vince and Hogan had become frequent and productive.

They also could not imagine that, in the years ahead, wrestling historians would repeatedly write that the Hulkster left for the WWF because Verne had been too stuck in the past to ever bestow the title on a sports entertainer.

But Greg insisted that the perception was wrong: "CBS came to Verne and they wanted to do a network TV show on a Saturday night. And they wanted Bockwinkel and Hogan in the main event. And Hogan was going to win. He didn't know anything about the CBS thing because Verne had signed a nondisclosure. We couldn't tell him."

There was another part of the arrangement that Greg claimed could also not be divulged: the battle royal standoffs with André would soon serve a purpose. "We were going to give Hogan the belt on that CBS thing, then come back in the fall with André challenging Hogan for the championship."

If the story is credible, it would suggest that Verne Gagne was envisioning the main event of *WrestleMania III* four years before it actually occurred.

CHAPTER 5

Hogan wasn't the only AWA name procured by Vince. The northeastern promoter was in the early stages of decimating Verne Gagne's roster and would soon boast an ensemble of such ex-AWA standouts as Jesse "The Body" Ventura, "Dr. D" David Schultz, Bobby "The Brain" Heenan, Mad Dog Vachon, Adrian Adonis, Ken Patera and Greg Gagne's tag team partner "Jumping" Jim Brunzell.

Brunzell would contend that, Hogan aside, Heenan and announcer Mean Gene Okerlund were the biggest losses. "First of all, Mean Gene was a student of the game. He knew what was going on with every rivalry. He knew what his job was — to get over the guy he was interviewing. He'd color the story a little bit, set you up not just with his words, but with the way his voice went up and down and his facial expressions. He was superior to every other announcer."

Okerlund had been directly recruited by Hogan, who was making an effort to persuade his favorite AWA performers to join him in the WWF. "He was filling everybody's head with how much money they were going to make," Greg Gagne said. "And Vince listened to him. He told Vince the best announcer was Gene Okerlund, and they came after him."

Out of everyone who left, Greg said that only two personalities gave the AWA notice beforehand: Vachon and Heenan. "Everybody else just walked out, even my partner. We were wrestling the Road Warriors in

Winnipeg and Jim just didn't show up. I think Vince wanted to hit people who were in the main events. Maybe he said he'd pay them more if they just left. He was killing us."

McMahon was generating uncertainty everywhere, including within the WWF.

Bob Backlund had held the WWF Heavyweight Championship since 1978 — save for a few days in 1979 when, in a title switch never acknowledged east of the Pacific, Antonio Inoki won the belt in Japan. Although Backlund was an exceptional athlete, his shy, earnest, Midwestern demeanor had prevented him from hitting the same nerve with northeastern crowds as predecessors Bruno Sammartino and Superstar Billy Graham. Anyway, he'd been Vincent James McMahon's pick. Now that Vincent Kennedy McMahon was in charge, Backlund's red buzzcut and singlet were not screaming "box office." It was time for Hulkamania to run wild.

But babyfaces rarely lost to babyfaces back then. So Vince came up with an interim champion. With his bald head, handlebar mustache and curl-toed boots, the Iranian-born Iron Sheik was a cartoon villain, waving a flag adorned with the face of Ayatollah Khomeini. When it came to amateur wrestling skill, though, he was no cartoon. After appearing in the Pan Am and World Games for Iran, he'd moved to Minnesota, won gold and silver medals in AAU competitions and served as an assistant coach for the US Olympic wrestling team in 1972 and 1976. While fans never would have guessed it, Backlund admired him — and the feeling was mutual. And if someone *had* to take away his championship, Backlund preferred they be a pure athlete rather than a bodybuilder and bass player.

The WWF was willing to create a backstory to help Backlund save face. On several occasions, the Iron Sheik had demonstrated his legitimate strength by swinging the heavy clubs that were part of the exercise regimen in Iran. Just before the title switch, he challenged Backlund to try his hand at the routine on TV.

Because of his conditioning, Backlund was actually one of the few WWF performers who *could* do this. But just to emphasize the difficulty of the task he was about to undertake, Backlund acted as if he was struggling with the clubs on the first two tries. When he finally demonstrated his mastery, the evil Persian jumped him, causing one of the heavy objects to hit him in the neck.

On the night after Christmas in 1983, the two squared off in Madison Square Garden. But announcers told cable TV viewers that the champ was entering the match at less than 100 percent. "He's favoring his left shoulder or his left arm," noted Pat Patterson.

Replied Gorilla Monsoon, "Well, he had that neck injury, Pat, here a week ago or so, that altercation that took place on television where he ended up with one of those Persian clubs wrapped around his neck and shoulder."

The moment the bell rang, the Sheik zoned in on his rival's neck. Throughout the match, even when Backlund would rally, he'd lift a hand and sell his neck injury. When the Sheik finally stood over Backlund and bent his body backwards in the Camel Clutch, the brave champion refused to submit. The Sheik arched his rival's frame further back. Time passed. Then, seemingly concerned for his charge's long-term health, Backlund's manager Arnold Skaaland threw in a white towel from ringside.

As fans looked on, stunned, the Sheik's manager, Freddie Blassie, placed the belt around his protégé's waist before the Sheik grabbed the microphone and heralded his win as a victory for Iran — the country where, starting in 1979, more than 50 hostages were held in the US embassy, the start of a humiliating episode of US history that lasted 444 days.

What was supposed to be a festive holiday season had now been darkened by the foreign menace. Fans waited for a ray of light to redeem their hopes, not realizing that it was coming by way of the AWA.

Bill Apter had been through this routine before.

In January 1971, he'd been working less than a year for the chain of magazines that would eventually include *Inside Wrestling*, *The Wrestler* and *Pro Wrestling Illustrated* (*PWI*), when his boss Stanley Weston summoned him out of the editorial room.

"I just got off the phone with Willie Gilzenberg," said Weston, referring to the WWWF's figurehead president. "I'm going to tell you something right now, but you've got to die with it."

Bruno Sammartino was scheduled to defend his WWWF Heavyweight Championship against the "Russian Bear" Ivan Koloff in Madison Square Garden. Bruno had held the belt since he dethroned the company's inaugural titlist "Nature Boy" Buddy Rogers in 1963, and a large share of the audience believed that he was infallible. Without providing specifics, Weston emphasized, "Make sure for the main event you have plenty of film."

Apter knew what that meant and, just to cover his bases, asked his father, a postal worker and sandlot baseball umpire, to accompany him to the Garden with an extra camera. It would be the senior Apter who'd fire off the shot of Koloff coming off the ropes just prior to his shocking win over the Italian Strongman.

Ever since that day, Apter generally expected to be positioned on the ring apron when a major title was supposed to change hands. But, on the afternoon before the Sheik won the championship, when Apter arrived at the WWF's makeshift headquarters at the Holland Hotel, Arnold Skaaland interrupted his card game to deliver an unexpected piece of news. Ringside credentials were no longer being issued.

With the exception of the WWF's own magazine, all wrestling publications were banned from events.

"We'll give you guys some seats if you want," Skaaland said apologetically.

Apter found the information difficult to grasp. Because he oversaw his magazines' rating system, he was in the habit of calling Vincent James's home weekly, sometimes engaging in small talk with Juanita McMahon when she answered the phone. But Apter knew that the edict didn't come from the father.

It came from the son.

Like Apter, fellow photographer George Napolitano, whose family of magazines included *Wrestling's Main Event*, *Wrestling All Stars* and *Wrestling Scene*, enjoyed a history with the McMahons. In fact, during a previous effort by the WWWF to create its own magazine — *Wrestling Action*, which appeared on newsstands between 1977 and 1979 — the Brooklyn native had been the chief photographer, dealing directly with Vincent Kennedy McMahon.

Napolitano's full-time gig was teaching junior high school in Brooklyn's Sunset Park neighborhood, particularly a photography class that was popular with students. Sometimes, after work, he rushed to the airport to catch a plane, banged out photos in some other city, then flew back to New York and returned to school before the first class began. While Apter was the better-known personality among fans, Napolitano was close with many of the industry's top names, hanging out with them on the road. In fact, during his WWWF Heavyweight Championship reign, there was a period when Superstar Billy Graham had his mail sent to Napolitano's house.

Among his better-known photos: André the Giant demonstrating his immense proportions by holding up a group of female wrestlers and stretching his long arms over Chief Jay Strongbow and fellow warriors Mike Pappas and Víctor Rivera.

As distressing as the WWF's magazine ban was for Napolitano, he was not shocked. "I knew it was coming. Even before Vince bought the company, the people I knew on the inside were telling me he was going to take over everything."

In retrospect, Apter concluded that he should have anticipated the situation as well. After Pedro Morales toppled Ivan Koloff for the championship, the company "did a test where we were not allowed at ringside. And I remember Pedro calling me and he was very, very, very upset. And he talked to Vince Sr. at that point because I think Vince Jr. was the one who put that idea in his head. And after two or three Garden shows, they let us shoot at ringside again."

From that point forward, the dynamic between the promotion and Apter, Napolitano and the other magazine photographers — including a teenage Paul Heyman, who insinuated himself into Garden culture to such a degree that he frequently hitched a ride to events with managers Freddie Blassie and Lou Albano — was generally friendly. But when Vince decided to launch *Victory Magazine*, the rules started to change.

At one industry function, Apter was chatting with a wrestler he knew when he spotted Vincent James McMahon. The photographer rose from his chair and offered a handshake. Instead, the promoter grabbed Apter's sleeve and scolded him. "I hear you're saying bad things about my son."

"I haven't said anything bad — except Vinnie is calling our distributors and telling them not to take our magazine."

Vincent James's tone switched from angry to sympathetic. "He told me, 'Just call Vinnie,'" Apter said. "'We'll work something out with you.' That never happened."

Interestingly, the younger Vince had phoned Apter prior to the publication of *Victory Magazine*, offering the affable photographer a job. "I told him, 'I'm flattered, but I work for Mr. Weston.'"

He was talking about his boss, Stanley Weston — a man both the older and younger McMahon knew well.

Although his name remains closely associated with wrestling publications, Weston's first great love was boxing. A gifted artist, Weston was still in his teens when he began colorizing black-and-white portraits with oil paint for *The Ring* magazine. In December 1939, at the age of 20, he painted the image of Light Heavyweight Champion Billy Conn that became the first of 57 covers he'd create for *The Ring*. He would also write books on boxing history, assemble one of the world's largest boxing memorabilia collections and, in 2006, be posthumously inducted into the International Boxing Hall of Fame.

In 1952, he expanded into wrestling, publishing *Boxing & Wrestling Magazine* during television's infancy when both pastimes were easy to produce for the fledgling medium. His first magazine devoted solely to the mat wars was *Wrestling Revue* in 1959.

Among the publication's avid readers was Bill Apter.

Growing up in Maspeth, a blue-collar section of Queens, Apter and his brother regularly watched wrestling on TV, reenacting the moves in impromptu matches in their bedroom. "I remember seeing Dick the Bruiser tear off the clothes of [interviewer] Lord Athol Layton and thinking, 'This is cool.' I wanted to have my legs insured like I heard Antonino Rocca did, and strut like Buddy Rogers."

At Maurice Park, he defended what he called the Maspeth Championship against all comers. "I only held it for two weeks because, when I had one of my opponents in a headlock, he bit my finger and I gave up."

In 1969, he started a wrestling radio show — paying for his time — on WHBI FM, making regular trips to Sunnyside Gardens in Queens to interview the performers. In between, he'd station himself at ringside and take photos of the action. At one point, he sent some pictures and an accompanying article to *Wrestling Revue* — now no longer in the hands of Weston. "They told me they'd pay $25 and I never saw the money."

But because his photos were in print, he was able to secure a meeting with Weston. "He said, 'How much did you make from *Wrestling Revue?*' and I told him, 'Zero.' He told me he needed somebody to keep the photo files for his boxing and wrestling magazines at his house on Long Island — for $25 a day, three days a week. I was in the basement. Upstairs was the art department. The editorial department was in one of the bedrooms."

Shortly after Apter started, Weston and his wife went on vacation for two weeks. "He told me, 'If any black-and-white film comes in, keep it on the side.' What he didn't know was that I was able to develop pictures. So when they got back from their trip, I had 25 rolls of film already processed and hanging up on the shower curtain."

Weston offered his ambitious employee a full-time job and gave him a Nikon camera to take to events. But he warned, "Don't ever take it to get fixed."

"Why?"

"It fell off a truck."

Although Apter was now being regularly invited to WWWF events, he quickly realized that Vincent James McMahon and Stanley Weston were not on the best of terms. The dispute apparently stemmed from a trip a photographer had made to Gorilla Monsoon's house, in which the leading heel proudly displayed his gun collection. When the pictures arrived in the office, a writer created a fictional tale based on the images — below a headline proclaiming that Monsoon intended to shoot Sammartino.

"The families went out of their minds," Apter said. "They were so pissed off because the Marellas [Monsoon's actual name was Robert Marella] and Sammartinos were like best friends. So I had to show Vince McMahon, Bruno Sammartino, Gorilla Monsoon and everybody else that I was going to do things differently. And that's how the door really opened for me."

No one was expecting serious journalism; after all, the quotes were largely made up. The point was to work the stories in a way that served the talent and promoters.

Still, Apter also knew how to promote himself and tie the publications to his personality. After Stan "The Man" Stasiak began beating rivals with the "heart punch," presumably cutting off the flow of blood to the heart with a mighty fist to the chest, a series of photos were published, showing the villain executing the move on the diminutive Apter.

"Mr. Weston loved those pictures. So I started going out of town, taking pictures of different guys attacking me."

The visibility not only raised Apter's status in the eyes of readers, wrestlers and promoters in practically every territory began reaching out to him to cover their events. "Bill was the man," future *PWI* managing editor-in-chief Craig Peters recalled. "He was absolutely and totally the conduit between our magazines and the business."

Hence, when absurdist comedian Andy Kaufman couldn't convince the WWF to fulfill his childhood fantasy by allowing him to participate in a wrestling angle, Apter knew a territory that would be far less cautious: Memphis, where headliner Jerry "The King" Lawler was willing to do just about anything to get himself on the cover of a national magazine.

Kaufman arrived in the Memphis territory, aggressively defending what he called the World Inter-Gender Wrestling Championship against women seemingly plucked from the audience. It was a routine he'd been doing for a while. In fact, in 1979, Vincent Kennedy McMahon interviewed him between matches at Madison Square Garden, holding back laughter when Kaufman offered $500 to any woman who could pin his shoulders to the mat. But that was as far as it went in the northeast. In Memphis, not only did Kaufman denigrate the female population, he mocked the entire community as bumbling hillbillies, imitating a southern drawl with an exaggerated accent. Finally, Lawler stepped forward to defend the pride of his home city. After weeks of buildup, the two squared off in the Mid-South Coliseum.

Both Lawler and Kaufman made sure that there were enough cameras around to chronicle the event, having no issue with the possibility that the attention might tempt a scribe into pondering the "real vs. fake" question. In reality, the pair had been thinking a few steps ahead of the press, practicing a series of maneuvers in Lawler's hotel room. At the conclusion of the match, The King turned Kaufman upside down and delivered a piledriver, seemingly breaking his neck.

Reporters returned to New York and Los Angeles, thoroughly worked.

According to the mainstream media, Kaufman's attention-grabbing deed had gotten him seriously injured.

But Kaufman and Lawler weren't finished. In July, the duo was at NBC's studios in New York as guests on David Letterman's popular late-night television show. Kaufman was in a neck brace and, as he and Lawler argued about what occurred at the Mid-South Coliseum, the King of Memphis Wrestling stood and appeared to knock Kaufman out of his chair with a hard slap. The chaos continued through the commercial break. Then, Kaufman splashed coffee in Lawler's face and unleashed a fusillade of on-air obscenities.

Although Letterman likely anticipated that there'd be some banter between the two, he never imagined how quickly the situation would degenerate. But Bill Apter knew, and both Lawler and Kaufman had ensured that their favorite wrestling reporter and Craig Peters were on set to photograph the exchange.

"I'll never forget, after the taping, running through the streets of New York," said Peters. "I can't remember if it was the *New York Post* or *Daily News*, but one of them had consented to let us use their darkroom and get the film developed. Bill shot color. I shot black-and-white. And it was one of my photos that went up on the front page the next day."

While Vincent Kennedy McMahon didn't publicly comment on the fanfare, there's no question that he was closely monitoring it.

Yet, just as McMahon was about to start generating the same kind of ballyhoo, the guy said to have matched Hulk Hogan with Stallone and Lawler with Kaufman would find himself iced out.

In years to come, Vince would impress upon Apter that the issue was never personal. But he already had his troops massed at the border. And even nice guys like Bill and George would be collateral damage in a long, protracted war about to claim many more casualties.

CHAPTER 6

During the brief period when he held the WWF Heavyweight Championship, the Iron Sheik did his best to exacerbate national and religious tensions. "I just call home a couple of days ago," he said on television. "I talk to Ayatollah Khomeini and I talk to the family. I heard there is a big celebration in Tehran, Iran . . . All the Muslims are happy about me."

To demonstrate that euphoria, he held up a Farsi-language newspaper with his photo on page one. He neglected to point out that this particular periodical was published not in Tehran but Los Angeles, where it primarily catered to the Persian Jewish community.

He wanted to be in a country where the populace was sophisticated enough to hail his attributes, he stressed — but not exactly in those words. So he was planning to take the belt and bring it back to Iran.

Faced with the possibility of having to apply for a visa and travel to Tabriz, Mashhad or Qom to see a title defense, fans cried out for someone to restore dignity to the Land of Liberty.

And they soon learned that it wouldn't be Backlund. But first, he needed to be written out of the plot.

The recently deposed titlist was in the ring at a TV taping when he found himself surrounded and menaced by all three Wild Samoans — Afa, Sika and Samula (later Samu) — as well as their manager "Captain"

Lou Albano. Suddenly, Backlund called for a time out, marched back to the dressing room and emerged with the Hulkster — clad in a tight red t-shirt with the words "American Made" stenciled across the front in white letters. Together, Backlund and Hogan unloaded on all four villains, sending them scurrying.

In case any Backlund loyalists had misgivings about the new arrival stepping into the top babyface slot, Hogan was endorsed by the ex-titlist in the interview that followed. "Everybody knows the Hulk," Backlund proclaimed, acknowledging that the last time Hogan had appeared in the WWF, he'd been a heel. "He's changed his ways."

Then, it was Hogan's turn to speak. With his body twitching and his throaty voice rising, he reminded the fans that Backlund himself was endorsing him. "I would like to thank Mr. Bob Backlund and the WWF for bringing the Hulkster back . . . This is a different Hulk Hogan, and Hulkamania is already running wild."

He would soon declare war on the Iron Sheik and all he represented, leaving the WWF with no choice but to announce that the two would battle for the crown at Madison Square Garden on January 23, 1984.

In Minnesota, Verne Gagne watched the development with horror, imagining the man who could never get the strap from Nick Bockwinkel blazing into Green Bay and Oshkosh, waving the mantle of the WWF. But Hogan didn't have the belt yet. And there was one competitor who could prevent him from acquiring it: the Iron Sheik.

Gagne and the Sheik had a deep history. After the real-life Khosrow Vaziri moved to the United States to join future Olympic wrestling coach Alan Rice's Minnesota Wrestling Club, the AWA took notice. In 1972, Verne invited him to train for the pros in an elite class that also included "Nature Boy" Ric Flair, Greg Gagne, "Jumping" Jim Brunzell, US Olympic weightlifter Ken Patera and ex–National Football League (NFL) line-backer Bob Bruggers — who'd leave the business in 1975 after surviving the plane crash that paralyzed headliner Johnny Valentine and almost canceled out Flair before his Hall of Fame career really kicked in.

Verne was an exacting taskmaster but Vaziri, accustomed to Olympic-level discipline, respected him — even if conditions at Gagne's training facility were inferior to anything the Sheik had ever encountered. Aspiring wrestlers were expected to show up in the dead of winter to an unheated barn on the promoter's farm in Chanhassen, Minnesota. The roof was faulty and sometimes snow had to be cleared from the ring before sessions could start. Livestock walked in and out of the building with such frequency that the Sheik compared the experience to training in a zoo.

Nonetheless, a total of 144 Gagne students would graduate to the pros — including Sergeant Slaughter, Ricky "The Dragon" Steamboat, "Mr. Perfect" Curt Hennig and Big Van Vader — even though the vast majority of invitees promptly quit. "After one day, most of the guys would throw up or pass out," Greg Gagne recalled. "And then, we'd never see them again."

Those who made it through each class, though, could enter the fraternity confident that they could hold their own, and probably win, if challenged to a shoot. "At the end of camp, Verne told us, 'You guys don't have to be afraid of anybody,'" Greg said. "'You can handle yourself under any circumstance.'"

Yet, the Sheik didn't always appreciate how the lessons were conveyed. Coach Billy Robinson had trained at the notorious Snake Pit in Wigan, in Greater Manchester, England. Under founder Billy Riley, the Snake Pit was known for teaching not just the traditional "catch as catch can" style of wrestling, but "hooking," applying illegal holds dangerous enough to end careers.

When pro wrestling was presented in carnivals, with the traveling strongman challenging people in the audience, hooks were sometimes necessary to ensure that the confrontations ended the way the promoter wanted. But Robinson, who would train both pro wrestlers and MMA fighters on three continents, enjoyed applying them to the point that, in England, the other performers called him "Billy the Bully."

"Verne was supposed to be our main instructor, but he was busy a lot of the time so Billy Robinson was in charge," Brunzell said. "Now, Billy's whole life revolved around hooking, submissions and all of that. He was very rough with us. He really was a sadist."

Yet, out of all the trainees, Vaziri was the most adept at holding his own. "I'll never forget one day," Brunzell said, "we're all of us in the ring, and he had Khos in the wrestler's position below him. Billy says, 'When I blow the whistle, try to get out.' But when he blew the whistle, Billy arched up and brought his knee down right below the buttocks in the meat of the thigh. This wasn't fair because Khos was kneeling, and Robinson gave him a terrible bone bruise. He probably had a charley horse for about three weeks.

"Then, Billy said, nice and casual, 'I'm sorry. But I was trying to explain what you can do in pro wrestling that you can't do in amateur wrestling. And there's no better way of explaining it to you than by showing you.'"

Having trained with some of the best amateur coaches on Earth, the student knew that a professional would never take advantage of a vulnerable understudy with a cheap shot. He vowed revenge on Robinson. In training, "he was also looking for the opportunity to get him back," Brunzell said.

News of the Sheik's resentment got back to Gagne, who asked the pupil to meet him one-on-one in a wrestling ring. As the pair grappled, Verne tried humbling Vaziri further, delivering a dropkick to the chest. Rather than faltering, the Sheik kept going after the multiple-time AWA champ.

That's when Gagne revealed the big secret: the business was a work, but you should always be alert in case of a double-cross. Vaziri was so shocked by this information that he later cried — unable to come to terms with the fact that becoming a pro wrestler would mean stepping away from legitimate competition. But first, Gagne had to extend an invitation to the closed society.

He did *that* with these words: "Be one of us."

In that moment, the bond between the two men was sealed.

But now, one week before the Madison Square Garden clash with Hogan, the WWF Heavyweight Champion was surprised to receive a call from the person who'd brought him into the business. "He said, 'Don't drop the belt to that bleached blond jabroni,'" the Sheik told me in 2013 in an article I wrote for *Bleacher Report*. "'He's a punk. I'll give you $100,000. You get in the ring with him at Madison Square Garden, you break his leg, take the belt and bring it to the AWA. We put Vince out of business.'"

The Sheik had no desire to hurt the McMahons, particularly after they'd just awarded him their championship. But he also knew that he *could* break Hulk Hogan's leg if he wished and understood that the anointment of the Hulkster would carry grave consequences for the Gagnes.

He refused to casually dismiss the request — especially since he viewed Verne as a great sportsman to whom he felt loyal. In fact, Vaziri's ties to the Gagne family were deep. Greg Gagne had been the best man when Khos married his Minnesota-bred wife, Caryl, and it was Verne's wife, Mary, who'd initially conceptualized the Iron Sheik character.

Feeling torn, Khos promised to call Gagne back within 24 hours and contacted Sergeant Slaughter — who, despite their bloody "Iran vs. USA" rivalry later on, was one of Vaziri's best friends. "I said, 'Oh, Mr. Sergeant, I have a problem . . .' He says, '$100,000 is nothing. We're going to make millions working with Vince.' So I told Mr. Gagne, 'No, I lose the match to Hulk Hogan.'"

He decided to keep the conversation a secret until he saw the McMahons at the Garden. The display of loyalty may have been one of the reasons that, even after the Iron Sheik developed a drug problem, Vincent Kennedy could never bring himself to permanently sever ties with him.

As Hogan entered the ring to the theme from *Rocky III*, "Eye of the Tiger," few in the capacity crowd were wondering how he'd fare in an actual shoot. Whether you believed it or not, this was sure to be a coronation. Although the Sheik had come to do the job, he performed the task with a dramatic flair, beating down the challenger before placing him in the Camel Clutch, the move that defeated Backlund. In a sight that would become common over the next few years, Hogan "Hulked up," his body shaking, fingers waving side to side, miraculously willing himself to rise from the mat with the Sheik desperately clinging to his back. Next, Hogan backed the Sheik into the corner, ramming his body against the turnbuckles. With the Iron Sheik helpless on the canvas, Hogan bounced off the ropes, leaped through the air and dropped a big knee on his antagonist.

Referee Jack Lotz banged his hand on the canvas — *one, two, three* — and the Garden erupted.

"Hulkamania is here!" Gorilla Monsoon shouted to TV viewers over the roar of the faithful.

Minutes later, the new titlist was being interviewed in the locker room by Mean Gene Okerlund when André the Giant suddenly lumbered into frame, dousing the victor with champagne and smiling broadly. "I am really proud of you," the Frenchman said in his deep voice.

In the run-up to *WrestleMania III*, this clip would be repeatedly shown to stress that, at one point, Hogan and André had been "like brothers."

When the fans filtered out of the Garden onto the streets of midtown Manhattan, reveling in the fact that they'd witnessed the start of a new era, Bill Apter pondered the situation from his apartment in Queens. One month after the ringside ban had been imposed, Apter knew that Vincent Kennedy McMahon was not going to change his mind. Still, he wanted some exclusive content of the new WWF kingpin.

"I call his hotel probably at one o'clock in the morning," Apter recounted. "They rang his room and he picked up — there were no cell phones. I told him what I wanted to do and he said, 'Where are you?' 'I'm home in Queens.' And he said, 'What time can you get here?' So I got on the subway and came to the hotel. I told him, 'You're going to get in trouble for doing this.' And he said, 'Just take the pictures.' I remember one shot I took of him, holding the belt and looking in the mirror.' It really captured something because it was the beginning of the whole Hulk Hogan period.

"When I spoke to him later, he said, 'You couldn't believe the damn heat I got from Vince for doing that.'"

CHAPTER 7

When Hogan returned to Madison Square Garden for his first title defense there against Paul "Mr. Wonderful" Orndorff, both Bill Apter and George Napolitano made sure that their magazines had a few freelance photographers hidden among the fans. "We had one guy from Britian who would wrap up a long lens in tin foil," Apter said. "When the usher asked him what it was, he'd say, 'It's a hero sandwich. I'm on a special diet and I can't eat the food here.'"

Occasionally, a security guard or WWF employee caught a shutterbug in the act and confiscated the film. But there were generally two or three others in the arena who escaped detection.

The Hulkster was already starting to generate mainstream interest, so the company was issuing credentials to photographers from the tabloids. "A lot of times, these guys would have a second camera to take extra pictures for us," Napolitano said. "I always knew who was shooting what, and where I could get extra pictures from."

Yet, because of their reputations within the industry, neither Bill nor George ever wanted to be seen firing off the clandestine photos themselves. "I just couldn't do that," Apter said. "It wouldn't make me look good. And, based on what his family created, I personally couldn't do that to Vince McMahon."

Outside the WWF, both wrestlers and promoters insisted that Vince had made a grave error by bestowing the championship on Hogan. A titlist was supposed to be a giant killer, the logic went, instilling hope in the fans by overcoming daunting challenges from much larger foes. Although the Hulkster looked great on the cover of a program, he was far better suited to be a number one contender. Booking him against smaller challengers would lead fans to believe that no one else could possibly win the belt. And that meant that the WWF's business was doomed to flounder.

At least, that's what these guys hoped.

Never once did McMahon buy into their fatalistic vision. He intended to blitz his rivals because *his* fans were investing in more than a championship. They were signing up for the cult of Hulkamania.

The rules about how things worked in the past were just that — the past. As Hogan would point out just prior to *WrestleMania III*, Hulkamania now stood as "the purest form of truth there is."

Within months of Hogan's victory, Ed Helinski had shifted over from editing the company's magazine to overseeing merchandising. "Everything was focused on Hogan," he recalled, "red and yellow, the headbands, the posters, the foam fingers. Everything."

All the company needed to induce sales was to hand out merch to fans in the first two rows at television tapings. "Once those shows aired, orders were flooding in left and right."

In Helinski's place at the magazine came Ed Ricciuti, an ex-Marine, martial artist and boxing champion at Notre Dame who'd spent much of his career writing about conservation issues in developing countries. He'd developed a strong rapport with a former editor at *Outdoor Life* who was now working as a magazine consultant. When the *WWF Magazine* put out the word that it needed a new editor, the consultant recommended Ricciuti, primarily because of his familiarity with combat sports.

There were some obstacles, though. Ricciuti had never followed pro wrestling — he had a vague memory of possibly seeing a clip of former boxing champ Primo Carnera taking bumps after the mob had picked his pockets clean, a sad descent that inspired the movie *Requiem for a Heavyweight* — and he and Vince McMahon instantly disliked each other.

"I went to the interview and it was like being on trial. Vince and the other executives were sitting at one table and I was in front of them in a chair. And the first thing he says is, 'We wear ties here.' I didn't have a tie. He didn't like my beard either, or the fact that I insisted on working freelance. I'm an independent contractor and was not going full-time with anybody.

"When the interview was over, I said to myself, 'There's no way in a million years I'm going to work for this guy.' But they hired me. I have no idea why, but always figured they must have had some lousy candidates."

At first, Ricciuti reported directly to Linda McMahon, who was overseeing both the *WWF Magazine* and program. "I thought the world of her. Sometimes, Vince would storm into the office while we were working on the magazine, acting unusually aggressive, ripping everything apart. And she was my offensive line so I wouldn't get tackled. She was a diplomat, always knew what she was talking about and kept him off my back."

Future Canadian Football League (CFL) Hall of Famer Angelo Mosca was at the tail end of his wrestling career and knew Ricciuti from when their paths had crossed at Notre Dame. The first time that the new editor entered the dressing room, Mosca gave him an advantage that neither Ed Helinski nor Steve Taylor ever enjoyed. "He put his arm around me and said to everybody, 'Be nice to this guy. He's been in the ring.' That made a huge difference."

The mission of the *WWF Magazine* was furthering the storylines that were unfolding on television, and while Ricciuti sought feedback from many of the wrestlers about their characters, he mainly consulted with the road agents and invented the majority of the quotes.

But during his visits to the office, he noticed a unique phenomenon: Hogan and Vince huddling together, sometimes for hours. "There was a lot of creativity going back and forth, as if they were co-creators of what the WWF was turning into.

"And I honestly believe they were. For all my ill feelings for the guy, I really think that Vince was a friggin' genius. Everything that the WWF became was because of him. But he never could have taken it as far without Hogan. The WWF might have called the wrestlers 'superstars,' but Hogan was on a level far above everybody."

With Hogan at the helm, Vince could make the full push into the rival territories, realizing Verne Gagne's worst fears when he asked the Iron Sheik to break the Hulkster's leg. "The WWF would come to Denver, and it looked more like the AWA than we did," Greg Gagne said.

"When you saw Vince's father's shows, they were top heavy — a lot of big names in the main matches," observed Jerry Brisco, the former co-holder of the NWA World Tag Team Championship now transitioning to a backstage role for the WWF. "Vince, almost from the opening match, was loaded. I'd never seen cards stacked with so many superstars in all my life."

And McMahon was just getting started.

Montreal had been a hotbed of wrestling since the time of the Great Depression, with French Greco-Roman gold medalist Henri Deglane winning a version of the world championship there in 1931 and the "French Canadian Lion" Yvon Robert drawing large crowds, starting in 1936. By the early 1970s, rival promotions All-Star and Grand Prix Wrestling — run respectively by prominent Quebecois families, the Rougeaus and Vachons — were each holding summer events at the home of baseball's Montreal Expos, Jarry Park. But, long-term, the overexposure ended up jeopardizing both companies and, within a few years, each was out of business.

In 1980, André the Giant, who'd embraced Montreal as his adopted home after leaving his native France, his real-life manager Frank Valois and local star Gino Brito started a group they called Promotions Varoussac, based on their actual last names — "va" for Valois, "rouss" for André Roussimoff and "ac" for Louis Gino Acocella. Playing off the same Quebec pride as their predecessors, major storylines often centered on international stars journeying to the province to clash with its best talent.

This included a collision between André and Hulk Hogan at the Paul Sauvé Arena in 1980, the promotion's first sellout, sparked after the Hulkster pulverized local icon Édouard Carpentier on Bastille Day in 30 seconds.

As Vince expanded, though, André sold his shares in Varoussac in 1984 to Quebec City–bred main-eventer Rick Martel and promoter Tony Mule. Brito's longtime tag team partner, Dino Bravo, owned another percentage. Under the new leadership, the company was renamed Lutte Internationale

(International Wrestling). But McMahon was never far from anybody's thoughts. For one thing, he ended the talent-sharing agreement that existed under his father. And before the end of 1984, the promotion's announcers Guy Hauray and Carpentier were snatched up by the WWF for its French-language broadcasts.

In May, Montreal-born wrestler, announcer and WWF power broker Pat Patterson organized a television taping in the Montreal suburb of Verdun, planting the company flag in the core of La Belle Province. Apparently, Gino Brito's late father, Jack Britton, who'd booked a traveling ensemble of midget wrestlers — the popular term at the time — had had a great deal of clout in the city, enabling his son to appeal to the management of Montreal Forum, home of hockey's Montreal Canadiens, to prevent a WWF incursion in the fabled building.

But Jacques Rougeau Jr. — whose father and uncle had run All-Star Wrestling — decided to appear on the renegade show. It stemmed from a falling out he'd had with Dino Bravo about the way he and his brother Ray were positioned on Lutte Internationale cards. "I thought Dino was misusing me. He was pushing himself and Rick Martel in main events, and Raymond and I were in the middle of the cards. They'd have us booked in the third or fourth match, but sometimes, on the night of the show, they'd switch us to the main event. But they still paid us third or fourth match money. So I got tired of it."

He'd quit and was wrestling in Mobile, Pensacola and other cities in the region for Southeastern Championship Wrestling when Patterson reached out and invited him to the Verdun event. "My dad was good friends with Gino and did not want Jacques wrestling for the opposition," Ray said. "He was afraid that eventually, yes, Vince would put the Montreal office out of business and take over."

When Jacques landed at Dorval airport, his father was waiting to drive him to the family home before the event. But even as they small-talked, the distress was evident in the senior Rougeau's voice. "He begged me not to do the match. 'You're going to kill the territory here.' I said, 'Well, the way I was being promoted by Dino, I was being killed anyway. Maybe now, I'll finally be promoted properly. I'm doing the match.'"

With the network of informants Vince had around the territories, the promoter knew that there were Jacques Rougeaus everywhere, just waiting for the opportunity to shine and be compensated for it. "Everybody said Vince stole talent," Brisco maintained. "He didn't steal anything. He went out, gave these guys an opportunity and paid them more money than they'd ever made in their lives. If that's stealing, I don't know. Maybe the other promoters should have just taken care of their talent."

CHAPTER 8

As the World Wrestling Federation office staff slowly grew, Vince impressed upon everyone that their success was predicated on the power of television. "I remember him telling me about how TV deals were done, and the importance of having a presence on the local stations in each market," Ed Helinski recounted. "He said, 'Give me three weeks of television and I can make a star out of anybody.'"

Considering the many performers who appeared on WWF television and did *not* transform into headliners, the statement reflects a degree of grandiosity. But for Jimmy Hart, the way Vince presented his talent placed him in a category separate from most other promoters. "You take a wrestler and put him on two different TV shows," said the manager. "He looks the same. He talks the same. He dresses the same. What's the difference? The production. Production can make you look bigger than life."

But production means little without exposure. And McMahon had no reluctance about spending money to get new eyes on his product. He particularly savored arrangements that undercut his rivals. "We had been working with a strong television station in San Francisco for three years," said the AWA's Greg Gagne. "It took us three years to really build up the interest, and we had a big show coming up. So we were planning to take six weeks of TV to really get the fans involved, slowly working up to the show.

We sent our tapes over ahead of time with our interviews just for the San Francisco market.

"We aired the first week of TV and announced a few matches. Then, the station manager calls me, 'Hey Greg, we got a call from Vince McMahon. He just bought the time slot. He's paying us two grand a month.'

"And I said, 'Wait, wait a minute. We're putting on this show, and we had an agreement.' 'Yeah, but you're not paying anything.' So I said, 'Give me a few minutes.'

"I called Verne and told him what was going on. And he said, 'Call him back and say, 'We'll give him $2,500.' And the guy agrees. Fifteen minutes later, I get another call and he says, 'Vince will do three grand.' I said, 'Okay, $3,500. Done. Done deal. Now, put our tapes on for next week.'

"But our TV show never played. Vince offered him five grand a month. And the station put on their show and took ours off and didn't even tell us."

Yet, Vince's expansion plans included more than syndicated television.

Although certain wrestling programs were seen in locations far from the respective promotion's home base, there had not been anything close to a national broadcast since 1955, when Chicago promoter Fred Kohler's *Wrestling from Marigold* last appeared on the old Dumont Network. The situation changed in 1976 when Georgia Championship Wrestling (GCW) began airing on Ted Turner's Atlanta-based satellite network WTCG (later TBS).

The coast-to-coast visibility made GCW one of the most desirable territories to work. "Promoters everywhere would take interest in you," Raymond Rougeau remembered. "And because everyone wanted to work there, you'd be in the dressing room with Dusty Rhodes, Thunderbolt Patterson, Ole Anderson, Dick Slater — the biggest superstars in the business. I wrestled [future WWWF Heavyweight Champion] Superstar Billy Graham in Atlanta when I was 21 years old and would work out with Ricky Steamboat when we were both in the territory after he graduated from Verne Gagne's wrestling school.

"Even though the TV was in a small studio, the fans were loud and everyone was really working because they wanted to impress all those people watching. So you always came back from Atlanta knowing something you didn't know before."

Interestingly, the influx of all that high-profile talent did not always suit the Georgia mainstays. "It was not really the best thing for the local talent," noted Jerry Brisco. "Because there were two hours of TV every Saturday and you could only put so many matches on. So if the other territories are flying in their stars, the local guys are missing their chance to get on TV and work the bigger cards. And you'd hear it. 'Why are you booking Jerry Lawler and the Von Erichs instead of me, when I'm the one who's here all the time, going up and down these roads? They're coming in for the big house and I'm sitting at home.'"

Of course, that didn't really concern Vince McMahon. He understood the strategic importance of TBS and was familiar with both the Georgia talent and the territory's history, particularly a previous wrestling war that led to the TV slot being extended from one hour to two.

In addition to being a longtime headliner, Ray Gunkel was a booker and partner in the territory when he died in the dressing room following a match with Ox Baker in 1972. Although the 48-year-old Gunkel suffered from arteriosclerosis, a vascular disease that includes obstructed blood flow due to the buildup of plaque in the arteries, Baker would capitalize on the mishap, boasting that his heart punch had killed his opponent.

The fact that another wrestler, Alberto Torres, had passed away following a match with Baker — also from heart disease — the year before prompted some promoters to depict the menacing heel as an unrepentant serial murderer.

Despite Gunkel's successful tag team with Buddy Fuller, the two were both partners in the territory and business rivals. In fact, on the afternoon of the funeral, Fuller and his uncle Lester Welch were alleged to have been part of a cabal plotting a way to take control of the company by denying Gunkel's widow, Ann, a percentage.

A former fashion model, Ann was accustomed to evading the machinations of devious men. So she broke away from the NWA-affiliated territory and started her own group, the All-South Wrestling Alliance, taking 25 wrestlers and announcer Ed Capral with her, among others. In her years with Ray, she had befriended promoters throughout the circuit and managed to secure dates in Athens, Augusta, Carrollton, Savannah, Statesboro and Waycross. And she played off her friendship with Ted Turner to gain a spot on his television station.

Her hour-long program ran back-to-back with the NWA territory's 60-minute show.

She knew that the various NWA territories were going to be sending in their top talent to headline rival cards and demoralize her. She'd also heard that her wrestlers had been threatened about being blacklisted across the continent. So she went to the media and depicted the wrestling war as a battle of the sexes. In the *Atlanta Journal-Constitution*, she said that the NWA was actually an abbreviation for "no women allowed."

For a while, Ann thrived, even running shows in Florida and North Carolina, to the point that the established promotion was forced to cut ticket prices. Still, the sheer number of forces aligned against her was formidable.

As a wrestler, Jerry Brisco was admired for his technical prowess. But his reputation was nowhere close to that of his brother, Jack. Universally considered wrestling royalty, Jack was an NCAA Division I National Champion as well as a future NWA World Heavyweight titlist. Now, the Georgia territory offered both Briscos a share of the company. "That's how they'd keep guys loyal," Brisco said, "by giving them a stake. And then, they were never going to work for an outlaw. It was a very unique system because the territories protected each other, but when it's over and you won, you better be ready to filter out your territory because all the guys who helped you want to use your wrestlers."

Promoter Jim Barnett was lured all the way from Australia in exchange for a 10 percent share in both Georgia and Florida. While the offer might have appeared excessive, Barnett was a true influence peddler in the sport of kings, a flamboyant gay man who managed to not only prosper in a homophobic environment but evoke fear in those he'd placed on his enemies list.

On a personal level, he had no issues with Ann Gunkel. In fact, it had been Barnett who'd introduced her to Ray.

His authority extended far beyond wrestling, as evidenced by President Jimmy Carter — who once posed for a photo grinning and holding Georgia star Mr. Wrestling II in a headlock — appointing Barnett a member of the National Endowment for the Arts (NEA) in 1980. Yet, wherever the One True Sport was experiencing a boom period, Barnett seemed to be involved.

The Oklahoman's first foray into pro wrestling occurred in 1949 when he began working for what is generally characterized as the first wrestling magazine in the US, *Wrestling As You Like It*, published by promoter Fred Kohler in conjunction with his show on the DuMont Network.

After learning the industry from Kohler, Barnett branched off on his own, becoming a co-owner of the NWA's Indianapolis territory in 1955, where he developed the first "studio wrestling" show, setting up a ring at the television station and surrounding it with a small, vocal group of fans.

In 1958, he formed a partnership with veteran promoter Johnny Doyle. Together, they invested in promotions in such cities as Denver, Detroit and Los Angeles. But when the press heard that Barnett might have been pimping out members of the University of Kentucky football team to a select clientele that included actor Rock Hudson, he and Doyle divested their Indianapolis and Detroit operations and shifted operations to Australia.

Far away from US investigators, the pair ran one of the most professional promotions in the world, cycling North American wrestlers in and out of the continent. The group, called World Championship Wrestling (WCW) — a name Barnett would bring back with him to the United States — flew its talent everywhere. After a large arena show in Melbourne each Saturday night, WCW taped a studio TV show in the city the next morning, then continued on to Perth on Monday, Adelaide on Tuesday and Brisbane on Wednesday, where they'd stay overnight. After taping another television program in Brisbane on Thursday, the crew flew to

Sydney for a Friday card, did TV there the next morning and started the routine all over again.

During its boom period, WCW sold out everywhere, and Barnett — who became the head of the company after Doyle retired in 1968 — ran tours of Indonesia, Singapore, Malaysia and Hong Kong, where the television stations dubbed the shows into the local language.

"I had some very strict rules," Barnett told Canadian journalist and author Greg Oliver. "They had to wear coats and ties on airplanes. They couldn't drink. They had to be gentlemen. They had to pay their bills . . . I wanted to make sure I had a promotion I could be proud of."

When a new government came in and mandated that Barnett take on Australian partners, though, he was ready to return to the US. As it turned out, this was the same period when Florida and Georgia promotions co-owner Eddie Graham contacted Barnett and asked for help against Ann Gunkel.

"Eddie Graham wanted Barnett there because he could do things politically that no one else could," said Cowboy Bill Watts, who also had a percentage of the Georgia territory.

Barnett utilized a multipronged approach to winning the wrestling war, relying on his wide network of contacts to bar Ann from arenas. Meanwhile, the GCW partners — who'd been flying in the biggest stars in the continent — not only restricted talent they knew from the other NWA territories from working for All-South but convinced wrestlers affiliated with outside promotions to stay away. In one instance, Bruno Sammartino was advertised to appear at an All-South show. But before he could board his flight, both Bill Watts and Vincent James McMahon reportedly beseeched him not to come.

When he didn't turn up, Ann was forced to refund thousands of dollars to disappointed attendees.

Soon, even members of the All-South roster were no-showing. After waging a spirited fight, Ann had little choice but to surrender in 1974, selling her assets to — who else? — Jim Barnett.

Most significantly, the back-to-back television programs on Ted Turner's station became one solid two-hour GCW bloc — a rarity in a time when few wrestling programs extended beyond 60 minutes. It would be a new decade before the slot on "America's Superstation" took on added worth when Vince McMahon decided to use every means at his disposal to grab it.

Of course, Jim Barnett was involved in *that*, too.

In 1982, GCW began expanding outside of its traditional territory, promoting cards in Ohio and Michigan — a region left largely unattended after the original Sheik Ed Farhat's promotion had flamed out.

"This was a big money drain," Jerry Brisco explained. "For us to get into a building, we'd have to pay back part of the money the Sheik owed them."

Because of the financial strain, the territory began attracting "lower-profile talent, not the top-tier talent like before. Our territory was hurting, and [booker] Ole Anderson was making a lot of excuses about why things weren't working. But Jack and I saw what was happening."

The departure of Rowdy Roddy Piper to the WWF in 1983 "had been a tipping point for us. Roddy was our money guy. We lost him and we knew we were going to have more troubles."

Even before Jack Brisco captured the NWA World Heavyweight Championship, the Briscos were accustomed to being farmed out around the country. "We didn't mind because we were getting sent to the big shows. So we did alright."

Now, as the pair worked the other regions, they inquired about whether anyone was interested in their Georgia points. They'd yet to receive a serious offer.

Simultaneously, Barnett — who was accustomed to coming out on the winning side of things — knew that his differences with Ole Anderson left him with little choice but to exit. While the Briscos imagined ambitious Charlotte promoter Jim Crockett Jr. playing savior, Barnett was eyeing Vince McMahon.

Privately, he made his own arrangement with the brash promoter but maintained back-channel communication with allies in Georgia. Since he was now part of the WWF, he wanted his new boss to gain control of the territory but understood that the deal could not go through unless Jack and Jerry were involved.

While cutting promos in Charlotte one day, the talent started gossiping about an injury Piper had recently sustained. "He went to grab a table or something, and back then, nothing was filed down," Brisco said. "He cut a couple of fingers right down to the bone. And we heard he might lose a finger."

But because Piper was traveling so often, none of the guys in Charlotte had been in touch with him since the episode occurred. As the Briscos discussed the matter in Jim Crockett's office, Jack offered a suggestion.

"Let's call Vince."

Crockett shook his head. "I'm not calling him."

"I will."

As it turned out, McMahon was sitting in his office when Jack phoned from Crockett's desk. "Jack explained that we were curious about Piper. Vince asked where we were, and Jack told him. And then, Vince said, 'Okay, just answer yes or no to my questions. Would you guys be interested in talking to me?' Because Vince knew we were shopping our stock. He was plugged into what was going on."

From his seat across from his brother, Jerry watched Jack's eyes light up.

On their day off the following week, the Briscos caught a flight to LaGuardia Airport, where McMahon was waiting for them. Right there, he made the offer to buy the pair's stock.

There was another loose end to clear up. Aging promoter Paul Jones — not to be confused with the wrestler of the same name — had been a partner in the Georgia office since 1944. Given his recent health ailments, his wife had power of attorney over his affairs. Back in Georgia, the brothers secretly met with the couple and brought up the financial issues they largely blamed on Ole. All agreed that if they didn't make a change, they'd lose whatever they invested. "Paul Jones was the key to the whole deal," Jerry said.

Before Ole realized what had occurred, Georgia had been sold out from under him.

Bizarrely, the Briscos were expected to honor their commitments for the next few weeks. "Even though we'd double-crossed them, they still expected us to finish out our dates. We heard our lives were in danger. We had a body shop in Tampa and someone called our partner there and said, 'Expect them to screw you, too.' And our wives got calls that we were having affairs and had kids all over the place."

While changing into their gear in Cleveland, prior to a match with the powerhouse tandem of the Road Warriors, the Briscos were interrupted by a referee who told Jerry that Joe Laurinaitis (Road Warrior Animal) wanted to speak to him. "We used to do everything to keep kayfabe," Brisco explained. "Heels got ready in one area, babyfaces in another. That's why he sent the referee and didn't come himself."

Fearing an attack, Jerry asked his brother to accompany him to the meeting spot. "When we got there, Joe was nervous. He said, 'Look, you guys have always treated us right and we respect you. So I want you to know what's going down. Guys are being offered bounties — three to five thousand dollars, depending on whether they break your arm or break your leg. Please don't tell anybody I told you this.'"

For the next few days, the Briscos were wary every time that they were in the ring. Was someone going to come out of the dressing room and interfere in the match, legitimately diving off the turnbuckles onto one of the brothers when he had a foe in the Figure Four? "From Cleveland, we went to Michigan. We worked that loop and then we worked the Carolinas. And then, we were done, and we went home. And then we went to work for Vince.

"Nothing happened to us."

The Briscos did not arrive in the WWF empty-handed. Jerry said that they brought along George Scott, the highly respected former booker in the Charlotte territory who'd play a mammoth role in forging allegiances, acquiring talent and creating storylines through the first *WrestleMania*. McMahon had also requested an announcer. But the legendary Gordon Solie — the play-by-play man in Georgia and Florida — resisted the overture. "God bless him, he was so loyal," Brisco said. "He told Jack straight out, 'I won't do it. I'm not making the jump.'"

Solie's announcing partner, Freddie Miller, had no such qualms. When the World Championship Wrestling logo — as previously mentioned, Barnett transported the name to Georgia following the Australia run — was shown on TBS on July 14, 1984, fans saw Miller's familiar face, stick mic in hand, enthusing, "On behalf of WTBS, it's a pleasure to welcome the World Wrestling Federation. Exciting new matches, great competitors from all over the world. And here's the man to tell you all about it, Vince McMahon."

Wearing a cream-colored windowpane check suit, McMahon lumbered into frame, shook hands with Miller and looked into the camera: "It is indeed a pleasure to be associated with TBS and we promise to bring you the greatest in professional wrestling entertainment."

Entertainment? In the northeast, the term made longtime fans bristle. In the South, it produced apoplexy.

It didn't matter that Paul "Mr. Wonderful" Orndorff, the Iron Sheik and "Dirty" Dick Murdoch had all spent significant time in Georgia; Orndorff and the Sheik still lived there, and Murdoch had been marketed as a babyface dubbed "Captain Redneck." By barging onto TBS and performing for Vince, they'd discarded their Confederate grays for Union blue.

So traumatic was Ted Turner's decision to allow McMahon onto his airwaves that fans below the Mason-Dixon line gave the incident a name: Black Saturday.

As TBS coped with a flood of angry calls, executives examined the content of the new program. Instead of the traditional studio wrestling show that followers loved, viewers saw taped WWF matches from various arenas. And Gordon Solie was nowhere to be found.

Turner tried allaying the anger by granting a new group run by Ole and Columbus, Georgia, promoter Fred Ward an early morning time slot on Saturday — featuring the beloved Solie doing the play-by-play. Cowboy Bill Watts's exciting Mid-South program also appeared on the Superstation, becoming one of the network's highest-rated programs.

McMahon was furious. When he signed a deal with Turner, he did not expect a rival program to also air on TBS. Now there were two. And his ratings sucked.

Looking to cut his losses, he turned to the man who'd spent his career thriving on this type of turmoil.

It was one of the reasons Vince had hired Jim Barnett, who promptly — and probably gleefully — reached out to Jim Crockett.

Jim Crockett Sr. and Vincent James McMahon had been both adversaries and allies. Now, their sons were doing business, but under the tensest of circumstances. In 1985, Jimmy — as the younger Crockett was colloquially known — signed over a check to Vince for a million dollars. Crockett got the two-hour slot. McMahon pledged to use the infusion of cash to destroy the Charlotte-based promoter.

No one was more stunned by the news than Bill Watts, who said he'd been given every indication that the success of the Mid-South show would lead to something permanent: "I made a deal with Turner to take over all wrestling on TBS. I even bought a bigger airplane so I could transport our key people back and forth. And then the next thing I know, Turner is loosey goosey, Crockett's got the deal, and I'm out."

Because of its roots in the carnival, pro wrestling had been the domain of cagey families like the McMahons, the Cricketts, the Gagnes, the Fullers, the Welches, the Rougeaus and the Von Erichs — men who not only worked the fans but manipulated each other. And now, here was Turner — an Ivy League–educated Episcopalian — out-carnying everyone.

But given McMahon's imperial designs, Jim Crockett's brother David argued that doing an end-run around Watts was the company's most logical option. "It was the only way we could truly survive."

The Black Saturday episode was one of the few during this period in which the McMahon playbook worked against him. As David Crockett noted, had Vince been able to successfully occupy Georgia, the other NWA promotions might have fallen quicker.

In terms of the pledge to annihilate Jim Crockett, the Charlotte promoter would not be neutralized to Vince's satisfaction until the aftermath of *WrestleMania III*.

CHAPTER 9

T hose who'd been watching the ascent of Jim Crockett Jr. were not surprised to see him take advantage of the Black Saturday controversy and emerge with the TBS slot. The irony was that his plan had never been to run Mid-Atlantic Wrestling, a.k.a. the Charlotte territory, at all. Everyone in the family understood that the spot was reserved for his brother-in-law, John Ringley. But Ringley's marriage to Jimmy's sister, Frances, hadn't lasted. And when the patriarch of the Crockett clan, Jim Sr. (or "Big Jim"), passed away in 1973, his 28-year-old son was handed the keys.

For someone who'd rarely expressed interest in professional wrestling, he became comfortable in his new position, savoring the way older veterans of the game treated him with the deference once reserved for his father. But he realized that he would not be able to hold onto that power without consistently earning their respect — an objective he accomplished by forming a bond with another young man who'd end up as his chief moneymaker. Not only could "Nature Boy" Ric Flair ignite an arena just by walking the aisle in his dazzling robe and throwing back his peroxide locks, but when he worked outside the territory, he was a great evangelist for Mid-Atlantic, convincing other major names to join the troupe.

Now that Jimmy had those two hours of Saturday TV, it appeared that Vincent Kennedy McMahon was not the only one capable of reinventing the industry. Regardless of where the business shifted within the next few years, it would clearly bear little resemblance to the worlds in which the two promoters came up.

Although Big Jim had also promoted minor league baseball and hockey, concerts and theater, he'd been involved in the wrestling business in the Carolinas and Virginia since 1933, when he purchased an old warehouse in Greensboro and renamed it the Sportsrena. In 1963, after Vincent James McMahon had splintered off from the NWA, the older Crockett attempted to raid New York City, holding cards at Sunnyside Garden in Queens headlined by his new business partner, Antonino Rocca. Rocca had been a Madison Square Garden main-eventer until being displaced at the top by Bruno Sammartino. Because of his Italian birth and Argentinian upbringing, he was a bona fide ethnic hero, the pride of both Italians and Latinos in the city. With a powerful sponsor, Schaefer Beer, and a strong TV station bolstering the promotion, events — consisting largely of Spanish speakers based in the New York area, Mid-Atlantic staples and former Capitol Wrestling stars like Cowboy Bob Ellis and Karl von Hess — drew interest for a brief period.

Unlike Ann Gunkel, who — despite her wits, ingenuity and exposure to the business through her husband — was very much a rookie when she went against the NWA, Vincent James McMahon was a true magnate who, in his understated way, could get people to do as he wished. In response to the threat from Big Jim, he loaded up his Madison Square Garden shows with such names as Gorilla Monsoon, Killer Kowalski, the Fabulous Kangaroos, Bobo Brazil, the Tolos Brothers, Pedro Morales and Miguel Pérez. By contrast, the Sunnyside Garden events were filled out with the likes of Pepe Figueroa, Gino Lanza and Freddie Ortiz, and the group quickly gained a reputation as a federation of jobbers.

It did not take Big Jim long to pull out, leaving Rocca treading water until he closed less than a year after he started.

Since it was the wrestling business — where everyone was trying to figure out an angle to fleece his buddy — the acrimony between Vincent James and Big Jim dissipated over time, leading to talent trades and declarations of solidarity.

Like Vincent Kennedy McMahon, Jim Crockett Jr. saw his stewardship of the family business as an opportunity to take the company to places his father couldn't fathom. He accomplished this by doling out another million dollars to purchase a mobile television production unit and packing theaters and arenas for the promotion's annual closed-circuit spectacular, *Starrcade*, starting in 1983 — two years before the first *WrestleMania*. In a forerunner to *WrestleMania 2* — which, as you'll read later, emanated from three separate venues — the 1985 version of *Starrcade*, headlined by Ric Flair defending his NWA World Heavyweight Championship against Dusty Rhodes, would be broadcast from both the Greensboro Coliseum in South Carolina and Omni in Atlanta.

The purchase of the TBS slot allowed Crockett and his booker Rhodes to consolidate the Charlotte and Atlanta promotions into one big territory and launch a yearly summer tour, the Great American Bash, across much of the collective real estate.

Given the hostility that southern fans had directed at the WWF following Black Saturday, the enlarged version of Jim Crockett Promotions (JCP) appeared fully capable of staving off whatever offensive Vince was planning. "We had stations in the Carolinas and Virginia that were very loyal to us," said Jimmy's brother David Crockett, an announcer on the Charlotte show. "We aired right before the local news and had fantastic ratings. Vince came in, offering them money, and they wouldn't budge."

To wrestling purists, the faster-paced JCP product was superior to the WWF's character-driven presentation. But Vince was working on cultivating a new type of wrestling fan whose tastes were predicated on factors besides work rate. "You'd think that if you were giving people better matches, it would pay off in the end," noted *Wrestling Observer Newsletter* founder Dave Meltzer. "I'd watch Ric Flair and it was usually a great match. Then, I would go to a Hulk Hogan match, and it wasn't great. Like, he couldn't go 30 minutes in the ring, non-stop, like Ric Flair. But the people would come back. And when the NWA would return to the same town, not as many people came back. And that's when it started hitting me that the WWF guys had star power, and the average person saw them as the major league."

And although Vince lost the most recent Battle of Atlanta, he'd been targeting Jimmy Crockett on multiple fronts. Yes, hitting him from the south turned out to be a miscalculation. But McMahon was also going after his rival's northern flank.

In 1983, longtime Toronto promoter Frank Tunney passed away during a leisure trip to Hong Kong. He'd soon be replaced by his nephew, Jack. This was an important development since, like Vince McMahon, Jimmy Crockett was very much a colonizer and had worked with Frank Tunney to build a base north of the border.

Just as Madison Square Garden was the crown jewel for the McMahons, Toronto's Maple Leaf Gardens was the focal point for all activity in the Tunney family empire. In the '40s and '50s, the territory was largely centered on local hero Whipper Billy Watson, a charismatic worker as well as a sharp businessman who owned pieces of other promotions. For an eight-month period in 1956, he toured everywhere as the NWA World Heavyweight Champion.

From a historical perspective, a far more important event occurred in Maple Leaf Gardens on January 24, 1963, when Lou Thesz defeated "Nature Boy" Buddy Rogers for the title. The switch was seen as an effort to chip away at the dominance of Vincent James McMahon and his partner Toots Mondt, since they managed Rogers's bookings and tended to keep him within the borders of their large territory.

Not willing to cede control, McMahon and Mondt spread the word that the title change didn't count since it occurred after a single fall rather than a two-out-of-three fall contest. The episode spurred the pair into quitting the NWA and recognizing Rogers as the first WWWF Heavyweight Champion.

Ironically, most of the new league's title matches were one-fall affairs.

Regardless, were it not for that one match in Toronto, the WWWF likely would not exist. Which, in terms of this book, means that there never would have been a *WrestleMania III*.

In time, Toronto served as a neutral zone where the NWA, AWA and WWF belts were all defended in Maple Leaf Gardens. In 1978, Frank

Tunney and Jim Crockett formed a partnership, with Charlotte booker George Scott — who'd grown up in Hamilton, Ontario — overseeing the plotlines in the territory and a sizeable share of the Mid-Atlantic talent flying in for shows. But the copasetic relationships with the other promotions also continued. At one point, Dino Bravo's Canadian Heavyweight Championship was recognized by the NWA, AWA and WWF. And in 1979, WWF titlist Bob Backlund and AWA kingpin Nick Bockwinkel battled to a double countout in Toronto in what was billed as a unification match.

Both Vincent Kennedy McMahon and Jim Crockett Jr. attended Frank Tunney's funeral. But the cordiality faded after Jack Tunney signed a deal with McMahon in 1984. On TV, he'd be anointed WWF president — a worked position — while legitimately serving as the head of the company's Canadian operations.

All he had to do was ditch Crockett.

While the Canadian Heavyweight Championship was vacated, the territory's television show, *Maple Leaf Wrestling*, continued, requiring the WWF wrestlers to travel to Ontario every three weeks for tapings. In 1986, the WWF simply aired matches from a mix of locations on the program, editing in a match or two from Maple Leaf Gardens as well as an update on the Canadian scene from Billy Red Lyons, a former wrestler who assisted Tunney in the Toronto office.

In Charlotte, the loss of an essential piece of the company's realm was deeply felt, leading JCP employees to second-guess Jimmy's plan to establish a foothold in other locales. "You couldn't just go into a place and tape TV," David said. "You'd need to have a couple of houses there to pay for it. And now, we were thinking, 'Someone's going to stick me in the back.' You get things going. And then, you worry about another guy like Tunney saying, 'I'm going with Vince now.'"

CHAPTER 10

With the exception of the Dallas Cowboys, in the early 1980s, no institution embodied Texas pride as much as World Class Championship Wrestling (WCCW).

Or, more specifically, the Von Erich brothers.

Initially known in wrestling as a goose-stepping Nazi in the decades after World War II, the patriarch of the clan, Fritz von Erich (his real name was Jack Adkisson), rebranded himself as a Scripture-quoting family man after purchasing a share of the promotion in 1966. Three years later, he became the sole owner of the operation as well as the company's home arena, the "world-famous Dallas Sportatorium."

There were six boys in the family. The first, Jack Jr., died in a freak accident in 1959 at age six in upstate New York, where Fritz was wrestling at the time. Knocked out by an electric jolt from a loose cable, the boy fell unconscious into a melting pile of snow and drowned. His brothers lived in the shadow of that trauma, reliving the pain through their parents' sorrow, although, on the surface, they seemed to push it behind them. In Fritz's native Texas, they thrived as high school athletes, living on a 115-acre spread Fritz had built for the family near Lake Dallas.

By the '80s, David, Kevin and Kerry von Erich were superstars in WCCW and celebrities throughout North Texas, with each assigned a specific role. "Kerry was a knockoff of Conan the Barbarian, with the hairdo and chiseled body like Arnold Schwarzenegger," remembered WCCW producer Keith Mitchell. "David was the Texas cowboy and actually lived the lifestyle, riding horses on his ranch. And Kevin wrestled barefoot and was like a jungle boy."

In a region peppered with churches, the fan base wholeheartedly believed — in the Lord and the One True Sport. "It was real wrestling to the fans," said WCCW television director Dan Bynum. "They were so rabid about the babyfaces that young girls would try to tear off their ring robes and grab them and kiss them. The heels needed bodyguards because they were literally in danger of being stabbed."

Both babyfaces and heels tended to be young, handsome and hard partying. Yet, for all the decadence that occurred after hours, there was an overall Christian tone to the show, with the Von Erichs telling interviewers about their personal relationships with God and an unofficial World Class chaplain, Gary Holder, backstage, leading prayers.

None of that was unusual for Bynum. The Dallas station that aired the show was owned by televangelist and Christian Broadcasting Network (CBN) founder Pat Robertson, who'd received it as a donation. While covering other sports for Channel 39, Bynum was accustomed to daily prayer meetings.

"One time, we were covering a Texas Tech basketball game. It was during the winter and there was an ice storm. On the way back from Lubbock, the driver rolled the production truck off the highway and totaled the truck. So when insurance paid up and a new, refurbished production truck arrived, we had to go out into the parking lot and stand in a circle around it and pray over it. That was the environment at the station."

But Bynum, a Methodist preacher's son from East Texas, knew that, professionally, he was moving in the direction he needed to go — since his first job in broadcast TV consisted of literally pulling camera cable through fresh manure at a rodeo. Before the cable television penetration that would define the early *WrestleMania* years, Channel 39 was one of just six stations in Dallas and commanded a large share of the market. There, Bynum honed his skills doing remote production for college football, basketball, baseball, track, swimming and gymnastics. "We always figured out where to put the cameras and the microphone so we could get the most impact for whatever sport we were covering."

When Fritz von Erich decided that he wanted a syndicated show to spread his following far outside of Dallas, he came to Channel 39, where "we had people with big ideas about how syndication should work."

The Sportatorium was a metallic, amphitheater-style building that had been the home to *Big D Jamboree*, a country music radio show from 1948 to 1966. "It was not air-conditioned at all and poorly heated," Bynum said. "So it was freezing in the winter and in the extremes of summer, they'd leave the doors open just to get some ventilation in there. But when they started having wrestling there on Friday nights, the fans didn't care. It was a huge success."

Bill Mercer, the station's general manager as well as a World Class announcer, encouraged the crew to capitalize on both the Sportatorium's homey optics and the enthusiasm of the faithful in the audience. "Mini cams had just come out," recalled Mitchell, who'd studied cinematography at Stephen F. Austin State University in Nacogdoches, Texas. "So we weren't restricted by just having one hard [stationary] camera on the ring. We did the wrestling show like any other sports production."

Between the innovative skills of the staff, the youth and exuberance of the roster and the creative mind of WCCW booker Gary Hart — a heel manager who tended to end up having his head squeezed in an iron claw delivered by one of the Von Erichs — the company was entering a boom period. One of the more memorable angles took place on Christmas night, 1982, when Kerry challenged Ric Flair for his NWA title at Dallas's Reunion Arena. The match had a compelling backstory. After retaining his championship through devious means in the past, the Nature Boy would be forced to face Von Erich in a steel cage. To further enhance the challenger's chances, the referee would be someone the fans selected in a write-in poll. By an overwhelming majority — or so followers were told anyway — Michael Hayes, leader of the popular trio the Freebirds, was appointed to the position.

Although the Freebirds and Von Erichs were allies, there appeared to be friction between Kerry and Hayes during the match — particularly after the arbiter encouraged the sportsmanlike contender to break the rules. Then, in a move few saw coming, Hayes's Freebird buddy Terry "Bam Bam" Gordy slammed the cage door on Kerry's head, rendering him unable to continue.

For the next few years, the Von Erichs and Freebirds would violently clash around the horn, maintaining fan interest by adding stipulations and nuances to the feud.

The rivalry was enriched by production elements that had not been widely seen in pro wrestling. News packages and vignettes were pre-produced and rolled into the show. "Just by having the ability to have a mini cam on someone's shoulder gave us a freedom of movement that added to the energy," Mitchell said.

Bynum described the two principal cameramen, Victor Sosa and Oswald Coleman, as "fearless" and "integral to the success of WCCW. They were able to stand on the lip of the ring apron and get these incredible shots. Of course, each handheld camera had a shotgun mic on it. We also had mics on all the corners and a microphone under the ring. When guys were slammed into the corners, you'd hear the turnbuckles rattling."

There was one more component that differentiated World Class from more archaic wrestling programs. "Since we were a TV station, we had a universal copyright license for music," noted Bynum. "Back then, if you used copyrighted music, all you had to do — since you paid the universal fee — was report what you used and the station paid the cumulative amount. So we were using popular music as entrance music."

That touch would be replicated in the WWF. Only Vince McMahon, in his zest to outdo what everyone else was doing, hired his own composers so the arrangements belonged to him.

World Class was so hot that McMahon dispatched Steve Taylor to Texas to work on a feature for the company's new magazine. "I spent a couple of days with the Von Erichs, in Fritz's house, hanging out with Kerry, taking pictures all around the farm," he recounted. "It was impressive. When we'd be anywhere in public, the Von Erichs were superheroes."

In this instance, Taylor was not given the special directions he'd received before his trip to Chicago to cover the AWA. He was simply informed that, since the WWF had a national magazine, they needed to cover the wrestling scene everywhere — no subterfuge necessary. Told years later that many suspected that Vince's true motive was ingratiating himself to Fritz and eventually luring the family into the WWF camp, the photographer replied, "Sounds right."

But, in World Class, a big piece of paradise was about to disappear.

Of all the Von Erichs, David was arguably the brother who'd taken best to the wrestling business. "He was probably the only one who really wanted to wrestle," said Mitchell. "Kevin was a great wrestler, but he wanted to move to Hawaii and snorkel. Kerry had the look and charisma, but I don't think he would have gone into the business on his own."

Behind the scenes, David also seemed to have the best understanding of how the industry worked. Unlike his brothers, he'd journeyed outside the Dallas market and worked as a heel in Florida. Since the heels generally led the babyfaces through their matches, the experience had turned him into an astute ring general, spontaneously calling the spots — the step-by-step maneuvers — to build to the climax.

"It was very easy to see him taking over the territory from Fritz one day," Mitchell said.

Within the dynamic of the family, the elder brother's wisdom was both acknowledged and accepted. "He was more levelheaded," Bynum observed, "a good advisor to his brothers. He kept them grounded."

Then, on February 10, 1984, shortly after arriving in Tokyo for a tour with the All Japan Pro Wrestling promotion, 25-year-old David died in his hotel room. The Consular Report of Death Abroad provided by the US embassy listed the cause as ruptured intestines due to acute enteritis. Although drug rumors circulated throughout the industry, officially at least, there was nothing suspicious in his system.

"I fully believe that he was being groomed to take the NWA title from Ric Flair," Bynum said. "And he was going to be a great NWA Champion and lead WCCW to a level of international domination. So to lose David was crushing, not only to the family, but World Class as well."

The Dallas Metroplex was overcome with grief. Although a cloud of misery had been hanging over the Von Erich family since the time of Jack Jr.'s death, David's passing pushed their anguish into the public eye, sparking the chain of catastrophes that would induce Hollywood to tell a film version of the clan's gloomy story in *The Iron Claw* in 2023.

"I almost blew my fuckin' head off when David died," Kerry told John Clark in the *On the Mat* newsletter in 1992. "In fact, I would have been happy to. My brother Kevin felt the same way. My brother David was our whole world."

Some 5,000 people turned up for the funeral. Mitchell tried to honor David by purchasing yellow roses — as in the yellow rose of Texas — but couldn't find any. "All over North Texas, they'd already been bought."

By this point, a fourth wrestling brother had debuted. In 1983, 19-year-old Mike von Erich teamed up with Kevin and Kerry against Freebirds' Michael Hayes, Terry Gordy and Buddy Roberts. He'd been slowly learning on the job. But David's death pushed him into a position of prominence for which he wasn't prepared.

"Mike had been my production assistant," Mitchell recalled. "He liked production and would have been very happy working in TV for his entire career. He did not want to be a wrestler. But after David died, Fritz said, 'He looks the most like his brother. He's going to take his place.'"

Mike's talents were not developed enough for him to work main events or believably pursue Ric Flair's title. That slot was designated for Kerry. For weeks, the World Class TV show built interest in the inevitable clash between the Nature Boy and the Modern Day Warrior. It occurred on May 6, 1984, at Texas Stadium. Despite the broiling heat, some 32,000 fans came out for what was billed as the David von Erich Memorial Parade of Champions.

"That was one of the most important shows I ever directed," Bynum said. "It was the apex of WCCW. Everybody was so invested in hoping that Kerry could do what his brother had been denied by death."

Much of the crowd wept as a 12-year-old fan belted out a tune entitled "Heaven Needed a Champion":

And the songs we sing will all be forgotten too
But even then, the memory
Of David von Erich
Will be fresh and sweet and ever new.

"Everybody knew Kerry was going to win," said *Pro Wrestling Illustrated*'s Craig Peters, who was stationed at ringside beside Bill Apter and George Napolitano. "There was a lot of Japanese press with us. It was all hands on deck. It was over 100 degrees at ringside, and the crowd was as hot as I'd ever seen, popping for every move, even during the undercard matches."

The bout culminated with "Slick Ric" making multiple attempts to place Kerry in the figure-four leglock. On each occasion, the challenger kicked him away. When Flair tried a hip toss, Von Erich blocked it, got behind the champion, hooked their arms together and rolled him onto the canvas for the three count.

Kevin, Mike and younger brother Chris led a procession of babyfaces through the ropes to help the new titlist celebrate, as yellow roses were tossed onto the mat from all directions.

"When Kerry took the belt and held it up, I remember turning around and just seeing people openly crying," Peters said.

"You can't have that impact anymore," Bynum said, "because it was real. It was real to the fans. It was real to me. I wanted it to be real."

Kerry's title run would last less than three weeks; he'd lose the belt back to Flair in Yokosuka, Japan. But he still returned to Texas as a hero. Attendance levels remained high in World Class. And few imagined that the far-away WWF would ever pose much of a danger.

CHAPTER 11

Despite his setback with TBS, McMahon enjoyed a strong presence on cable due to his budding relationship with the USA Network. There, he hosted a unique program called *Tuesday Night Titans* (*TNT*), a spoof of a late-night talk show. Vince sat in the main chair with British-born retired grappler and announcer Lord Alfred Hayes playing his sidekick. Wrestlers and managers cycled through, cutting promos and performing skits, some of them so absurdly corny that viewers kept tuning in just to make sure the stuff they saw last time hadn't been part of a dream.

"It had all the earmarks of being a garden-variety talk show," said the WWF's vice president of television production, Nelson Sweglar. "Vince saw it as a nice promotional vehicle."

The show was shot at a studio Sweglar ran in the suburbs of Baltimore. The facility was also responsible for editing down matches from different arenas for the syndicated programs. When McMahon decided to open his own production space near his Connecticut headquarters, he persuaded Sweglar to come, too.

"He made me an offer I couldn't afford to refuse. So I was hired away from my own company."

Interestingly, at this stage, McMahon was so focused on luring people to his wrestling product that Sweglar said the promoter occasionally missed other revenue-gaining opportunities. "I noticed that we had some time available in the body of each of our syndicated shows that we could use to sell commercials. I sat down with him and said, 'There's three or four minutes every week that are yours. Sell the time. You can make money in each market.' And he wasn't interested. He said, 'We're in the wrestling business, not the TV business.' He was young and was trying to do so much at once. I guess he just didn't have the time to stop and even consider it."

He would not adhere to that philosophy for long.

The change came about as McMahon brought in employees from a variety of backgrounds and made himself amenable to their suggestions. As part of his larger plan, he was also doing business with people from outside industries who turned him on to their monetizing models.

And while he rejected allegiances with traditional wrestling promoters, he welcomed collaborations with executives who'd been successful in other forms of entertainment.

Most notably the music industry.

Together, they'd disrupt the landscape with a movement that became known as the Rock 'n' Wrestling Connection.

It all started on a flight to Puerto Rico, when singer Cyndi Lauper — whose 1983 debut solo album, *She's So Unusual*, was a worldwide hit — found herself beside "manager of champions" Captain Lou Albano. Unlike many of her peers, the Queens-bred Lauper viewed wrestling as physical theater and the performers as artists no different than herself. Her first video, "Girls Just Want to Have Fun," was about to be cast, and Lauper determined that Albano would be the ideal character to play her father alongside her real-life mother, Catrine.

In those days, one of the only places to see a music video was MTV, the music television network. "Girls Just Want to Have Fun" would win MTV's Best Female Video award in 1984, with Albano's prominence thrilling wrestling fans accustomed to the people they watched each week being relegated to the fringes of pop culture.

Not anymore.

Lauper was at the height of her fame, appearing twice on the cover of *People* magazine in 1984 and 1985, as well as the covers of *Rolling Stone*, *Time* and *Newsweek*. And she took pro wrestling along with her.

Or, more specifically, she took the WWF. For fans of MTV just discovering the sport of kings, Verne Gagne, Bill Watts and Jim Crockett Jr. might as well have not existed.

In May 1984, WWF fans were told that Lauper was going to make an appearance on Rowdy Roddy Piper's interview segment, "Piper's Pit," alongside Albano. When the world-famous singer actually showed up at Agricultural Hall in Allentown, fans collectively gasped and looked on in wonder.

At first, the villainous Piper showed surprising grace, complimenting Lauper on both her talents and appeal. But Albano changed the mood by boasting that, as her manager, he'd taken Cyndi "from nothing" to the heights of stardom.

"I love Lou," she corrected, looking over at Piper, "but he's not my manager."

Like any good wrestling angle, it all devolved from there.

Not only had Albano discovered Lauper in Queens, he insisted, but he'd written the lyrics of her hits "Girls Just Want to Have Fun" and "Time After Time."

Once again, Cyndi denied Albano's claims, triggering a sexist rant about how women like her belonged in the kitchen and pregnant. "No woman's ever accomplished anything without a man behind her."

When Piper reinforced the Captain's claims, Lauper had no apparent choice but to resort to violence. The segment ended with her tearing Hot Rod's shirt and hitting Albano over the head with her purse.

And that was just the beginning.

On July 23, 1984, Cyndi Lauper led Wendi Richter to the ring in Madison Square Garden to challenge the perennial Women's Champion, the Fabulous Moolah, in what was dubbed *The Brawl to End It All*. Of course, Moolah was managed by Albano. Lauper's involvement prompted MTV to broadcast the match live, enabling Vince to show non-fans all the fun they'd been missing.

"What other sport lets you kick a guy when he's down?" Bobby "The Brain" Heenan would ask *Sports Illustrated* in 1985.

Sports Illustrated? Bill Apter and George Napolitano might no longer have been welcome at ringside, but Vince made sure that the national and international press were treated as honored visitors.

Needless to say, everyone wanted to see the songstress get involved in the action, and she didn't disappoint, once again using her purse as a weapon, this time on Moolah. Just before the special went off the air, Cyndi and Richter were seen celebrating Wendi's title victory.

For those who hadn't bothered with professional wrestling before, a whole new world was opening up. And Lauper was doing her best to kick the door open a little wider.

When she accepted her Grammy for Best New Artist in 1985, she brought a special guest onstage, her "bodyguard" Hulk Hogan in a sleeveless tuxedo variation.

"Rock 'n' wrestling," he'd tell the media. "It's not a dream. It's the way we live."

Whether the Hulkster was shooting or working, Steve Taylor was certainly enjoying the ride that came with watching Vince live out the vision he'd described at their first meeting. "In those days, Vince would say to me, 'If we're not still having fun, we're getting out of this.' We didn't always have fun back then. But we definitely had a lot of it."

It wasn't fun for everybody.

The Brawl to End It All deeply rattled Jimmy Crockett at a time when McMahon was targeting both his syndicated network and talent. As previously mentioned, Crockett was more than willing to spend a few dollars to fight Vince but realized that he needed allies with the same goals. So together with Verne Gagne, Memphis promoter Jerry Jarrett and others, he founded a group called Pro Wrestling USA, staging super shows with their enlarged troupe of wrestlers.

Chicago White Sox minority owner Eddie Einhorn, who'd been involved in a previous effort to start a national pro wrestling league, lent his name to the project and arranged for the group to purchase a time slot on New York's WPIX TV.

"The logic behind it was all these promoters would get together and create these massive cards with all the stars we had," said Greg Gagne.

Collectively, they reasoned, they could neutralize Vince McMahon.

"We were at a meeting of all the non-WWE promoters," said announcer Jim "J.R." Ross. "We had a break and I headed off to the men's room. The rest of the guys followed suit a few minutes later. No one knew I was in the bathroom stall. They were all talking about the problems they had with Vince McMahon and one of the guys who shall remain nameless said, 'We can have him killed for several hundred thousand dollars.' Nobody else thought that was a great idea, obviously. They were looking for a solution to their problem and that was not a good one."

McMahon was accustomed to hearing about death threats and took them as seriously as his rivals' promises to work together. "In their first meeting, they all agreed they hated me and would do everything they could to put me out of business," he said at the time. "The second meeting, they couldn't even agree on where they should order lunch."

Still, the company's first show, a September 18, 1984, television taping in Memphis, did feature an impressive array of talent. "And then, it just all unraveled," said Pro Wrestling USA's live events promoter Gary Juster.

While not exactly born into the wrestling business, the circumstances of his birth kind of made Juster's later choices inevitable. As he left his mother's womb, his first encounter was with her OBGYN, Dr. Richard Reid Fliehr, father of Richard Morgan Fliehr — a.k.a. "The Nature Boy."

Growing up in the Twin Cities area, Juster became engrossed in the televised interactions between Verne Gagne, the Crusher, Mad Dog Vachon, the Kalmikoff Brothers, Stan "The Big K" Kowalski and Tiny Mills.

"They only had about four or five stations back then, and the show from Minneapolis drew very good ratings," he recalled. "What they would then do was they would bicycle the tapes, as they used to call it, to, say, a station in Milwaukee. And the station in Milwaukee would air the show about a week later, and then, bicycle the tape to Madison. So everything was like a week behind the other one. Milwaukee was a week behind Minneapolis. Madison was a week behind Milwaukee."

The fans never knew, unless a kid from Milwaukee was visiting his grandmother in Madison and began calling the spots and the finishes from her living room couch.

At age 15, Juster came up with a novel concept for raising money for his Jewish youth group: contacting the AWA and working out a deal for the promotion to stage a fundraising event at a local school. The show worked out so well that the next year, as junior class president of Golden Valley High School, he promoted a second card.

"I was the ring announcer. There was no way they were going to let me into the dressing room with them."

Still, the kid hadn't skimmed a dime, which apparently made him an exception in the business he aspired to enter. He continued monitoring the AWA closely, waiting for the next opportunity to arise.

It came when he was 19, home for the summer from George Washington University and glancing through the Minneapolis Twins yearbook. "One page would have a picture of Harmon Killebrew and a short description, and then there'd be another page for Bob Allison, and I thought, 'Why not do this for wrestling?' I took the idea to my uncle, who was a printer, and he volunteered and did a sample page for me."

By now, he'd managed to befriend Nick Bockwinkel and, when they next saw each other at a TV taping at the WTCN studio, Juster handed him the mock-up. "He thought it was a great idea. But everything was strictly kayfabe back then, and he didn't even want to tell me that Verne owned the territory. He just said, 'You need to present this to Verne Gagne because he's the World Champion. He has a lot of influence around here.' And Verne took a liking to me and a buddy of mine who had a camera, and we did the yearbook."

When he returned to college in Washington, DC — where the WWWF was headquartered at the time — he contacted Gagne about making an introduction to Vincent James McMahon. Gagne obliged, and "I did a WWWF yearbook with a very talented friend from Minneapolis I convinced to come out for a few weeks. He liked it so much that he never went back."

And while he quickly left the wrestling business, the friend, Gary Halvorson, did become a well-known entity in the entertainment field, directing simulcasts of the New York Metropolitan Opera, the Macy's Thanksgiving Day Parade and episodes of *Friends* and *Everybody Loves Raymond*.

Juster kept his focus on wrestling. After graduating from law school, he reached out to the elder McMahon for a job. In a fatherly manner, the promoter lectured, "Stay away from wrestling. Practice law. Wrestling is like drugs, prostitution and pornography. You should do better things."

The recent graduate knew McMahon was right. But he was too strung out on the One True Sport to even consider detoxification.

He practiced law but didn't really like it. Then, in the early '80s, upon learning about a new television station starting in Baltimore, he met with the program director and suggested a wrestling show for the noon spot on Saturday. Not having much else to showcase, the program director agreed. At first, Juster arranged for Joe Blachard's San Antonio–based Southwest Championship Wrestling (SWCW) — the group that preceded the WWF on the USA Network — to supply the content. Then, he replaced it with Ole Anderson's tapes from Georgia. But this was just a start. What Juster really wanted to do was apply for a promoter's license and run a card at the Baltimore Civic Center.

The arena's management was less than receptive. The WWF ran the building multiple times a year. How much more wrestling did they need? "I threatened to sue them. I said, 'You're a public, city-owned and operated facility. This is a violation of the Sherman Anti-Trust Act.' And they bought it and gave me a date."

For Juster, the timing couldn't have been better. This was the period when Georgia Championship Wrestling (GCW) was expanding into Maryland and needed someone with a local promoter's license. The first show, on February 18, 1984, featuring wrestlers and storylines fans already knew from TBS, drew 8,000. The next card in April — headlined by Flair defending his title against Jack Brisco just before the challenger and his brother departed for the WWF — attracted even more spectators.

When Pro Wrestling USA launched a few months later, Juster was tasked with booking and promoting the buildings while making sure that the AWA and JCP were equally represented on the syndicated television show. "I was getting three matches from Verne and three from Crockett."

Behind the scenes, though, the camaraderie between the promoters was non-existent. "I don't know if you'd call Pro Wrestling USA an alliance," said David Crockett. "There were too many chiefs. Everyone wanted to control everything. If an NWA guy was wrestling an AWA guy, who was going to lay on his back for who? When we took over TBS, everyone else wanted their talent on the Superstation. But what were they doing for us?"

All Vince had to do was sit back and watch his adversaries cannibalize each other. "The promoters in the territories always said they'd share talent," noted Jerry Brisco. "But they never wanted to let a top talent get out of their sight. They knew the other promoter would do everything he could to steal him."

All of this was very distracting, forcing promoters to divert their energy from building on the goodwill in the towns where they'd been successful. "During this time, the idea shifted from 'let's take care of our own territory' to 'let's go fight Vince,'" said Bruce Prichard, who watched the wrestling war from the Houston branch of Bill Watts's Mid-South promotion. "'By god, let's go to New York. Let's go to LA. Let's go to St. Louis, and then we'll go to Chicago.' They took their eyes off their home territories."

David Crockett grew to believe that JCP would have been better off fortifying what they had. "We were sending talent away from us to help other people. We should have kept them around and put on better shows in Charlotte and Greensboro and Atlanta and Richmond. But so much of our attention was up north."

Even when Pro Wrestling USA made an impressive showing, the dynamics between the partners did not allow anyone to savor it. This was evident when Crockett, Gagne and Fritz von Erich worked together on *SuperClash '85 — The Night of Champions* in the wake of the first *WrestleMania* at Comiskey Park in Chicago. "Jimmy did not like Verne at all," Juster said. "And the feeling was mutual. They weren't even talking after a while."

Although the announced attendance of 25,000 was exaggerated, more than 20,000 legitimately turned up at the White Sox's home stadium for a show that saw Ric Flair retain the NWA World Heavyweight Championship over Magnum T.A., AWA World Heavyweight kingpin Rick Martel battle Stan Hansen to a double disqualification and WCCW Texas Champion Kerry von Erich beat Jimmy Garvin with the Iron Claw. But Jimmy Crockett and Verne Gagne disagreed over the live gate. With each accusing the other of skimming, Crockett refused to fulfill a promise to send NWA stars to upcoming AWA events.

"There was quite a bit of that," said David Crockett. "You have a bunch of thieves, and we're all out for number one."

Greg Gagne maintained that, on the night of the event, David Crockett was sighted "walking around with contracts, trying to sign our people."

Crockett insisted that the charge was false. "I might have said, 'You know, if you're ever looking to make a move, let us know.' I was not buttonholing people. But if you carry on a conversation and it comes up, you're going to say, 'How long are you going to be with these guys?' Or 'you might like the weather our way.'"

What made the situation worse was that Pro Wrestling USA's spot shows — cards in smaller arenas — barely drew. "We tried," Juster said, "but we were in the heart of WWF territory a lot of the time. Some of the houses were horrible, maybe 100 people. We had a couple of big shows, but other than that, it never got off the ground."

As McMahon predicted, the axis folded, and promoters returned to their territories, weaker for the experience.

In the AWA, a contract Gagne secured with ESPN should have helped. But network support was minimal. Broadcasts were often shown in the afternoon when most fans were at work or school, and there was virtually no publicity urging viewers to tune in.

"The shows were disorganized," said Juster. "Verne was fading as a booker. A lot of stuff was done on the fly."

During one broadcast Gagne was running, Juster said, a match started before the referee had a chance to enter the ring. "Someone had to say, 'Verne, Verne, there's no referee.'"

As the AWA continued to falter, Jimmy Crockett managed to poach Juster from the Midwestern league. "Verne was livid," Juster said. "He'd been my mentor and really felt betrayed. My favorite part of it was that his daughter was a flight attendant for Northwest Airlines. And shortly after this happened, I was flying to Minneapolis. They were coming down the aisle with the beverage service. She comes to my row, takes one look at me and keeps going.

"She loved her father and was very loyal to him. From what I understand, when Verne died, she didn't want Gene Okerlund giving the eulogy because he'd left to work for Vince."

By then, a lot of people she knew had also been employed by McMahon, including her brother, Greg. But at the time of Pro Wrestling USA's demise, that possibility seemed remote, as Verne and his peers continued to find ways to stay in the game, and Vince McMahon devised new methods to torture them.

CHAPTER 12

A mong the many advantages McMahon enjoyed was having the most calculating mind in wrestling at his side. Although Jim Barnett's official title was senior vice president at Titan Sports, the WWF's corporate name at the time, he commanded a power far beyond most other employees. His shrewdness and cunning had enabled him to insinuate himself into every important promotion in the industry. Yet, because his homosexuality had led to a degree of exclusion, he'd observed the various promoters as an outsider, taking notes of their eccentricities and weaknesses. This placed him in the unique position of being able to tell Vince how his enemies thought and the way they operated their respective companies.

The Georgia deal had also brought the Briscos to the WWF. Since they'd toured every significant territory, they'd enjoyed relationships not only with the promoters but the people who ran the important arenas. "Vince wanted to start promoting the South," said Jerry. "But the NWA still had that wall up. You know, a building is usually owned by a management corporation. If you can't get into one building, you usually can't get into their other buildings. But I'd made a lot of friends when I had pieces of Georgia and Florida, people who'd moved up the ladder in corporate management. So I could get them to change their minds about who they should be doing business with."

Since the Briscos were ending their active careers — Jack would quit the business in February 1985 after a particularly grueling tour, becoming, at age 43, one of the few to never return — McMahon asked Jerry to begin promoting for the WWF in Florida, Georgia and the Carolinas. His territory would soon expand to include Virginia, Alabama and Mississippi.

Vince needed those markets since he was planning an event to eclipse everything that came before.

"I was in the conference room when Vince was talking about having the greatest wrestling show ever," said Ed Helinski. "And I remember [ring announcer] Howard Finkel saying, 'We all know about Beatlemania. Why don't we call it *WrestleMania*?'"

It was not McMahon's first choice. "Vince wanted to call the event The Colossal Tussle," booker Geroge Scott told me in the 2013 article I wrote for *Bleacher Report*. "I thought that was really stupid. So I started flapping my arms and skipping around the room, going, 'Oh, the Colossal Tussle, the Colossal Tussle.' I was doing a little imitation of Jim Barnett. . . . I skipped out the door and Vince yelled, 'Get back in here. We're calling it *WrestleMania*.'"

Now, his rivals had something *else* to worry about. "We're on this journey that had not been traveled before," said Jim Ross. "I think everybody was kind of curious as to where this thing was going to end."

Vince began setting the stage for the event three months beforehand. On December 28, 1984, Dick Clark, host of iconic music show *American Bandstand*, presided over a ceremony in the center ring at Madison Square Garden, presenting Cyndi Lauper — seconded by Hulk Hogan and Wendi Richter — with a trophy for her contributions to women's wrestling. She then announced that she wanted to mend fences with Lou Albano, citing his legitimate charitable work and outsized role in creating the Rock 'n' Wrestling Connection. For the first time anyone could remember, the manager entered the ring to almost universal applause as Cyndi awarded him with a gold record.

To further establish Albano as a babyface, Rowdy Roddy Piper then stepped into the ring, took the mic from the Captain's hand and declared, "It was me who set this up. It was me who started it. I want to present you with . . ." He suddenly raised the record and cracked it over Albano's head.

As Albano flopped onto his back on the canvas, dribble bubbling from his mouth, Lauper tried shielding him with her body. Using his boot, Piper swiped her to the side and continued the assault. Hogan had left the ring at this point, but he rushed back, chasing Piper away.

All was in place for the next WWF encounter to be televised on MTV: *The War to Settle the Score*, featuring Piper and Hogan in the main event.

As with *The Brawl to End It All*, the February 18, 1985, show took place in Madison Square Garden and only the main event was broadcast. That was what the new breed of fans wanted to see since it was inevitable that Lauper would somehow get involved.

Not only that, Mr. T, who'd appeared with Hogan in *Rocky III* and now starred in the wildly popular action-adventure TV series *The A-Team*, was strategically positioned in the front row.

In the final moments of the match, Hogan appeared to be cruising to another successful title defense when Piper's confederates, "Cowboy" Bob Orton Jr. and Paul "Mr. Wonderful" Orndorff, interceded on the challengers' behalf. Lauper rushed the ring to aid her friend — and was quickly *kicked in the head* by the Rowdy Scot.

The stunning lack of chivalry compelled Mr. T to hop the barricade and brawl with the villains.

No two celebrities of this magnitude had ever been so enmeshed in a wrestling angle, and Vince had truly accomplished his objective of getting the non-wrestling public interested. When the WWF announced that Mr. T had volunteered to be Hogan's tag team partner at the first *WrestleMania* on March 31 against the duo of Piper and Orndorff — with Orton in their corner — no one who followed pop culture wanted to miss it.

In Minnesota, Verne Gagne was even more revolted than he'd been by McMahon's decision to bestow his title on a bodybuilder and bass player. "I can't speak real highly of his caliber of wrestlers if in two weeks an actor like Mr. T can be transformed into someone capable of taking on his top pros," he told *Sports Illustrated*.

Incredibly, many in the WWF kind of agreed with him.

"The wrestlers whose minds worked old-school, they didn't like Mr. T," Nikolai Volkoff told me. "They felt he didn't belong there."

His backstage demeanor didn't help. "Mr. T could rub anyone the wrong way," observed "Mean" Gene Okerlund.

Some of the on-air personalities also grumbled that Hogan — with his eye perhaps on his post-wrestling career — seemed to treat his tag team partner with a deference he had not earned. The actor "was leading Hogan around by the arm," Okerlund said, "when it should have been the other way around."

If Mr. T expected to coast through the *WrestleMania* main event, the pledge went, no one was going to make it easy for him.

"There was a big difference between Cyndi Lauper and Mr. T," Piper told me. "While Cyndi came into our business not to take anything out, Mr. T thought, 'What can I do for Mr. T?'"

During a press conference at Rockefeller Center to publicize the event, Mr. T suddenly dove onto Piper "out of nowhere . . . no discussion about it beforehand. He didn't have any respect."

As the main event participants continued their press tour, live events executive Ed Cohen received a call reporting that Mr. T had fired a member of the office staff. Aware of the value that the actor was bringing to the brand, Cohen laughed the whole thing off.

"Keep the guy away from T," he instructed. "Let him think he's really fired."

Although few knew exactly how much the outsider would earn, it was easy to surmise that it would be more than the WWF regulars. And he appeared to have no issue with spending the rest of the company's money. "Mr. T ran up like $22,000 in expenses in one week," said George Scott. "I think that kind of freaked Vince out. He told me if *WrestleMania* wasn't successful, he'd go bankrupt."

Was this thing really going to work?

"You had the feeling that everything was on the line," said Ed Helinski.

"The company was still having growing pains," photographer Steve Taylor remembered. "Financially, we were trying to do a lot of things to expand. You never felt totally secure that the company was going to make it."

Hogan said that he worried about *WrestleMania* failing and the participants being blacklisted from the other promotions.

"No one knew if *WrestleMania* would fly," Okerlund told me. "And it flew. It flew like nothing else."

Either the tales about the anxiety never reached Jimmy "The Mouth of the South" Hart in the Memphis territory, or he chose to simply ignore them. One month before *WrestleMania*, he was written off Memphis television and left to join the WWF caravan.

For weeks, both Vince and George Scott had been trying to reach the manager, but Hart never phoned them back. "I'd be on the road and go to a pay phone to call my wife. 'Hey, you got a call from George Scott.' 'Oh, that wasn't George Scott. That was [Memphis star] Austin Idol trying to rib me.' Same thing with Vince McMahon. 'Hey, you got a message from Vince McMahon.' I didn't believe it."

Finally, WWF wrestler Hillbilly Jim, who'd worked in Memphis as Harley Davidson, managed to get Jimmy on the phone. "'You know, they're trying to reach you in New York.'" Even though the company's office was located in Connecticut, performers often referred to the promotion as "New York." "'They got a big show coming to Madison Square Garden called *WrestleMania*. Howard Finkel's been watching all your tapes and they love your interviews.'"

Hart immediately agreed. But he knew that, until everything was officially lined up, he'd need to kayfabe.

The territory had been run since the 1940s in parts of Tennessee, Kentucky, Indiana, Alabama, Arkansas, West Virginia, Ohio and Mississippi by Nashville-based Nick Gulas and partner Roy Welch — of the large southern wrestling family that also included performers with such surnames as Fuller, Golden, Fields and Hatfield. By the early 1970s, Christine "Teeny" Jarrett — who'd started working in the territory by selling tickets in the back of a Nashville shoe store — was promoting such cities as Louisville and Lexington, Kentucky, Evansville, Indiana and Columbia, Tennessee.

Her son, Jerry, made his in-ring debut in 1965 and was one of the territory's top stars. But like his mother, he found that promoting pro wrestling came naturally. In 1977, he and headliner Jerry "The King" Lawler staged a coup — allegedly in response to Nick Gulas's decision to feature his awkward son, Geroge, in main events — claiming the part of the territory that included its key city, Memphis, by, among other maneuvers, persuading popular announcers Dave Brown and Lance Russell to decamp with them. Within three years, Jarrett and Lawler had the whole thing.

The promotion was known for outlandish stunts like the scaffold match, the Tupelo concession stand brawl and comedian Andy Kaufman's feud with Lawler.

In 1985, the Saturday morning Memphis wrestling show was the number three television program in the market, trailing only prime-time soap operas *Dallas* and *Dynasty*.

"The thing I learned from my grandmother and my father is, first and foremost, this is a business," said Jerry Jarrett's son, Jeff. "You can come up with the most creative ideas in the world, maybe the most outlandish, big, broad and bold ideas, but at the end of the day, is cash going to come in? Are you going to get the return on your investment? If the answer is no, it's truly all for naught."

Jimmy Hart made money for the territory. Prior to entering the wrestling business in 1978, he was already locally known through his band, the Gentrys, which had sold more than a million copies of their hit "Keep on Dancing" in 1965. As a manager, he paid attention to every part of his presentation. "I'd go to the fun shop and get these crazy-looking ties, a big giant bowtie maybe to wear one week. I bought glitter to put on my shoes. I had a cane back then, and I'd take tape and wrap it around the cane like a barber pole. If I wore a blue outfit, I'd use blue tape."

When confronted by the babyfaces, Hart would speak nervously in a high-pitched voice: *"You're going to give me a heart attack if you don't quit talking to me like that."* "Here's this squeaky little voice that God gave me, but I'd exaggerate it. And the people would get even more mad at me because it was like fingernails on a chalkboard."

Hart felt an allegiance to both Jerry Jarrett and Lawler and wanted to be the one to inform them that he was leaving for the WWF. But at the time, Lawler happened to be touring Japan and Jarrett was away on a hunting trip.

Unable to reach them, he did the next best thing. "I told Plowboy Frazier [who'd later play Hillbilly Jim's "Uncle Elmer" in the WWF] that I was putting my band back together and I was leaving wrestling. Because I knew Plowboy, who I loved, was a blabbermouth. Lawler called me as soon as he got off the plane from Japan. 'What's this about the band getting back together?' So I was able to tell him personally."

With Jerry Jarrett still away, the manager was allowed to write himself off the Memphis TV show. Beloved announcer Lance Russell set up the angle by telling viewers that, because the promoter wasn't there, he'd been granted the authority to hire and fire people. Later on, in the midst of a heated interview segment, Hart dumped a 20-pound bag of flour over Russell's head. Shaking the powder from his hair, Russell announced the suspension: "This is the lowest thing you've ever pulled. Get out! Get out of here!"

"What gives you the authority? Maybe I'll suspend *you*," Hart screamed.

Eventually, the manager scampered under the ring and hid — until security dragged him out of the building.

Memphis was a notoriously poor-paying territory, so the promotion was used for talent departing for bigger opportunities. Regardless, "people like Jerry Lawler, Superstar Bill Dundee, Dutch Mantel and a few others were household names and huge ticket sellers," Jeff Jarrett said. "Even with Vince McMahon and Jim Crockett doing a lot of national expansion, our business was built to weather a lot of storms."

For one thing, the promotion assumed that someone like Vince McMahon was not interested in running cities like Chattanooga and Johnson City. "We'd been in the same time slots in those places for years, and our TV was so strong. That's where our money was made and that's where our survival was."

Either way, Hart felt as though he'd graduated from the bush leagues. On TV days, McMahon arranged for his talent to have catered meals backstage, a scenario that would have been unthinkable in Memphis. "You had to eat before you got there."

As much as he wished his old employer well, he now viewed his job as helping McMahon realize his goals. "I don't do drugs or anything," he assured the promoter in their first meeting. "I'll always be on time for you. I'm sure you heard that before, but I mean it. Whatever you want, I'll do it. If you want to paint me yellow, I'll bring the paint. If you need a whipping boy, I'll bring the belt. I'm grateful to be here."

In fact, Hart did have a skill that went beyond his zeal for being humiliated by babyfaces. As a former recording artist, he was a capable songwriter — having inherited the trait from his mother, Sadie Sallis, credited with penning "Enclosed One Broken Heart" for Eddy Arnold, a tune that hit number six on the *Billboard* country chart in 1950.

In the age of the Rock 'n' Wrestling Connection and beyond, he'd be called upon to compose the entrance themes for numerous performers.

In time, fans would grow accustomed to seeing the Mouth of the South coming to the ring several times a night, each time with a different protégé, a situation that bewildered some of the more established managers. "They said, 'How can you let the babyfaces knock you around three or four times a night?' We go out once, walk our guy to the ring and never get touched.'

"I told them that each time I go out, I make myself into a different character. I change my jacket for everybody. I use different phrases. I wanted Vince McMahon to look at me and say, 'Look at Jimmy Hart. He manages so many people. He doesn't bitch and complain. He takes bumps for everybody. He entertains people.'

"'If I only last a week,' I told them, 'it'll be the greatest week of my life.'"

But both Hart and McMahon understood that he was going to last much longer than a week. Despite his inexperience in the WWF system, Hart was instantly slotted into *WrestleMania*, playing the cornerman for King Kong Bundy, billed at 458 pounds. With the Mouth of the South cheering him on from ringside, Bundy would claim a piece of history, setting what may have been the first in-ring record at *WrestleMania*, squashing journeyman S.D. Jones in what was reported as nine seconds.

CHAPTER 13

Everything seemed to be in place for *WrestleMania*, but there were still some uncomfortable moments along the way.

"Dr. D" David Schultz, who'd been feuding with Hogan in the AWA before absconding with him to the WWF, had already sparked a lawsuit on the night of *The Brawl to End It All* by slapping an ABC News reporter who dared to ask the real vs. fake question. He was suspended, but since he'd been defending the business — and the reporter *was* acting like a dick — the company quickly brought him back.

That didn't mean that everyone in the WWF was entirely at ease having him around. The very sight of Mr. T backstage — a place that was supposed to be off-limits to marks, the pejorative term for the suckers who belonged in the stands — antagonized Schultz, and he let the actor — and everyone else within earshot — know it. As he'd already demonstrated, Dr. D was not beyond using his hands to remedy annoyances, igniting fears that it was just a matter of time before he had a physical confrontation with the Hollywood star. In fact, Schultz said that he was specifically warned to leave Mr. T alone but chose to ignore the admonishment.

During a match at the LA Forum, Dr. D spotted Mr. T sitting at ringside with legendary wrestler Professor Toru Tanaka and belligerently approached, shouting and threatening. Hulk Hogan later claimed that Schultz "bitch-slapped the hell out of" the actor, but there's no account of this. What is true is that road agent Chief Jay Strongbow was nervous enough to get the cops involved. Swooping in, they handcuffed Schultz and expelled him from the arena.

He was banished from the company, as well.

Yet, there was something about Mr. T that seemed to trigger these types of incidents.

Four days before the big event, Hogan and the actor were being interviewed by comedian Richard Belzer on his television show, *Hot Properties*. Jokingly, Belzer asked Hogan to put him in a wrestling hold. It was a dare that wrestlers did not appreciate, usually delivered by someone who imagined that, since pro wrestling was sports entertainment, the moves couldn't possibly hurt. To this day, no one is sure if Belzer's intention was to demean or stay true to the show business spirit that McMahon was promoting. Regardless, Hogan clamped on a front face lock and squeezed.

Said Mr. T, "Keep him in that for a little while."

The Hulkster amped up the pressure.

"I'd never seen him do that to anyone before," Hogan's close friend, Brutus Beefcake, told me in 2013. "But Mr. T was prodding him. 'Do it. Do it.' And when Hulk let go, Belzer fell down and split his head open on the stage floor. If someone challenges your livelihood, you answer. I'm not sure if it was good or it was bad. If anything, it might have gotten a few more people interested in seeing *WrestleMania*."

Indeed, rather than being ostracized for brutalizing a TV personality, Hogan continued to be courted by the media. On the night before *WrestleMania*, he and Mr. T were invited to host NBC's *Saturday Night Live*, a scenario that would have been unimaginable in the days when Killer Kowalski, Skull Murphy and Haystacks Calhoun were headliners in New York.

According to the WWF, the company had achieved its goal of breaking through to a different audience, an assertion Bruce Newman in *Sports Illustrated* did not completely accept. "Somehow McMahon and his WWF have convinced a good part of the press that the knuckledraggers who traditionally made up wrestling crowds have been booted out of the bleachers and replaced by Wharton graduates," he wrote.

The truth was that, in addition to reaching out to newer fans, the organization still hoped to entice traditional ones to turn up for *WrestleMania*.

Jerry Brisco promoted the closed-circuit venues in 35 cities in seven southern states. "I didn't know jack crap about promotion," he said. "Even though I'd owned parts of promotions, I was a wrestler. In our day, promotion was you bought a newspaper ad and that was it. Now, we had to get creative to get the local radio stations and TV stations to talk about the show. The whole thing was new to me."

As it was to everyone else.

As he pondered the enormity of the event, Steve Taylor realized that he'd need some help and recruited his friend Tom Buchanan. The two had worked together as staff photographers at the *Auburn Citizen*, and Tom was currently employed by the *Utica Observer-Dispatch*. The *WrestleMania* gig was a freelance project — he would not become staff at the WWF until after *WrestleMania III* — and the meticulous Buchanan could not chance anything going wrong. So the week before, he was flown to Toronto to practice at a WWF show there.

"I needed to figure out the timing of wrestling. Every sport has different timing. When do you push the button? Where's the action going to be? How do you focus? Who do you follow? Where do I stand? So I learned all of that very quickly in Toronto.

"I realized that the best thing for me to do was move around inside the barricade and shoot under the ropes. We were shooting mostly with the flash on. So I had to figure out where the ropes were and how to manage the flash with that, how to focus from different distances, how to stay out of the public's way."

Given the attention that *WrestleMania* was receiving, the stakes were high. "There were hard cameras [stationary cameras situated in the stands and focused on the ring], so that was considered the front of the stage. You don't want to get in the way, but you could work the sides of the ring or the back of the ring. And that's where I mostly shot at *WrestleMania*."

As he positioned himself at ringside, Steve Taylor felt a surge of fear. "This was going to be one of the biggest things I'd ever photograph in my career. There was a lot of pressure on me. And we were shooting slides. It wasn't like today. *Oh, this is what the picture looks like.* I didn't know what I had until it was sent to the lab and developed."

In years to come, Buchanan would find many of the photos he took that day unacceptable. "I shot *WrestleMania* as a newspaper photographer, with my flash on the camera and 100 speed film. Just basic photography. When you're shooting under the ring with the flash, you get shadows. It's pretty ugly."

Then again, the entire setup was unsophisticated. "The first *WrestleMania* looked like a house show," Taylor said, referring to an untelevised wrestling event. "Only there were television cameras there."

Similarly, *WWF Magazine* editor Ed Ricciuti viewed the show as not much different than any major WWF card at the time. The one exception was that celebrities were involved. "The whole idea of how to really present *WrestleMania*, at least in my mind, wasn't crystallized."

From ringside, Ricciuti predicted that the event wouldn't last beyond *WrestleMania III*. "One more year for the trend to go up," he theorized, "another year for it to go down."

More than 35 years later, he'd reflect, "I guess I was wrong."

Liberace, the flamboyant, jewelry-clad pianist and singer, was more associated with his Las Vegas residencies than the edginess of New York City. But his shows at Radio City Music Hall drew the same types of middle-American tourists as his concerts on the Strip. He also grew up as a wrestling fan in Milwaukee and appreciated the excessive and theatrical aspects of the art form. Not only was he the guest timekeeper for the *WrestleMania* main event, he made as grand an entrance as the combatants, doing a high-stepping dance in the ring, arms linked with the Radio City Rockettes.

"Now, the Rockettes probably don't mean jack shit to someone today," "Mean" Gene Okerlund told me in 2013. "But back then, man, wrestling had never seen anything like this, and it meant something."

Yet, everyone conceded that there may not have been a *WrestleMania* were it not for Lauper. To set up the women's *WrestleMania* clash, Wendi Richter had dropped her title to Moolah protégé Leilani Kai at *The War to*

Settle the Score. In the weeks since, Cyndi and Richter had vowed revenge at *WrestleMania.* They received it when the challenger once again captured the gold, and the pair exulted in the ring for the international press.

For a period, Richter was depicted as a female equivalent of Hulk Hogan, but the relationship with the WWF would quickly break down, primarily over compensation. In November 1985, Richter showed up at the Garden to wrestle a masked woman billed as the Spider. It was Moolah under a mask. Moolah had trained the champion for the squared circle and knew every deviant carny tactic in the trade. Not long into the match, she double-crossed her former student, rolling her up in a small package, as referee Jack Lotz — who was part of the plot — delivered a fast count. Infuriated, Richter pulled off her opponent's mask, revealing Moolah's face, delivered a backbreaker, and covered her rival. But the bell had already rung, and the title switch was official.

Richter was so upset that she stormed out of the building in her ring gear, refusing to ever speak to Moolah again.

But none of that could have been foreseen at *WrestleMania.* Instead, fans basked in the sight of Wendi and Cyndi celebrating their win, expectations soaring as the time to witness Hogan and Mr. T as tag team partners drew closer.

Muhammad Ali had been announced as the special referee and seemed excited to take part in the spectacle. In the run-up to *WrestleMania,* though, it became clear to people in the company that the boxing legend was suffering from cognitive damage likely related to his career. The day before the show, for instance, McMahon called Ed Cohen and said that Ali had not gotten around to picking up a referee's outfit.

Cohen ran out to the sporting goods store and purchased one, accurately guessing the sizes of the pants, shirt and shoes.

Recalled Roddy Piper in the 2013 article I wrote for *Bleacher Report,* "I really wanted to work with Ali at *WrestleMania.* But . . . we realized it could get very ugly, and he could get hurt, without some control. So we made Ali a special official at ringside."

While Ali would primarily stay outside the ring, McMahon confidant Pat Patterson was the arbiter between the ropes, a wise move since, as a backstage coach, he could subtly deliver instructions as the action progressed.

There was a lot to manage. When Piper and Paul "Mr. Wonderful" Orndorff stepped into the ring for the main event, Hot Rod was already angry about events that preceded *WrestleMania*. He'd previously wanted to win the WWF World Heavyweight Championship, albeit under questionable circumstances, and build a program — or ongoing saga — featuring the Hulkster chasing the heel for the prize. After all, Leilani Kai was allowed to win the women's title at *The War to Settle the Score*. Even though the understanding was that she'd drop the strap pretty quickly, for the rest of her life, she'd be able to call herself a champion. With all Piper had contributed, wasn't he worthy of the same thing?

McMahon apparently did not believe so. Now, Roddy was slated to be on the losing side against Hogan and Mr. T. As the participants — including Piper's "bodyguard" "Cowboy" Bob Orton Jr., who wore a perennial cast on his forearm to protect an injury that never seemed to heal — went over the details of the encounter, the actor "wanted to treat our match like a cartoon and bang the heels' heads together," Hot Rod told me in 2013. "And I laid down the law that I would not let Mr. T pin my shoulders. I wasn't being difficult. I'm not going to let someone come into my business and treat me like a clown."

Once the bell rang, Orndorff found himself equally resentful of Mr. T. "I thought he was a piece of shit. He wasn't that good of an athlete, and I had to go out there and make him look like King Kong. He didn't sweat. I did."

As Piper and the television star tangled, the wrestler tried confining their exchanges to maneuvers largely based on amateur wrestling. "I wouldn't let him throw a punch. At one point, he tried to get cute, and I got him in a front facelock just for a second, to put him in his place.

"But when I saw him bend forward, I knew what I needed to do to make it look good. I told him to drape me over his shoulders and pick me up. He held me there, like a fireman's carry, and stopped until I told him to spin me around. That's the photo that went all over the world — me getting the airplane spin from Mr. T."

At the end of the contest, Orton snuck up the turnbuckles and dove off, aiming his cast at Hogan as Mr. Wonderful held him in place. The Hulkster quickly moved, and Orndorff took the blow, falling to the mat so Hogan could finish him off and send everyone home in a state of ecstasy.

Seemingly disgusted with their ally, Piper and Orton left Orndorff in the ring and headed to the dressing room, turning him babyface and setting up a rivalry between the partners.

Orndorff told me, "I knew a lot of new fans were watching so I didn't make the match too complicated. They remembered the finish and they knew what it meant. That's all that mattered."

Jerry Brisco watched the show at the closed-circuit location in Kissimmee, Florida, spending much of the event phoning the other venues he'd been assigned to check on attendance figures and possible technical glitches. "I was worried about the feeds because it wasn't like today. At each place, you had a truck with all kinds of equipment. So it was a complicated deal. I was a complete novice but got my education that day."

Remarkably, he only had issues at a facility in Alabama. "There were about 900 people there at this place in a little town and the equipment didn't work. So we sent them home and refunded them all. That was the only catastrophe."

As it was, the entire state of Alabama had drawn particularly poorly. "I think the largest crowd was Dothan, and that was probably about 1,500 people."

Georgia did not fare much better. While the northeast and west coasts were hailing the WWF, the fans partial to Jim Crockett's product seemed satisfied with what was already there. "We had the old auditorium in Atlanta, and we lost our ass. It sucked. We knew it with the ticket sales going in. But the company didn't want to cancel. I was pissed. I felt like I didn't do a good enough job of convincing the people that the old way was over with, and this was a new era. But when we added up everything together from all over the country, we had exceeded all calculations. Even in the places I thought were bad, when the percentages were broken down, the company was happy."

Bruce Prichard attended a telecast at the Astro Arena in Houston, where he'd been working for Paul Boesch, a promoter who had the rare reputation of doling out generous payoffs and was currently aligned with Cowboy Bill Watts's Mid-South territory.

Although just 22 years old, Prichard was not just a backstage employee but a cunning operative. And as he studied the details of the locally advertised event, he found a flaw that could potentially be exploited to reduce McMahon's closed-circuit success.

"They started out promoting a start-time at one o'clock, and they promoted it that way nationwide. So if you were in LA, the start time would have been one o'clock. If you were in Chicago, it would have been one o'clock. If you were on the east coast, it would have been one o'clock. But they also said the show was supposed to be live. Which wasn't true because by one o'clock in Houston, they would have been an hour into the show. So I went to the commission and told them, and WWE had to change all the advertising and start the *WrestleMania* feed in Texas at noon."

Prichard and the commissioner of the Texas Department of Labor and Standards, which oversaw wrestling and boxing regulation, attended the closed-circuit card together. "I went in with the commissioner. I didn't buy a ticket."

He was stunned by what he witnessed. "The first thing I noticed when I walked into the Astro Arena was the entire floor filled with people that were coming to watch a giant screen. That was an eye opener for me, like, 'Holy shit, this many people coming to watch what's basically a film.'"

Throughout the event, he was taken by the audience involvement. "People were shouting at the screen and wearing Hulkamania shirts. And people were purchasing merchandise. They were lined up to purchase merchandise like they were watching live. And they left satisfied, like they'd really been to something special, even though they'd just seen a broadcast of it."

If you worked for the WWF, the train seemed to be moving in the proper direction. And that was before executives even considered the surprising response to the event on pay-per-view. As cable television penetration increased, the first pay-per-view channels were created the same year as *WrestleMania*. As an afterthought, the WWF included the option for fans who wanted to watch the show at home.

Reportedly, more than 100,000 households capitalized on the convenience, enabling Vince McMahon to take credit for opening yet another frontier.

CHAPTER 14

Even Bill Apter had to concede that McMahon had put on a good show. "I was blown away," the photographer said, "and very pissed off that I wasn't there, shooting."

But George Napolitano realized that, unintentionally, Vince had given him a gift. "*WrestleMania* made wrestling itself become something bigger than it had been before. It opened up a lot of doors for me. Suddenly, people from outside of wrestling were looking to buy pictures."

And, unlike Apter and Craig Peters, whose photos were owned by publisher Stanley Weston, George could sell any picture he took.

Even the widespread acceptance of the *WWF Magazine* seemed to benefit the competition. "We were cranking out six or seven magazines a month," Peters said, "and we never missed a deadline."

At that point, the territory system — while threatened — very much existed. "I still had plenty of work," Napolitano said. "I liked coming to the Garden every month and the WWF TVs, I also liked going to Atlanta, going to Charlotte, going to Greesboro, going to Texas, going to Florida."

Although Vince had taken some of the brightest names in the industry, Jim Crockett Promotions (JCP) could still offer its fans a roster of genuine stars. "Besides Ric and Arn Anderson and Tully Blanchard and Dusty and Magnum T.A., we had incredible tag teams like the Rock 'n'

Roll Express and the Midnight Express," said David Crockett. "With the syndicated show and TBS, we were just blowing the doors off and having fun doing it."

Although the WWF arguably received the most prominent coverage in the newsstand magazines, there were lots of other pages to fill. For many fans just learning about pro wrestling, the publications exposed them to a range of talent about whom they'd otherwise be unaware. "The promoters were really happy to have us, and we could pretty much do whatever we wanted in those places," Apter noted.

"I felt like Jim Crockett Jr. made me one of the boys. He gave me rides to the different shows on his private plane. It was wonderful."

Among Crockett's many goals, he told Apter, was making the genial New Yorker famous. On a regular basis, Apter and Peters appeared on TBS, interviewing Crockett's stars on a segment called "Pro Wrestling Illustrated Press Conference."

"You won't be able to walk down the street in New York without being recognized," Crockett lavishly predicted.

For Apter's part, he intended to make JCP and other groups "look as big or maybe bigger than the WWF."

When it came to storytelling, few territories were as absorbing as Cowboy Bill Watts's Mid-South promotion.

"Bill didn't have a lot of pomp and circumstance," said Bruce Prichard. "He believed in believability, credibility."

Matches were physical and athletic, often centered around a simple theme like revenge, a vicious grudge or a war to determine which competitor was the toughest. His episodic, reality-based television show almost certainly had an influence on the WWF. But even Watts conceded that that didn't make Vince unique. "Everybody took from everyone else. If something worked somewhere else, of course you would take it."

The cowboy "was the master of the cliffhanger," Prichard said. "Guys would be brawling in the ring and you'd hear, 'Oh my god. Everything is breaking down. We're out of time. See you next week, folks.'"

The Oklahoma-based territory had a long reputation for featuring former amateur wrestling standouts as well as its junior heavyweight division. After NWA Junior Heavyweight Champion Leroy McGuirk was blinded in a car accident in 1950, he began working full-time in the local wrestling office, eventually becoming the primary owner.

In 1974, while attending Northeastern State University in the foothills of the Ozark Mountains, Jim "J.R." Ross filled a broadcast position on the company's show. He also began touring the circuit as a referee. After Watts, a headliner in both North America and Japan, purchased the league in 1979, Ross would be promoted to the lead play-by-play announcer as well as the company's vice president of marketing.

Under Watts, Mid-South promoted shows around Oklahoma along with parts of Arkansas, Louisiana and Mississippi. "As a wrestler, I knew I could draw money," he said. "At first, I felt that the only person I could count on was myself. But I learned how to build others.

"The first guy to pass me in the Oklahoma territory was Dick Murdoch. I'll never forget coming out of the building in Shreveport and seeing all the fans hanging back by the cars, waiting for Dick Murdoch. And I thought, 'I'll show them who the star is!' But then, when I sat in the motel room, I said, 'You big dummy. Let's think about what happened. You built someone up who can help you carry the load, so you don't have to be there every night for the show to be a success. Now, go out and build another star.'"

And after that guy was built, Watts would need another main-eventer just behind him. Because even though he considered Murdoch a friend, Watts couldn't chance the possibility of a star holding him up for money — threatening to no-show without a significant pay bump.

In his time — working against Bruno Sammartino in Madison Square Garden, Harley Race in Tampa, Mr. Wrestling II in Atlanta and Verne Gagne in the AWA — Watts had been around enough dressing rooms to determine what he wanted and didn't want in his. "You had to be in the arena an hour before the bell. All cards had to be put away — no gambling within an hour before the first bell. Because I'd seen guys who were in the middle of poker games running out, just barely getting to the ring. They were so involved in their game, their mind was still on their losses and they screwed up the match and everything else.

"If a wrestler told me, 'The motel forgot to wake me up for an early flight,' that's not my problem. That's your problem. I'm still fining you for being late.

"The wrestling business is my business, and I'm not going to let you destroy it."

Weather notwithstanding, there were no excuses for ever missing a town. "One time, I was supposed to be in Jackson, Mississippi. We sold the place out, but all the flights were canceled because of a bunch of storms. I chartered a single-engine Bonanza and we flew through a tornado storm alert area. I landed and the cops were waiting, and I changed into my wrestling gear in the back of the cop car. Got there, worked two-out-of-three falls with double juice [both wrestlers bleeding]. And we never even got to talk about what we were going to do. We just did it in the ring."

During those instances when a participant decided that he didn't want to sell — or register pain — it was incumbent on his rival to get the reaction the hard way. "I was partners with Frank Goodish [Bruiser Brody] in Fort Smith, Arkansas, of all the stupid places. [Former Olympic silver medalist] Danny Hodge was on the other team, and Goodish decided that he didn't want to make him look too good."

Goodish was seasoned enough to know that, because of the double tendons in his hand, Hodge had freakish strength and regularly crushed apples in televised demonstrations. Rather than reminding his partner of this, Watts let him suffer for his arrogance. "I told Frank, 'Go ahead. I wouldn't sell for him, either. Let's see what happens.'

"They barely started the match and, pretty soon, Frank is screaming out there. And I said, 'Go ahead, Frank. Show him how strong you are. Show him how well-built you are. Show him how you don't want to sell.' And as soon as he could, he was tagging me in and saying, 'Bill, I don't want any part of this.'"

Outside the arena, losing a bar fight meant instant termination, and Watts couldn't risk word spreading that a farmer or carpenter had manhandled one of his wrestlers. "I told the guys, 'If you're going to hang out in bars and you're going to get into a fight, you better damn sure win it.'"

When B. Brian Blair appeared in Mid-South in the early 1980s, the logistics of car travel preoccupied the wrestlers as much as their performances in the ring. "If you were wrestling in Oklahoma City on a Friday night, you'd have to leave after the show and go 375 miles to Shreveport for TV the next morning."

Blair often caught rides with journeyman "Quickdraw" Rick McGraw, who'd purchased a van and collected gas money from his passengers. "He could haul six people around and make enough money to pay his expenses. When we finally got to town, Rick would sleep in the van. Paul Orndorff and I always rented a room. We knew in advance which motels had two beds in the room. Then, one guy would check in and the other guy would sneak in. We called it 'heeling a room.'

"There were women in every town and you could spend the night with them. Once you were established, it was like having a bed and breakfast everywhere. The only issue was that there would sometimes be heat between the different women. Because maybe one week, you wanted to stay with this one, and another week, you wanted to stay with another one in the same town. But I don't know if I'd really call it a problem. We were very happy in that territory."

Of all the characters Watts developed in Mid-South, he was proudest of the Junkyard Dog (JYD). Mississippian Sylvester Ritter had worked Memphis as Leroy Rochester and Calgary as "Big Daddy" Ritter. But neither character received a great deal of acclaim. Recognizing Ritter's charisma, Watts rebranded him the "Junkyard Dog" — after the line from the 1973 Jim Croce song "Bad, Bad Leroy Brown" about the subject being "meaner than a junkyard dog." To play up the gimmick, the Dog came to the ring in a dog collar and long chain.

If any offense was taken by the sight of a Black man in the South in this type of restraint, no one voiced it. African American fans flooded to Mid-South cards to cheer on the Dog, and white fans were right next to them, shouting just as loudly. Despite warnings from other promoters about building his territory around an African American star, Watts believed that he understood the demographics and was giving his audience something that enlivened them.

As an athlete, Ritter bore little resemblance to prior Oklahoma territory headliners like Leroy McGuirk, Danny Hodge and Jack Brisco. But as with Vince McMahon later on, Watts was playing to fan tastes. "I knew JYD couldn't work. But he was a great interview and projected so well."

After a card in St. Bernard Parish in Louisiana, Watts received a call from his booker, Ernie Ladd.

"He can't carry it," an exasperated Ladd reported.

Ladd had been instructed to oversee a 20-minute Broadway — or match that seems to be coming to a conclusion when the bell suddenly rings, leaving fans anxious to witness a rematch — between the Dog and Super Destroyer (Scott "Hogg" Irwin, not Hulk Hogan). "He's out of shape," Ladd said. "His tongue was hanging out. I don't think we can do much with this guy."

Watts threatened to fire Ladd over the phone. "I didn't send you down there for you to see what he couldn't do. I sent you down there to see what he *could* do. You're missing the point."

Ladd called back a few minutes later. "I got the message."

In 1980, JYD and Buck Robley were the Mid-South Tag Team Champions, pitted against Terry Gordy and Buddy Roberts of the Freebirds. Not only was the title at stake, but the rules of the match stipulated that whoever suffered the pinfall would lose his hair.

After being relentlessly double-teamed by his foes, Robley went down for the three count, and Freebirds leader Michael Hayes entered the ring with what he said was a hair-removing potion. When the Junkyard Dog attempted to protect his partner, Hayes hurled the substance at the star, hitting his eyes and apparently blinding him.

"We made sure that Hayes said that the blinding was an accident," Watts recounted, "even though everyone knew he did it deliberately. Because if I allowed the heels to blind JYD purposefully, how could we continue as a promotion? We'd be co-conspirators in a crime."

Conveniently, the Junkyard Dog's wife was pregnant at the time. When she finally gave birth, Watts made sure to send a television crew to his star's house. As JYD pointed at his new daughter, his wife had to redirect his hand toward the child.

In keeping with kayfabe, the Dog would be led around by his wife whenever they left home. Even in the house, he would not remove his eye coverings unless the blinds were drawn.

Fans completely bought into the story, while Hayes fed their anger by mocking his opponent on television, wearing sunglasses and carrying a cane. Eventually, JYD said that, blind or not, he needed to take revenge. But because of his compromised vision, he and Hayes would be connected by — what else — a dog collar in the grudge match.

The pair also met in a cage to ensure that the other Freebirds would not interfere. As soon as the chokers were affixed, though, the Junkyard Dog tore off his blindfold, revealing that his eyesight had returned, and beat his tormentor bloody.

"We had some great soap operas," said J.R.

Although Mid-South talent had been regularly showcased at Paul Boesch's high-profile events at the Sam Houston Coliseum, the relationship took on a more permanent air when Watts purchased a third of the operation. Still, Houston remained its own entity. "We'd have shows in Angleton, Rosenberg, Galveston, places like that within 100 miles of Houston," said Prichard.

Prichard had been a fan of Houston wrestling his entire life, watching champions from the NWA, AWA and even the WWWF appear on the biweekly Friday night Coliseum cards, along with legends from Mexico. "My brother [future WWF wrestler and trainer Dr. Tom Prichard] and I had a very understanding mother, who would take us to the Houston wrestling office to buy tickets. Paul Boesch would come out from his office to get his mail around 9:30 in the morning, so we always made sure to be there by then. The front part of the ticket office was full of pictures and memorabilia. But then, Paul started bringing us back to his office, where there were pictures on the wall from the 1920s and '30s. We'd find something new every time we'd go there."

By 14, Tom was helping Boesch add to the collection by taking photos at ringside. One day, he told his younger brother that the promotion needed some kids to sell posters that night. Ten-year-old Bruce volunteered as soon as he realized that he'd receive a quarter for every poster sold.

"We were each given four posters and sections of the Coliseum to work. I sold my posters out pretty quickly and grabbed more. While the other kids were standing around and watching the matches, I was up in the balcony, as high as you could go. I think there were 100 posters in total and I sold 60 of them and made twelve dollars. In 1973, at ten years old, that was a big deal."

At the next card, he returned to the Coliseum to repeat the task. Over time, he befriended ring announcer Boyd Pierce and was given a microphone to plug his posters. He became so adept at doing this that, when Boyd failed to show up one night when Prichard was 14, the teenager did the ring announcing himself.

"At 16, I started refereeing, and by 18, I'd done so many jobs, I felt like I was running the place."

After Watts's involvement increased, Prichard felt as though he was witnessing the golden age of Mid-South from the inside. "We had a great run from 1983 to '85, even though we did some hotshotting I didn't like."

This was exemplified by another angle that involved a participant losing his hair. "They advertised a match between 'Hacksaw' Jim Duggan and Hercules Hernandez, and told the fans that if Hernandez lost, his manager, Jim Cornette, would get his head shaved. They did it in Baton Rouge on Thursday and they had it booked on a Sunday show in Houston. Exact same match, exact same stipulation.

"Well, Hernandez lost in Baton Rouge and they gave Cornette a buzz cut. So now, they're screwing over Houston. Cornette came in the ring, wearing a mask with a guy from Tennessee no one ever saw before. Cornette introduced him as his cousin and they shaved the guy's head.

"So go ahead — say Vince McMahon hurt the credibility of the business. The other promotions weren't doing things any better."

Regardless, ticket sales were strong, even when the Junkyard Dog unexpectedly departed for the WWF in the summer of 1984. "Vince later told me he never asked JYD to walk out on us, but I didn't believe that. I took it personally. Because I had given JYD his gimmick. I'd taught him and I coached him and I made him a superstar. When he needed money, I gave him two loans, one in cash, one by check. And he broke our trust and walked out on everybody."

Jim Ross considered JYD "the heart and soul of the team. Everything was built around him. There was a lot of time and a lot of money invested in him. A top guy should never leave without notice and when he did that, it was crippling.

"It also sent a bad message to the other guys: *Hey, if the Dog can just leave, then I can do it, too.*"

This became a greater possibility after JYD was catapulted to the spotlight in the WWF, wrestling Intercontinental Champion Greg "The Hammer" Valentine at *WrestleMania* and winning via countout without the title changing hands.

In Oklahoma, Ross couldn't help but feel satisfaction in the achievements of the performer he'd grown to know in Mid-South.

Watts was also left with a sense of gratification. But that was because, while the rest of the wrestling world was buzzing about *WrestleMania*, the intractable promoter hadn't even bothered to watch.

CHAPTER 15

In New York that day, no one was thinking about Bill Watts.

After completing his photography assignment at the Garden, Tom Buchanan tagged along for the *WrestleMania* after-party at the Rainbow Room in Rockefeller Center. There, wrestlers mingled with journalists, celebrities and New York business insiders. Some of the guests had been encouraged to bring their kids and expose them to the repackaged entertainment option. Wrestling icons like "Classy" Freddie Blassie and "Golden Boy" Arnold Skaaland sat with their wives, greeting well-wishers. A beaming André the Giant posed for photos and animatedly chatted with Vince's eight-year-old daughter, Stephanie. "I was used to working for newspapers and newspapers were notoriously cheap," Buchanan said. "This was a huge, high-end affair, and it said a lot about how the company saw itself and where it was going."

Amid the exuberance, WWF employees were receiving periodic updates on ticket sales at the closed-circuit locations. By the next day, the Associated Press reported that more than a million people had watched.

For Ed Helinski in merchandise marketing, the popularity presented new challenges. "We couldn't keep the Hogan merchandise in stock. Sometimes, we'd have to hold back on the mail orders because having the merchandise at the venues took precedence. We thought if people came to a show and saw the merchandise, we had that one shot of selling to them. The mail orders could wait a little bit longer."

In June 1985, Basil Devito Jr. was hired as director of promotions. A short time later, before a television taping at the Mid-Hudson Civic Center in Poughkeepsie, New York, he and Vince McMahon walked onto the stage overlooking the ring. "The house was only about a third filled, which was disappointing," Devito said, "and people were being moved around so the building could look full in front of the cameras." McMahon explained how the three weeks of television that would be shot that day were going to provide "three weeks of advertising for us all over the country." Fixing a hard stare at Devito, the owner continued, "I don't ever want to see an empty seat again. And those empty seats are your responsibility."

Devito was joining a growing list of employees who hadn't been fans growing up. But he had a master's degree in sports management and work experience that included the National Basketball Association (NBA), NFL and 1984 Olympics. He and McMahon immediately liked each other, and Devito was hired after one meeting.

"I went to work for WWE on one rented floor in a building on Holly Hill Lane in Greenwich and shared an office with three other people. I had no institutional knowledge of the industry or the organization."

This wasn't necessarily a negative. As an outsider, Devito hadn't absorbed the backwards logic prevalent in the wrestling trade. "The old territory guys rarely brought in anybody who wasn't connected to the business," said former Pro Wrestling USA live events promoter Gary Juster. "Everything was kayfabe and they ran their business out of their back pockets. There weren't the systems in place you had in the real business world."

Once, while discussing long-term storylines, McMahon asked if it would help Devito to know the planned outcomes of certain angles. "I told him him 'no,'" Devito recounted. "You can market the Super Bowl without knowing who's going to win. It made no difference to me. I didn't want to be that kind of insider."

What he cared about was finding employees motivated to help the company grow. Mike Weber had been in the graduate program at Ohio

University, studying sports administration, when Devito contacted professor Charles "Doc" Higgins, looking for interns. Higgins thought that the 27-year-old Weber, who'd previously run youth programs for the YMCA, would be a good fit.

Although Weber knew little about professional wrestling, Devito made him feel excited about the opportunity he was about to receive: "If you intern with an NBA team, you're going to work in one city, and learn a little bit about ticket sales and group sales and maybe some PR. Major League Baseball — same thing. You come here for three months, I guarantee you that you will do events in at least ten different markets, you'll travel, you'll promote and if you're any good, you'll get a job."

That was no exaggeration. Of the dozen or so interns Devito brought to the WWF, he estimated that ten received full-time positions. Before Weber's apprenticeship even ended, he'd been hired as the company's head of public relations.

"Basil had unbelievable organizational skills," Weber said. "I remember it being a big deal when he got us computers at our desks. He wanted to show that we weren't a bunch of wrestling guys smoking cigars in a back room, but an actual business."

McMahon trusted Devito's judgment, and Devito understood that one costly mistake was all it took to be exiled. "Vince knew exactly where he wanted to go and what he wanted to do," noted Dick Glover, the organization's vice president of business affairs starting in 1986. "Then, he went about trying to put together a group of people in each of the various disciplines who could do it with him and for him."

It was not just the caliber of the people McMahon hired, Devito insisted, but the owner's overall vision that was moving the company forward. "If he was matched up against an NBA coach, and Vince took five players and the coach took five players, Vince would find a way to win with zero doubt."

"*WrestleMania 1* was very good for WWE," Nikolai Volkoff told me in a *Bleacher Report* article in 2013. "For everybody else, it was no good. It's

Mother Nature. The big fish eats the small fish. You cannot go against the laws of Mother Nature."

The shift was only partially due to the fact that McMahon was willing to spend more money than his competitors. "Vince would plan," said David Crockett. "We were like, 'Oh, we gotta hurry up and do this. Spin the wheel, make the deal.'"

The inclusion of country star David Allan Coe in the 1985 Great American Bash tour exemplified the promotion's shortcomings, Crockett asserted. "Why not just have a rock show or a country show? We're a wrestling event."

Unquestionably, Jimmy Crockett was trying to prove that he wasn't the only promoter who could feature celebrities on his cards. But while McMahon had had his guests interwoven throughout the *WrestleMania* broadcast, JCP staged a concert at the conclusion of the show, attempting to establish a tie to the promotion by having Ric Flair, Dusty Rhodes, Magnum T.A. and Jimmy Valiant join the singer onstage.

Bill Apter and George Napolitano's magazines ran photos of the moment. The *New York Times* and *Sports Illustrated* did not.

One flaw was the selection of Coe himself, who'd charted high on the country charts but had none of the mainstream appeal of Cyndi Lauper and Mr. T. It seemed like, in his zeal to compete with McMahon, Jim Crockett Jr. had affirmed his northeastern rival's claim that JCP was B-level and chicken-fried.

"We spent so much money on the fireworks laser show," David Crockett complained. "The stage cost and entertainment costs were ridiculous. But [booker] Dusty Rhodes was a country guy. He wanted it. And it wasn't his money. It was the company's money. And Dusty didn't think about money, per se, when he wanted something."

With *WrestleMania* behind him, Vince continued building out his roster and transforming established wrestlers into different versions of themselves. In a play on their similar initials, "Jumping" Jim Brunzell and B. Brian Blair were paired up as the Killer Bees in June 1985, competing in trunks ornamented in yellow and black stripes, like the winged insect.

Brunzell had been an important part of the AWA, training for pro wrestling in the class that included Ric Flair and the Iron Sheik, teaming with Greg Gagne in a unit called the High Flyers, and winning the territory's World Tag Team Championship twice. "Teaming with Greg was like a day off every night," Brunzell said. "We wrestled incredible teams — Ray Stevens and Nick Bockwinkel, Bobby Duncum and Blackjack Lanza, Jesse Ventura and Adrian Adonis — and made good money. Even though Greg was a little underweight, he was an outstanding worker, a good talker and had great timing."

But after the departure of Hogan, attendance plunged. "I had my own gym two blocks from my house in White Bear Lake [Minnesota] and needed my wrestling money to cover some bills. So I went to Verne and said, 'I love the AWA and want to continue to be Greg's partner. But financially, I can't do it. I need you to give me a guarantee I'll always make a certain minimum of money.'"

He claimed that the promoter denied the request. "The next week, I was in New York. Hulk spoke up for me. He knew I could work. Vince could have cared less. All he saw was that if I left the High Flyers, it was another nail in Verne's coffin."

Before he was even partnered with Blair, Brunzell was asked to do a TV interview while McMahon looked on. "He sort of turned his head and said to himself, 'We've got another Bob Backlund.' I knew what that meant. Bob was a great wrestler, but he didn't have the fire you needed for a good interview. He was too much of a babyface. And I think that was probably the beginning of my in and out with Vince. I could never trust him. I thought he was a manipulator. He just rubbed me the wrong way."

Regardless, McMahon was confident that Brunzell would do fine if allied with Blair.

Raised in Tampa, Blair grew up watching the University of Tampa football team and Eddie Graham's Championship Wrestling from Florida (CWF) promotion. During a summer break from the University of

Louisville, where he'd been awarded a football scholarship, he came home to train under Graham's enforcer, Hiro Matsuda, alongside Hulk Hogan.

In addition to presenting both highly technical matches and brutal bloodbaths, Graham was known for creative, long-term booking and was a promotional mentor to Bill Watts. "Eddie once said to me, 'You're a college man,'" Watts recalled. "'I never even finished high school. Why would you come down here?' And I said, 'I came to get my PhD.' And I did. Eddie Graham was so sharp. He taught me so much."

Watts was booking for Graham when they came up with arguably the best-remembered angle in the Florida territory. It unfolded in 1974, during a match pitting heels Dusty Rhodes and "The Korean Assassin" Pak Song against Eddie Graham and his son, Mike. As Rhodes held the promoter in place so Song could deliver a chop, Eddie moved out of the way and Dusty took the blow, falling out of the ring.

Meanwhile, Mike was tied up in the ropes and attacked by heel manager Gary Hart, as Song turned his attention to beating up on Eddie. When Rhodes came back to the ring and saw the father and son in distress, he shocked the audience by assaulting the villains. But Hart and Song soon double-teamed Dusty, prompting Mike — who'd been freed by the referee — to save his former enemy.

On TV, Rhodes would declare that the encounter proved to him that Mike was no longer a boy but a man. Florida fans were so heartened, they never booed Rhodes again.

He'd emerge from the story as "The American Dream" — the moniker that would grace his grave marker. But none of that would have been possible had Eddie Graham not recreated him as a babyface in Florida.

An astute businessman, Graham played a hand in a number of decisions that would have a wide impact on the industry. Just before lobbying for Jack Brisco to win the NWA World Heavyweight Championship in 1973, Graham offered the Native American star a percentage of the territory, ensuring that he'd return and headline after the reign ended. Four years later, Graham and Vincent James McMahon plotted out the precise timeline for Superstar Billy Graham to defeat Bruno Sammartino for the WWWF Heavyweight title and lose it to Bob Backlund.

Like Verne Gagne, Bill Watts and other promoters of the era, Eddie Graham expected his performers to be genuine shooters capable of punishing anybody who dared challenge them. In training, Matsuda abused aspirants, hoping to run off everyone but the strongest candidates.

"We started out doing 100 Hindu squats and 100 push-ups with either 30 seconds or a minute rest until we did 500 of each," Blair said. "Then, we'd go to the ring and amateur wrestle for ten minutes straight. Ten minutes is a long time to wrestle after you're gassed from doing so many Hindu squats and push-ups. So the first two days, I'd just roll out of the ring and puke.

"On the third day, I rolled out of the ring and I was trying my best not to puke. I felt like I was going to, but I didn't. And Hiro grabbed my face and said, 'Hey boy, why you no puke?' I said, 'Well, Mr. Matsuda, I haven't eaten since the last time I puked.' And he turned his head and I saw his ears go up, so I figured he was smiling.

"After that, he would take me to my limit. But he would say, 'Good job.' He started encouraging me."

Eventually, Blair dropped out of school to fill in as a referee and continue his training.

Over the years, he'd be considered such a reliable athlete that before *WrestleMania*, he and Tito Santana were tasked with wrestling Paul Orndorff around the horn and preparing him for the main event.

It was a thrill for Blair, who, as a 13-year-old soft drink vendor at Tampa Stadium, idolized the future Mr. Wonderful when he played football for the University of Tampa. "Paul was so strong, man. I couldn't stretch him. We'd do submission wrestling, amateur wrestling. He was the toughest guy."

Once the Killer Bees started, Canadian announcer Billy Red Lyons came up with the concept of the tandem donning identical masks in the course of their match and befuddling opponents. Said Blair, "He told me that he and the Destroyer had done it when they were a tag team, since they were around the same size and wore the same trunks. But they did 'masked confusion' as heels. The way we pulled it off as babyfaces was we'd say that the heels were always cheating, so we had to do something to make it even.

"We took Billy's idea and ran with it. And since I always love making a little money, I said, 'Man, we can even sell masks.'"

Because Blair and Brunzell both had amateur backgrounds and been trained by two of the toughest shooters in the business, the pair had a fluid ring style and worked well together. The only issue was that Brunzell did not like McMahon and had heat with others in important positions. "[Booker] George Scott had fired him in the Carolinas, so he was working with a handicap already," Blair said. "But we were together because he was friends with Terry [Bollea] in the AWA and I was friends with Terry from Tampa, and Vince wanted this tag team."

In fact, as interest in the WWF widened, the company issued a Killer Bees t-shirt. "I remember the first time Vince showed it to us," Blair said. "He was really excited. Now, if your boss is excited, you better be excited, too, right? At least, that's my philosophy. But Jimmy makes a face and says, 'What is that?' And I'm like, 'Oh my gosh, why is he saying this?'"

Brunzell insisted that the figures in the drawing did not look like bees. "I thought they turned us into butterflies and Vince did it just for a joke. That's really what I thought. And I wouldn't put that past Vince. Would you?"

CHAPTER 16

Business was so good, few others in the WWF had the same jaundiced view of the owner.

"There weren't really budgets or anything like that," said photographer Tom Buchanan. "I remember going to a budget meeting for the magazine and Linda McMahon was there because she was running publications at the time. And she said, 'Tom, just treat my money like it's your money. Respect it. Buy what you need. Please don't waste it.' And that was the rule I lived by."

"Brooklyn Brawler" Steve Lombardi regarded Vince as "one of the boys, a good guy we could all talk to, a guy who liked to joke around and laugh with us."

As late as 1993, Lombardi would be able to knock on the door of the office the owner set up at each arena and pitch concepts. It was his idea, for instance, to briefly wrestle under the name Abe "Knuckleball" Schwartz, coming to the ring in a baseball uniform, swathed in white pancake makeup with seams drawn across his face — like members of the fictitious Furies gang in the 1979 movie *The Warriors*.

"I told him, 'I want to be a wrestling baseball player,' and he looked right at me and said in his deep voice, 'Is that so?' Just like that, we were getting ready to shoot vignettes — without any show writers, without any corporate stuff, just a conversation between him and me."

When WWF employees gathered outside of work, sometimes the McMahons joined them. "Vince played on the [WWF] softball team with us," said Mike Weber, the company's head of public relations. "He was only in his early forties then and a heck of an athlete."

At company parties, Vince would go out of his way to dance with workers' wives while, in the office, Weber and Linda occasionally spoke about their elementary school-age daughters. "I remember Stephanie running up and down the hallways, just having fun, and Linda asking me to give advice to [her son] Shane that it would probably be a good idea to go to college."

When the McMahons purchased a new dining room table, Linda asked if anyone needed their old one. "I rented a U-Haul and came to their house and picked it up," Weber said. "It was just a lot of personal interaction through and through, a real family affair, a great atmosphere, and it made you feel like you wanted to work harder for these people you liked so much."

Later, when Basil Devito's sons were born, the McMahons told him that they were happy to welcome the first twins in the office family. "Vince and Linda were the first two people at the hospital."

Likewise, Hulk Hogan also established a rapport with employees with whom he often dealt. "We were constantly on planes together and sharing cars together," Steve Taylor recalled. "One of the funniest times was when I flew down to Tampa to do a photo shoot at his house, and he picked me up at the airport. I wait at the curb and he pulls up, gives me a big hand-shake, grabs my bags and puts them in the trunk. And the people are just standing there, staring at me, thinking, 'Who could this guy possibly be?'"

In 1986, future WWE Hall of Famer Ernie "The Big Cat" Ladd joined the company as a color commentator. "The wrestling war is over," Ladd told intimates. "But the other guys don't know it yet."

In pro wrestling, few competitors carried the authority of Ladd.

At 6'9" and 290 pounds, he'd been one of the largest players in the old American Football League (AFL), supplementing his income by wrestling in the off-season. In 1969, he determined that the One True Sport paid better and committed himself to it wholeheartedly, main-eventing in every major territory. Because of his size, he was the ideal heel contender, casting a literal shadow over the champion and seemingly forcing him to fight for his life to protect the gold. He particularly stood out in front of a microphone, cutting promos that were both engrossing and entertaining.

"Don't give me that smirky look on your face," he'd said in one 1976 exchange, staring down at a microphone-wielding Vince McMahon. "You're just a TV announcer. I know I burn you up every time I look at you, TV announcer. It make you sick, don't it? Don't it, boy? . . . Look at you, you wish you could do something about it, don't you? Well, put some tights on, Mr. TV announcer . . . Boy, I know I have you bad."

Recently, Ladd had been the booker for Mid-South Wrestling, one of the few Black men to ever rise to that type of position behind the scenes. Bill Watts was proud to have elevated his friend to a job that required him to use his fertile imagination rather than simply rely on his physicality and felt that Mid-South was setting a standard for other promotions to follow.

Now, Ladd had gone north and joined the WWF, and, in this case, it wasn't entirely Vince's fault.

In 1986, the oil crash hit the very states where Bill Watts promoted. "All my main arenas were in what you call the oil states of Louisiana, Texas, Oklahoma and Arkansas," Watts said. "Every business was almost ancillary to the oil industry. So you could read your business in an area. If the oil business there was going up or going flat, that's how your business was going to go.

"All entertainment was affected — rock 'n' roll shows, country shows. Bourbon Street [in New Orleans] was almost deserted. You couldn't find a hooker. One of my employees loved calling the dating services. Back then, the escort services would take out quarter-page ads in the yellow pages. He went through pages and pages of these ads and said they were all closed. There was no money being spent.

"We had one of our best cards at the Superdome. Our gate was generally three times our advance sale. This time, all we did was our advance sale and nothing on top of it."

Oddly, Houston, which had already weathered a similar trend in 1984 and '85, continued to flourish, reportedly selling out 50 shows in a row at the Sam Houston Coliseum during that period. While the 1986 oil crisis was impacting the Von Erichs' World Class cards in Texas, Houston remained untouched.

But virtually every place else in the Mid-South territory suffered, according to Watts. "Everybody was going broke, and we were forced to expand our tours just to get our reach out there and expose our product to new people."

The strategy forced the company to stretch its resources even thinner.

Naturally, McMahon was also doing his best to exacerbate the agony. As with Verne Gagne and the AWA, Vince began paying stations in the market for the time slots Watts had negotiated for a trade-out of some sort. "He was buying up my time and replacing it with his shows. We could have filed a federal antitrust suit and probably done well, but that would have taken years and tons of money I didn't have."

Once the Junkyard Dog departed, Watts knew that McMahon would be back to cherry-pick the best of the Mid-South roster. "He had the money to buy your talent and he had the big population centers where they could get the exposure they wanted. We didn't have a single city that could match New York or Boston or Philadelphia."

Over the next few years, certain Mid-South names would become firmly entrenched in the WWF, including JYD, Hacksaw Jim Duggan, "The Million Dollar Man" Ted DiBiase, the Big Boss Man, One Man Gang (a.k.a. Akeem), the Bushwackers, "The Red Rooster" Terry Taylor and Jake "The Snake" Roberts.

Bruce Prichard watched the changes unfold in Houston. "People were seeing the guys in New York making several thousand dollars a night instead of maybe $1,000 a week in the territories. Then, there was the lure of Madison Square Garden, the lure of traveling the entire country and making a lot more money, having your own action figure, being part of a Saturday morning cartoon. [*Hulk Hogan's Rock 'n' Wrestling* animated series ran from 1985 to 1987.] That was something none of the regional territories could offer."

At the time of Roberts's departure in February 1986, the promotion's top title, the North American Heavyweight Championship, was held up following his inconclusive clash with the titlist, Dick Slater in Houston. Despite the primitive technology of the time, word-of-mouth gossip had spread that Jake was headed to the WWF. As a result, the so-called smart fans of Mid-South were convinced that Slater would decisively win the belt during the Valentine's Day rematch. Instead, after a thrilling back and forth, Roberts managed to pull out a win with a DDT.

"Everybody expected one finish and I didn't do it," Watts said. "Because Jake told me he wouldn't just leave as the champion and I believed his word."

The belt would go to Slater on February 23 in Oklahoma City. "Jake did exactly what he promised to do."

Still, realizing that the territory system was fading, Watts took the dramatic step of trying to get national recognition himself, by changing the name of Mid-South Wrestling to the Universal Wrestling Federation (UWF) in April 1986 and awarding the main title to the territory's last North American kingpin, Duggan.

As part of the expansion, Watts secured two hour-long syndicated slots and improved the feel of the TV show.

Four years earlier, he'd upgraded from the studio in Shreveport to an arena at the Irish McNeel Sports for Boys Club on the grounds of the Louisiana State Fairgrounds. "We wanted to have a bigger crowd," announcer Jim Ross said, "with a better atmosphere."

Since then, the company had continued to refine its production values, and Watts was confident that, like the quality of his wrestling, the feel of the show was as good as anyone's in the business.

The more attractive presentation conjured up hopes in the group's followers that the company's rebranding as a national promotion was going to work. Yet, the decision was also evidence that McMahon's Machiavellian plans were working. Around North America, the wrestling community appeared to be more balkanized than it had been since the days prior to the formation of the NWA.

Jim Crockett Jr. purchased the Kansas City territory — also known as Central States Wrestling or Heart of America Sports Attractions — in 1986, hoping to send JCP talent there for seasoning and to keep them fresh.

Central States had been one of the original NWA affiliates; its two main partners, Pinkie George and Orville Brown, attended the conclave that formed the organization in 1948. Since 1963, promoter Bob Geigel had primarily been the face of the territory, serving three terms as NWA president. It was largely Geigel's influence that led to promotional partner Harley Race winning his first NWA World Heavyweight Championship in 1973.

But as the wrestling war took its toll, Race found himself more than $500,000 in debt and divested from the league, and he jumped to the WWF in 1986. On television, McMahon made it a point to never mention the star's numerous NWA title reigns. The *WWF Magazine was* allowed to say that he'd been a champion "all over the world," and the company acknowledged his import by dressing him in a crown and cape and rebranding him "The King."

Back in Kansas City, the relationship between Crockett and Geigel imploded almost as soon as the sale was consummated. "It was a one-sided partnership," David Crockett maintained. "We go to Kansas City and have a show, promote off our syndicated television and TBS and send talent. They sit back. It might have helped somebody's ego, but that doesn't translate to the bottom line."

When Jimmy Crockett attempted to feature Central States matches on JCP television, the encounters were so poorly lit that they detracted from the rest of the program.

In 1987, Crockett pulled out of the deal, calling his talent home, while Geigel stepped down as head of the NWA and started a group called the World Wrestling Alliance (WWA), consisting primarily of the aging Kansas City roster that preceded the Crockett purchase and a handful of inexperienced talent.

Competitors exchanged shoulder blocks and clotheslines in an antiquated ring since Crockett had also recalled his equipment.

The one thing he kept, however, was the territory's timeslot in St. Louis.

For a period, the WWA attempted to co-promote with World Class and the AWA, but the allegiances fared worse than Pro Wrestling USA. In 1988 — the year that Trump Plaza Hotel and Casino sponsored *WrestleMania IV* in Atlantic City — the experiment ended, and Geigel quietly left the business, taking a security job instead at the Woodlands racetrack in Kansas City.

CHAPTER 17

Back in Stamford, Basil Devito struggled to maintain a grasp on not only the codes of the pro wrestling subculture but the many changes that were occurring within the company. "We were adding live events," he said. "We were doing double shots [sending the same wrestlers to two separate shows] on Saturdays. We were still learning how this should all be done. The awesome, well-oiled machine would come later."

At one employee party, Vince McMahon scanned the room, leaned into Steve Taylor and mumbled, "Who are all these people?"

"They work for you."

Vince shook his head. "I know. Amazing."

When Mike Weber arrived in 1986, he estimated that there were approximately 60 people on staff. Space was running out in the office the McMahons had rented in Greenwich, and Weber shared a work area in a coffee room with ring announcer Howard Finkel. When the media called, there was one consistent request: "Would it be possible to interview Hulk?"

Weber would write down the outlets interested in grabbing a few minutes with the company's most famous performer, then go directly to McMahon. "Hulk Hogan couldn't do anything without Vince's approval — and rightfully so. So there was a lot of communication about whether Hogan should do a certain interview. As in, 'How does it benefit what we're trying to portray?'"

As more talent joined the roster, Weber's options increased. "If a reporter couldn't get Hogan, we might provide Randy Savage or Jake 'The Snake' Roberts or Jimmy Hart or Bobby Heenan — guys who were smart and could really talk. It didn't matter if they were babyfaces or heels. They took a lot of Hogan's media requests and turned them into gold."

Having survived the anxiety of presenting the first *WrestleMania*, the organization was barreling ahead. "There was sort of this optimistic energy," recalled vice president of business affairs Dick Glover. "People from outside the wrestling environment were joining as part of the senior-level team. We were all there because we believed we would be successful."

Although there were the inevitable office rivalries, the staff tended to be tight-knit and supportive of each other, Weber said. "We were all getting our feet on the ground together with a company that was getting its feet on the ground. I'd walk by Dick Glover's office and he'd wave me in. He had a popcorn popper and people would just come by and help themselves and shoot the breeze. He encouraged it. For a guy in such an important position, he was so positive and down-to-earth."

Shortly after Glover's arrival, the WWF took out an ad in one of the trade publications featuring Hulk Hogan spreading his arms across two pages. "We were literally trying to show the company's reach to the mainstream business community," he said, "that working with us would be an opportunity you shouldn't miss. We had this fantastic audience already and all these growth plans."

Understanding that the traditionalists on the wrestling end found the changes threatening, McMahon occasionally tried to mollify them. Before one television taping, Vince sat at a table in front of the well-groomed, recent hires as well as the road agents with bleached hair and scarred foreheads, blocking out the night's events. "After we were finished with the logistics," Devito said, "he looked over at our side of the room and said, more or less, 'Okay, now you guys in the jackets and ties can leave.' And then, they had the rest of their meeting."

Because he spent so much time on the road, Taylor understood both the resentments of the wrestling people as well as the frustrations felt by the office guys who wanted to pull the company up from its carny past. "It was really like two different companies. You even saw it in the way Vince was treated. Some office people might go, 'Oh, there's Mr. McMahon, the business genius who created this phenomenon.' And the rest of us, who traveled with him, were like, 'Yo, Vince, I have a question for you. You got a minute?' And I think he appreciated how we could be informal — at least then, before the company got bigger and bigger."

To be sure, Vince was anxious for more growth and constantly coming up with plans to reach the next level. After digesting the surprising pay-per-view numbers for *WrestleMania*, "Vince wanted to do a pay-per-view exclusive event as soon as possible," Devito said.

On November 7, 1985, the WWF staged something called *The Wrestling Classic* from the Rosemont Horizon outside Chicago solely for pay-per-view customers. McMahon announced that this would be the first of five such airings under the banner of what he called "WrestleVision."

"We didn't know anything about pay-per-view," Devito admitted. "I don't think anybody did back then."

The show featured a 16-man tournament culminating in a finale between the Junkyard Dog and Savage. The forgettable and unsatisfying finish involved JYD flipping his opponent over the ropes with a high back body drop. Savage was unable to return, and the ref counted him out.

Fans also saw another collision between Hogan and "Rowdy" Roddy Piper. As with the tournament climax, it ended clumsily. After the referee was knocked down, Piper battered Hogan with a chair, but the champion fought back and clamped on a sleeper hold. Before Roddy could conk out, his "bodyguard" Cowboy Bob Orton Jr. used his signature cast to bash the Hulkster. Coming to his senses, the arbiter disqualified the challenger. Yet Piper and Orton continued to gang up on Hogan until the villains' former ally, Paul "Mr. Wonderful" Orndorff, stormed the ring and made the save.

McMahon would later describe *The Wrestling Classic* as "a dud," telling *Electronic Media*, "All of our guns weren't loaded for WrestleVision as they were for *WrestleMania*."

The subsequent four events were canceled, and concentration shifted back to the company's dependable franchise.

McMahon wanted *WrestleMania 2* to somehow take the company past the point where *WrestleMania 1* had stopped. Since the inaugural event had been in Madison Square Garden, where most of the WWF's major shows had occurred up until that point, he proposed presenting matches in three separate locations: the New York and Chicago metropolitan areas and Los Angeles. "Three different time zones," said Devito, "three different buildings."

The decision would buttress the WWF's reputation as a national, rather than a northeastern, organization, with the selections reminding the public that the company had a presence in all three major US population centers.

"It was part of Vince's plan to make the WWF the only wrestling company anyone would know," observed Bill Apter.

For those who kept track of such things — and McMahon certainly did — the event would erase the novelty of Jim Crockett Jr. staging the 1985 *Starrcade* in Atlanta and Greensboro. It would also provoke the Charlotte-based promoter into keeping pace, forcing him to abandon Greensboro for Chicago in 1987 — as you'll read later — alienating fans in South Carolina.

At the time of *WrestleMania 2*, Crockett was looking to establish a beachhead in the Windy City — officially, this was AWA territory, but Jimmy couldn't have cared less — and entered into discussions with the Rosemont Horizon. As he had in the past, McMahon turned to Jim Barnett, who secured the building for the WWF for *WrestleMania 2* on April 7, 1986.

The other locations would be the Nassau Coliseum, outside New York City on Long Island, and the Los Angeles Memorial Sports Arena.

McMahon's staff worried about the plan. Devito acknowledged that the three locations required three times as many celebrities, three times as much money and three times the work.

"It probably wasn't the best idea," conceded Taylor. "One show — you had to worry about putting that together. Three shows meant three times as many problems."

Vice president for television production Nelson Sweglar had a difficult time locating production people with the appropriate product knowledge. "One of the pitfalls," he said, "was finding the kind of experienced wrestling staff in three different cities to make that work properly. What you want is, from a programming standpoint, some kind of continuity. And there wasn't really the staff to do it. We had to coordinate three sets of commentators in the different time zones. I'm amazed to this day that it came off."

In New York, where Mr. T — whose star had waned in the year since the first *WrestleMania* — beat Roddy Piper via disqualification in a worked boxing match, Vince was paired at the announce table with actress Susan Saint James, wife of the owner's close ally, sports executive Dick Ebersol.

"She didn't know anything about wrestling," Sweglar said, "and didn't have time to learn."

Bill Apter watched the show. The New York portion of the telecast aired first, followed by the matches from suburban Chicago and then Los Angeles, while fans at the venues followed along on large screens. Bill Apter watched as a spectator in the Nassau Coliseum, having received a complimentary seat from friends at the company producing the WWF action figures. "It was very, very weird. I was a guest, but the WWF didn't invite me. And, once in a while, I'd see people from the WWF walking by me to make sure I wasn't taking pictures or anything."

Craig Peters was bewildered by the selection of celebrities. "It was like they were throwing spaghetti against the wall. I mean, look who they had? [Watergate conspirator] G. Gordon Liddy, Ray Charles, Joan Rivers, Ozzy Osbourne, Cab Calloway, for god's sake."

In Los Angeles, where Hulk Hogan retained his crown over King Kong Bundy in a cage match, announcers Jesse Ventura and Lord Alfred Hayes did engage in some amusing exchanges with guest commentator Elvira, a horror movie TV hostess whose transition to the wrestling environment was seamless.

Although Tom Buchanan was stationed in Long Island, he was impressed by the lighting setup in LA. "We hired some *Sports Illustrated* shooters and they hung remote strobes from the trusses that were triggered by their cameras. If you look at the photos from all three locations, you really see the difference. Their pictures were spectacularly better and, almost immediately we bought a system that did the same thing."

In the time since he'd received his first assignment with the WWF, Buchanan's understanding of the business had deepened, thanks largely to a routine he developed with "Macho Man" Randy Savage.

"He taught me how wrestling works," Buchanan recounted. "It started in Toronto, where I was shooting one of his matches and my task for the show was getting photos of [Savage's manager and real-life wife] Elizabeth."

While other female managers and valets were depicted as brash vixens, Elizabeth appeared demure and vulnerable. Fans were led to believe that Savage was insanely possessive of her — an allegation several of his peers described as a shoot. Once the bell rang, he never seemed to take his eyes off the nervous woman in his corner.

"I start shooting Elizabeth during the match, and Randy stops wrestling, looks at me and points. 'What are you doing? Don't take her picture.' I back off a little, shoot the match, but I still have to get my photos of Elizabeth. So I turn the camera back to her, and Randy stops his match again, comes over to the ropes and yells, 'I told you not to take her picture.' And I'm scared because I don't know what's going on.

"I back off again, then shoot Elizabeth when I think Randy isn't looking. This time, he jumps over the ropes, onto the floor and chases me over the barricade, and I hide behind the cop while he's screaming at me.

"So I go backstage afterwards and talk to [local promoter and figure-head WWF president] Jack Tunney. And he tells me Randy is very jealous and I should take him seriously. 'You've got a problem.'"

For the next few days, every time Buchanan walked into an airport, rental car office or hotel, he had his eye out for Savage. Eventually, they were booked on the same card again and the photographer deliberately sought out the star. "I had to deal with this."

The two repaired to a private room backstage. "I said, 'Look, I was the photographer in Toronto.' And Randy's saying to himself, 'Toronto? Toronto?' And I say, 'Was there a problem?' And he thinks about it some more and goes, 'Oh yeah. You run fast. That was good.'"

From that point forward, they'd repeat the act whenever they were on the same show, refining it along the way. In time, they grew to regard each other as friends. "He showed me how stories get created, how spots get created."

Much of the mainstream attention surrounding *WrestleMania 2* focused on the main event in Chicago, a 20-man battle royal involving both WWF stars and NFL players, including the most popular personality in American football at the time, 300-plus-pound Chicago Bears lineman William "The Refrigerator" Perry.

Although Perry was reportedly respectful to everyone he met, he still engendered a great deal of resentment. At one point, after seeing the NFL players featured on the cover of the *Chicago Sun-Times*, an irate Big John Studd slammed Basil Devito into a wall.

"You're an idiot," Studd growled. "Don't you know who sells the tickets? It's us. It ain't them. We're the business, not them."

The WWF further enflamed the wrestlers by placing mats around the ring to protect the guest athletes. Since this was not yet standard procedure in the sport of kings, members of the ring crew were dispatched to a local elementary school to procure the coverings from the gymnasium walls. "I remember the wrestlers looking at the mats on the TV monitor and saying, 'What wussies,'" Weber said. "'Oh, we have mats now?'"

"Jumping" Jim Brunzell was particularly annoyed that so many outsiders were going to be exposed to how the business operated. "Smartening up those football players was the biggest sacrilege of all," he said.

André the Giant angrily proclaimed that he expected to win the battle royal, telling friends, "I'm not putting over a football player."

André received his wish, ironically, after Big John Studd was the one who played the fool for the Refrigerator. After Studd deposited Perry over the top rope, the NFL star stood and reached up to the ring, extending a hand in friendship. That Studd, a heel, would have reciprocated defied logic. But this was sports entertainment, not the Snake Pit in Wigan. So Studd accepted the gesture and was pulled over the top rope onto the arena floor.

This was kind of a violation of the rules. Since Perry had already been eliminated, he had no authority to continue participating in the match, and Studd should have been allowed to continue. Plus, even if Big John had been feeling magnanimous enough to take Perry's hand, wouldn't the ropes have prevented him from somersaulting to ringside?

McMahon did not expect fans to scrutinize this point and few, if any, did. The match continued until André was left alone with Bret "Hit Man" Hart and his tag team partner and real-life brother-in-law, Jim "The Anvil" Neidhart.

Both had been headliners in Stampede Wrestling, the Calgary-based territory run by Bret's father, Stu Hart. But a series of back-and-forth deals with McMahon had brought the tandem to the WWF. Aware of what they each had to do, Hart and Neidhart gave the Giant the finish he wanted.

First, André knocked Bret down with a big boot to the face, then rammed his head into Neidhart's in what announcer Gorilla Monsoon termed a "double noggin knocker." A kick from the Giant sent Neidhart over the ropes. André then hurled Bret to ringside as well, plunking him on top of the Anvil.

In Chicago, the only thing that mattered was that André the Giant had proven that even a large contingent of NFL players could not stop "the Eighth Wonder of the World." To the Hart clan in Calgary, though, the selection of the Giant's final two opponents in such a high-profile setting resonated strongly.

Maybe that deal they'd made with McMahon wasn't such a bad thing after all.

CHAPTER 18

L egendary shooter Stu Hart and his wife, Helen, met while he was wrestling in New York, introduced by future Houston promoter Paul Boesch, who knew Helen and her sister from the Long Island beach where he worked as a lifeguard. Within hours of their wedding, the couple was just north of the city in White Plains, where Stu wrestled "Golden Boy" Arnold Skaaland.

If Helen had any questions about the life she'd be leading, his choice that night answered everything.

Within a year of the marriage, the two had settled in Calgary, where, in 1948, Stu founded the company that became Stampede Wrestling with Al Oeming, a wrestler who owned North America's largest game farm, loaning out rare and endangered animals for Disney movies. By the time Stu became the sole owner of Stampede in 1959, the territory covered a wide chunk of western Canada. Eventually, it would stretch from British Columbia through Alberta and Saskatchewan into Manitoba, as well as small slivers of northern Montana and North Dakota.

Meanwhile, Stu and Helen raised 12 children; at some point, all the boys wrestled professionally and all the girls married wrestlers. In the Hart household, a 20-room Victorian mansion overlooking the city of Calgary, Helen ran the financial end of the territory while Stu cooked for his large brood and trained aspiring wrestlers in the notorious "dungeon" downstairs.

He seemed to take perverse pleasure in finding a bodybuilder or football player who thought he was tough enough to be a wrestler. Almost unanimously, members of the family described hearing terrified shrieks emanating from the dungeon and occasionally seeing a trainee running away, terrified, in the snow.

"Stampede Wrestling really consumed our lives," recalled Ross Hart, Stu and Helen's tenth child and the family historian. "It was part of everything I did. I learned writing skills corresponding with the different wrestling magazines and sending them match results and updates. And I'd get the programs from the different territories in the mail.

"At the Friday night shows [at Calgary's Victoria Pavilion], I'd bring some friends with me and we'd sell programs. But we'd always be done in time to see the semi-final and main event."

Even around family, Stu conducted himself as if the battles in the ring were legitimate, confusing his children when his hated enemies stopped by the house to chat with Helen and pick up their checks. "Everything was very kayfabe," Ross said. "It wasn't until I was 13 or 14 that my mother had to explain to me that it wasn't exactly real. 'Dad got cut by Abdullah the Butcher, but he's going to be alright. It was kind of staged to create an angle and draw a crowd.'

"Once I knew the truth, I still protected the business. I would never think of exposing it."

He was regularly provoked to do so, particularly at school when other kids challenged the game's authenticity. "I'd hear that all the wrestlers were a bunch of phony actors who used fake blood or whatever. And then, the fight was on. I had to defend my dad's honor."

A front facelock generally ended the teasing. "My dad taught us a lot of moves. We did amateur wrestling, too, but dad showed us some extra things to use as self-defense." It was a skill the boys needed. "A lot of kids thought they could make a name for themselves by beating up a Hart. We had to always be on guard — not just for us, but for our sisters, too. When they were targeted, it was up to the boys to protect them."

As each son transitioned into the business, Stu made sure that their training was versatile, mandating that they work out with visiting wrestlers from Mexico, Japan, the United Kingdom and Germany, acquiring a dexterity that would enable them to work anywhere.

They also learned quite a bit at the dining room table, listening to Stu and his guests discuss both the politics of the industry and mechanics of the ring. With his scratchy voice and tendency to punctuate sentences with long pauses, Stu became one of the most imitated men in pro wrestling — along with Jim Barnett.

But, within the business, he was internationally respected. Often, when one of the Hart kids arrived in a foreign locale to work a match, he'd discover that the fans were already familiar with his style since Stampede Wrestling was syndicated around the world.

Announcer Ed Whalen was almost as famous as the wrestlers, the host of the promotion's television programs since 1962 as well as a mainstream sports and news personality in Calgary. Although his approach to the action was generally serious — by many accounts, he was something of a true believer and was known to become as emotional as the fans — he coined such playful phrases as "it's going to be a ring-a-ding-dong dandy," and his sign-off, "in the meantime and in-between time . . ."

During the Calgary Stampede, the rodeo, exhibition and festival held each summer, Stu would fly up the biggest stars he could find, showcasing them in the "wrestling float" in the jubilee's opening parade. "We'd usually bring in André the Giant," Ross remembered, "and whoever the world champion was at the time. We generally brought in the NWA champion because we were part of the NWA. But there were times when my father wasn't a member for different reasons, so I remember Bruno Sammartino defending the WWWF title one time and Nick Bockwinkel coming in as the AWA Champion."

After high school, Ross went on the road with Stampede, driving the icy roads to places like Moose Jaw, Manitoba; Wetaskiwin, Alberta; and Great Falls, Montana, booking shows and contacting the media about local cards. "I think I had a hand in everything from setting up rings to refereeing to training guys."

When business was good, the territory's major shows had genuine star power. "When business was down, it was terrible."

Stampede's most calamitous incident occurred on December 2, 1983, at the Victoria Pavilion. Archie "The Stomper" Gouldie was the rare former football player who'd been tortured by Stu Hart in the dungeon and ended up in the industry — after first returning to the Hart Mansion and begging forgiveness for taking the business lightly. Although he was billed as the Mongolian Stomper elsewhere and pretended not to speak English, in the Calgary territory, everyone knew that he was raised in Carbon, Alberta, and he didn't bother to hide it. On the mic, he would mesmerize fans with his heel promos and, for years, was considered the promotion's top villain.

When he was ready for a face turn, Stu came up with an angle involving a gimmick son named "Jeff Gouldie." At the pavilion, the two were partnered with Bad News Allen — Allen Coage, who'd won a bronze medal for the US in judo at the 1976 Summer Olympics and would later appear in the WWF as Bad News Brown — against Bret Hart, future British Bulldog Davey Boy Smith and Sonny Two Rivers, a Japanese wrestler playing a First Nations character. As the match progressed, tension on the heel team was evident and Bad News stunned the crowd by piledriving Jeff Gouldie onto the arena floor.

"Apparently, his neck was broken and the fans went nuts," Ross said. "It was just so effective. They really believed. Archie Gouldie was going berserk and people were hurling chairs. Some were trying to get closer to the wrestlers and attack Bad News and some were fleeing in panic." In the chaos, one woman was trampled and an elderly man battered Allen with his cane.

"Bad News lost his temper and grabbed the guy and assaulted him. The guy had hit him first, but the local media was there and it never looks good when one of your wrestlers attacks a senior citizen."

Concerned about his own reputation, Ed Whalen quit the promotion on the air, refusing to be associated with this level of violence.

"The following week, on the day that Bad News was supposed to fight the Stomper, there's like 2,500 people lined up outside the pavilion in minus 35 degrees. But literally hours before the show, the Calgary Boxing and Wrestling Commission suspended my dad's license. We couldn't have a match anywhere in the city. We had to relocate to a Native reserve outside Calgary where there was no public transportation and you couldn't get there unless you went by car.

"Unfortunately, what should have made us money for a long time kind of lost all its steam and went nowhere. By the time my dad got his license back, the riot and all the negative publicity killed the drawing power of the angle."

What made matters worse was that Whalen's replacement, retired wrestler and veteran announcer Sam Menacker, could not adequately fill the spot. "He might have been a good host at one time, but he couldn't remember angles or names or speak fast enough to keep up with what was going on. So the viewing audience really dropped."

In the aftermath of the incident, Stu Hart and Vince McMahon began talking about the WWF taking over the territory. "He'd already kind of set up a Canadian operation, working with Jack Tunney in Toronto," Ross said. "We knew it was a matter of time before they expanded across Canada."

The agreement — overseen by Jim Barnett, who couldn't resist getting involved in this stuff — was formalized in August 1984. "They got all of my dad's wrestling rings, along with his TV slots and access to his top talent."

Every one of those talents had some tie to the Hart family. Bret's tag team partner in the Hart Foundation, Jim "The Anvil" Neidhart, was married to the Hit Man's sister, Ellie. For a period, their chief opponents in the WWF would be the British Bulldogs, consisting of Davey Boy Smith, who was married to Bret's sister Diana, and "Dynamite Kid" Tom Billington, who was married to the sister of Bret's wife at the time, Julie.

The other names in Calgary seemed to be cut out of the equation. "It was kind of disappointing for the people who didn't have anyplace to work," Ross said.

This prompted one of the brothers, Bruce Hart, to begin promoting cards with wrestlers who hadn't been picked up by the WWF. "He went behind our back," Ross insisted. "He was basically going to run opposition to the WWF. He was talking to a local TV affiliate. It hurt my dad's credibility because the WWF either thought we were involved or that Stu didn't have control over Bruce."

It didn't matter that Bruce's outlaw federation closed after a few shows. The effort "was considered a violation of the agreement the WWF had with my dad," Ross said, "and it nullified the deal."

In October 1985, Stampede Wrestling was sold back to the Harts.

Although the WWF maintained its grip on the territory's traditional TV slots, Stu was quickly promoting again, with Bruce running much of the day-to-day activities. Unlike others in that position, he chose not to revert back to the old headliners but harvest a new crop of talent and create a version of Stampede Wrestling that would be fondly remembered. Among its stars: the comedic Makhan Singh (Mike Shaw, who'd later appear in World Championship Wrestling as Norman the Lunatic and the WWF as Bastion Booger), Owen Hart, Chris Benoit, future Japanese legends Jushin "Thunder" Liger and Hiroshi Hase, and the team of Bad Company, Bruce Hart and Brian Pillman.

Despite the misunderstandings, Stu Hart maintained cordial, if not warm, relations with Vince McMahon, never burning the bridge to what the old shooter knew was going to be history's most influential promotion. For his part, McMahon did not seem to direct any animosity toward the Hart family members on his roster. In fact, he appeared quite taken with them and had the British Bulldogs win the WWF World Tag Team Championship at *WrestleMania 2* from the Dream Team of Brutus Beefcake and Greg Valentine.

And while the Hart Foundation was ascending as a tag team, Stu was confident that, down the line, Bret's natural athleticism and ability to connect to an audience was going to propel him to the top. When that day occurred, it would be better for the Hit Man to be performing in the WWF rather than in Red Deer or Medicine Hat.

CHAPTER 19

With each territory breached, the WWF footprint expanded, and the travel grew more exhausting.

"Working for the company meant you were never home," remembered photographer Tom Buchanan. "I'd be on the road for three or four weeks at a time."

Because McMahon had compiled such a large roster, he could run as many as three shows a day with separate crews. "For three-and-a-half years, I was on the road an average of 27 days a month," said Jumping Jim Brunzell. "This is the gospel truth. I wrote my schedule in datebooks, and I still have the books to show you."

The late Tom Zenk, who formed a tag team with Rick Martel in the WWF called the Can-Am Connection, remembered flying into towns on the first flight of the day, grabbing a workout, tanning, cutting promos at the arena, wrestling, returning to the hotel, bleaching his white ring gear in the sink, then leaving the next morning on the earliest plane out.

"We became slaves of the machine," said Jacques Rougeau. "We were living in bags in arenas, hotels and airports. You'd go home for three days to see your family, and then you were back on the road. You're not a normal human being. You lose track of time. It was so demanding mentally to be on that loop with that group of people, and you didn't have ties to anybody outside the business."

Once, as his family said goodbye to him at the airport, one of Rougeau's young sons asked, "Why don't you want to be with us?"

Yet when Jacques and his brother, Raymond, officially signed with the company in 1986, each felt grateful for the opportunity to earn more money — and receive more visibility — than ever before. Raymond believed that Vince viewed the signing of the two French-speaking babyfaces as an opportunity to conquer not just Quebec but, eventually, markets like France, Belgium, Switzerland and Francophone sections of Africa.

Following Jacques's fallout with Lutte Internationale co-owner Dino Bravo, the Rougeaus had returned to the territory, captured the Canadian International Tag Team titles and engaged in a three-month feud with Ronnie and Jim Garvin. Although the Garvins were portrayed as brothers, Ronnie was actually Jimmy's stepfather. He also happened to be from Montreal, which meant that the rivalry with the Rougeaus had resonance in La Belle Province.

Although Jacques Rougeau Sr. was still suspicious of McMahon, on the surface, the WWF and Lutte Internationale had a working relationship. As the deal with Stu Hart in western Canada was falling apart in 1985, Vince worked out an arrangement with Lutte Internationale that granted his company exclusive rights to Le Colisée in Quebec City. In exchange, he agreed to stage a series of interpromotional cards at the Montreal Forum, each of which drew a minimum of 15,000 spectators.

"You have to understand that companies had been running joint shows for decades," Raymond said. "So it didn't seem as strange as it would later on."

In total, the two promotions promoted six events together, enabling the management of the Montreal Forum to personally experience the WWF's star power. It was so impressive that, in February 1986, McMahon signed an exclusive contract with the building, leaving Lutte Internationale out in the Canadian cold.

Much like Calgary, the WWF had its pick of who it wanted in the territory, and the Rougeaus ranked high on the list. "We had to wait to get our working papers in the United States," Jacques said, "but they had a tour coming up of Australia and we started there."

By the end of the year, Dino Bravo would be wrestling for Vince as well.

Given the way that the territory system worked, the Rougeaus were accustomed to working far from home. But Jacques had always been able to return to Quebec to recharge and connect with loved ones. Now, he was barely in the province at all and struggled to maintain a sense of home by fraternizing with French-speaking talent. He tried packing in family activities during his visits to Quebec but, in the long term, it would not be enough to salvage his marriage.

"At first, after being on the road for so long, when I'd come home, it was like I was falling in love again, and I was so happy," he reflected. "But then when I had to leave, I was so sad. Eventually, what happened was that I'd close my feelings up when I was home, so it wouldn't hurt when I left again. But the pain was always there and my ex-wife and kids suffered the collateral damage."

Two years after Kerry von Erich's epic NWA World Heavyweight Championship win at Texas Stadium, WCCW was imploding.

Like Bill Watts, Fritz von Erich had made the decision to withdraw from the NWA. In February 1986, World Class Championship Wrestling American Heavyweight Champion Rick Rude was announced as the company's new world titlist before a television taping. In an effort to distinguish the promotion from its competitors, WCCW declared that its world championship could change hands via disqualification or referee's decision.

Fans were indifferent, if not outright disappointed, that the NWA kingpin would no longer be swinging through the territory.

The same month, top heel Gino Hernandez died at 28 years old. "He was the first person I ever heard of overdosing on cocaine," said World Class producer Keith Mitchell. "As stupid as it sounds, I didn't even know that you could. It wasn't something that really happened in my sphere."

Kerry von Erich didn't seem to be doing much better. On June 4, 1986, he was speeding down a highway on his motorcycle in Argyle, Texas, weaving in and out of traffic. Suddenly, the Modern Day Warrior lost control, crashed into the back of a police car and skidded across the pavement. He suffered internal injuries in addition to dislocating his ankle and hip and badly injuring his right leg.

Three weeks after the mishap, Kerry spoke to his fans on WCCW television, urging them to avoid the mistake he'd made. "Motorcycles are silly," he advised, reclining in a tracksuit. "I'd stay away from them."

Dr. William Sutker admitted that "his foot was in really pathetic shape when he came in, and we were all worried that he had a really good chance of losing his foot." Surgeons had reportedly managed to save the limb by fortifying it with muscle from other parts of the athlete's body.

But, according to Kevin von Erich, while training for his return to the ring, Kerry tried walking on the foot prematurely and reinjured it. As a result, part of the limb was amputated.

Still, Kerry adhered to his pledge to continue his wrestling career. Only now, he had a prosthetic foot, kayfabing to such an extent backstage that he kept on his boot while showering.

Prior to the accident, the wrestler had developed a dependence on pain killers. As Von Erich tried hiding his amputation and dealing with the pressure of winning back declining audiences, his addiction issues increased.

By the time of the crash, much of the dressing room was struggling with similar vices. At the end of June, "Gentleman" Chris Adams — who'd been feuding with Gino Hernandez at the time of his death — became enraged on an American Airlines flight when the crew stopped serving him alcohol. Kevin von Erich was among those who had to restrain the leading babyface after he punched a male flight attendant and headbutted the pilot three times.

Regardless, Fritz programmed Adams to win the World Class belt at the Reunion Arena on July 4 — a championship he'd have to relinquish after he was sentenced to 90 days in jail in September.

Behind the scenes, people gossiped that business would have been better if David were still around. Although he liked to party himself, he had the capacity to control his brothers as well as the other young wrestlers who looked up to him. And production people were certain that David could have convinced his father to present their special events on pay-per-view. But Fritz resisted all efforts. "He was so old school," noted

WCCW television director Dan Bynum, who'd left the promotion in late 1984 but maintained close ties. "He felt that it would kill the house, kill ticket sales. Above and beyond the psychological breakdowns that ensued in the family, it was Fritz's inability to see the future of wrestling that prevented World Class from enjoying the possibility of greater riches."

Certainly, David's death had forced Mike von Erich to be pushed beyond his abilities. Naturally slender, Mike bulked up on steroids, sparking mood swings and violent eruptions that were inconsistent with his personality.

Because of the family's deep Christian beliefs, the Von Erichs were ardent supporters of Israel, where their show was immensely popular. During an August 1985 tour of the Holy Land, Mike was awarded the newly created WCCW Middle Eastern Championship after defeating Hernandez in Tel Aviv. Before returning to Texas, he took a hard fall outside the ring, dislocating his shoulder. The family decided to delay surgery until he returned to Dallas. There, he developed a high fever, estimated at between 106 to 107 degrees Fahrenheit, after the operation and was diagnosed with toxic shock syndrome.

Rumors circulated that he was a victim of medical negligence. "I had heard that the doctors had left gauze or something like that inside of him," said WCCW producer Keith Mitchell. "When I went to visit Mike in the hospital, I remember a doctor being on pins and needles around Fritz. You could tell he was terrified of being blamed for the damage to his son and being physically attacked."

The life-threatening combination of bacterial infections caused organ failure and very likely brain damage. But Kerry assured fans that his sibling was training for a comeback: "My little brother Mike is in better shape than he's ever been in his life, which is a miracle right there, thanks to your prayers."

Because Fritz liked his cards loaded with Von Erichs, Kevin and Kerry were often wrestling two or three times a day. To relieve the burden, another member of the clan was introduced to World Class — cousin Lance, said to be the offspring of Fritz's gimmick sibling, Waldo von Erich. Later, after a business fallout, the owner would go on television and admit that the real-life Kevin Vaughan had no connection to the family and was commissioned to use a name that Fritz had trademarked.

For someone who protected kayfabe, this revelation exposed the business more than anything Vince McMahon was doing at the time.

As promised, Mike did wrestle again. But he was suffering from depression and substance abuse problems. Said Mitchell, "It was so sad. They continued to push him and he could not handle it."

A month after his return, he totaled his car on Highway 121 in Lewisville, Texas, sustaining minor head injuries. Then, in May 1986, he was arrested for drunk and disorderly conduct.

If things could not get any worse, Fritz's booker, Ken Mantell, left for the UWF when Watts attempted to go national, taking Chris Adams, Missy Hyatt, the Freebirds, One Man Gang and Kamala the Ugandan Giant with him.

After years of swiping talent and television slots, it seemed like McMahon could focus most of his energy on building his product as the fractured remnants of the territories continued to collapse.

Even before the WWF invasion, some of Verne Gagne's moves in the AWA had insiders questioning his judgment.

In August 1982, Austrian wrestler and promoter Otto Wanz had beaten Nick Bockwinkel for the AWA World Heavyweight Championship in St. Paul, Minnesota. Since world titles changed hands so infrequently, the spectators went wild, thrilled to see history unfold. But the selection of Wanz was a confusing one since the hefty strongman was unknown in North America. Some observers argued that if the AWA title was truly a "world" championship, it made sense to put the belt on an international figure. But the 41-day reign occurred during a period when the company's most popular performer, Hulk Hogan, was continuously being screwed out of the championship, and hoisting the strap on an outsider left a segment of the fan base uncomfortable.

After Hogan and his allies left, Japanese star Jumbo Tsuruta won the belt in Tokyo in 1984. The scenario was fairly common in wrestling. Through some business arrangement with a Japanese promotion, a Nipponese headliner would briefly capture the championship when a US titlist was touring, adding to the local hero's legend. Hence, Giant Baba had fleeting runs with the NWA crown in 1973 and 1979. Also in 1979, Antonio Inoki held the WWF Championship in a reign not recognized outside Japan. Unlike Wanz, Tsuruta was one of the biggest names in the business. And in the AWA, he graciously dropped the title to 28-year-old Rick Martel after three months.

Gagne was apparently investing in youth. But since Vince McMahon and his allies at MTV were developing the Rock'n'Wrestling Connection at the same time, Verne seemed to be missing something.

He tried, though. With the handsome Martel as his lynchpin, Gagne signed a deal with the Remco toy company and released a line of AWA action figures. These included the Road Warriors, Fabulous Ones (Steve Keirn and Stan Lane) and Baron von Raschke in 1984, and the Freebirds, "Gorgeous" Jimmy Garvin and the future "Mr. Perfect" Curt Hennig in 1985. On television, Verne pushed newcomers like Scott Hall, Bull Power (Big Van Vader) and the Nasty Boys (Brian Knobbs and Jerry Sags) — all of whom would achieve greater fame in the WWF and WCW in the 1990s.

In late 1985, the AWA completed its Rick Martel experiment and programmed him to drop the championship to rugged Stan Hansen, whose crazed American cowboy gimmick and believable matches had turned him into a true superstar in Japan. Very quickly, Hansen and Gagne differed on creative direction and the new titlist absconded with the AWA World Heavyweight Championship. Touching down in the Land of the Rising Sun, he defended the gold around the island nation, while back in the AWA, Bockwinkel — who'd been hastily gifted another title reign — was relegated to coming to the ring with one of the tag team belts.

Gagne argued that the AWA owned the title and Hansen should return it or face legal consequences. So Hansen did, sticking the belt in the mail after first running it over with his truck.

"The belt was beat up. That's all I got to say," he told the Hannibal TV website.

When Gagne received it, there were reportedly mud tracks on the main plate.

CHAPTER 20

As much of the rest of the wrestling community loaded their guns and waited in the dark for Vince McMahon to raid them, Florida promoter Eddie Graham seemed unconcerned. Graham and the McMahon family had a warm history dating back to the 1950s when he and gimmick brother Jerry were headlining Madison Square Garden. When other promoters despaired over Vince's intentions, Eddie was known to retort, "He'd never do that to me."

By the mid-1980s, though, Graham was preoccupied with other issues. He'd made bad investments and, after years of sobriety, resumed drinking, blacking out for long stretches. Wrestlers who visited his Tampa office would sometimes find the door closed but hear him arguing inside with his business partners.

What few people in wrestling realized was that suicide ran in Graham's family. Both his father and brother killed themselves and his son, Mike, and grandson, Stephen, would also take their own lives. Sadly, Eddie kept the thread intact, dying from a self-inflicted gunshot wound on January 21, 1985.

With *WrestleMania 1* two months away, there was other wrestling news obscuring the tragedy. But JCP booker Dusty Rhodes, who owned a stake in the Florida territory, felt that action needed to be taken and, by 1987, for all intents and purposes, Florida was part of Jim Crockett Jr.'s expanding empire. "Dusty bends Jimmy's ear, 'We've got to help out,'" recalled David Crockett. "So we started sending people down there."

As with Central States and Pro Wrestling USA, David believed that his brother was spreading himself too thin. "We should have just taken care of ourselves and, maybe four times a year, gone somewhere else that wasn't in our area, but done that very carefully."

Jimmy saw it differently. With Dusty's encouragement, the Charlotte boss was determined to keep pace with Vince McMahon. "We tried to help Florida, but Eddie Graham still had partners and everyone had different ideas about how it should be run," said David. "Baltimore and Philadelphia drew good crowds, but, with the union costs and transportation costs, it's expensive, unless you hit other towns on the way up and on the way back. We promoted at the Olympic Auditorium in Los Angeles a couple of times because we had all that exposure on TBS. Did we make money? No."

By early 1987, a group of rival promoters — Duke Keomuka from Florida, Bob Geigel from Kansas City, the Fuller family from Knoxville and Fritz von Erich — spoke about forming their own version of Pro Wrestling USA to go against not McMahon but Crockett. Said Dave Meltzer in the *Wrestling Observer Newsletter*, "Working together is not one of the strongest qualities afforded to wrestling promoters."

Crockett channeled McMahon by drawing strength from the opposition. Unlike with the WWF, though, something in JCP inevitably went wrong.

With his good looks and charming persona, Terry Allen — nicknamed Magnum T.A. due to look-alike Tom Selleck's hit TV show *Magnum, P.I.* — had been programmed to win the NWA World Heavyweight Championship. But in October 1986, while driving home in the rain, his Porsche skidded into a telephone pole in Charlotte. Temporarily paralyzed on his right side, he was hospitalized for five months, his wrestling career finished.

Dusty came up with a plan to fill Magnum's slot by turning Soviet heel Nikita Koloff into a babyface who suddenly appreciated the opportunities he'd been given in the United States. A *Starrcade* match against champion Ric Flair drew fan interest, particularly after Nikita announced that he planned to win the title for Magnum. But the strap stayed with Flair after both competitors manhandled the referee and were disqualified, and the NWA had to scramble to come up with its next hero.

In previous years, Bill Watts's Superdome cards drew more than 20,000 fans. But in 1987 — on a show featuring Rick Steiner vs. Chris Adams in a taped fist match; Dusty Rhodes and Steve "Dr. Death" Williams vs. Dick Murdoch and Eddie Gilbert in a bullrope match; and the Freebirds vs. Black Bart, Big Bubba Rogers (the future Big Boss Man) and the Terminator (Marcus Laurinaitis, brother of Road Warrior Animal) in a clash that saw competitors eliminated as soon as they bled — only 3,000 bothered to turn up.

Most of those spectators were unaware that, two days earlier, Watts had sold the UWF to Crockett.

"I was losing $50,000 a week," Watts explained. "I decided, 'I've had enough. I had a great ride.' I tried to get Vince to buy me. He wouldn't do it. So I played Crockett a little bit and said, 'Vince wants to buy my business.' And so Jimmy came to the table."

UWF announcer Jim Ross helped engineer the purchase. "I was meeting with Crockett on another matter [a dual show], and I brought up the fact that Cowboy was burned out and ready to get out of the wrestling business. And if he wanted, he could buy the company. So that's how that started."

As part of the deal, J.R. went to JCP, doing color commentary beside David Crockett and Tony Schiavone. "It was sad for me," Ross said. "I loved Mid-South. I helped build it. And then, I helped sell it. But Cowboy was tired and didn't want to fight anymore."

Other additions to Crockett's roster included Gilbert, Steiner, Ron Simmons, Missy Hyatt, Terry Taylor, Shane Douglas, Big Bubba and Sting.

As had occurred before in wrestling, when one promotion purchased another one, the owner buried much of the incoming talent — to prove his group was superior all along. "It was all ego-based," Watts said.

J.R. did not blame Crockett. "It was a Dusty decision, and Crockett wasn't going to go against his booker. The JCP incumbents weren't comfortable with the guys they were getting, so there was a lot of politics involved."

Still, the infusion of UWF wrestlers *did* kindle interest in the NWA at a time when it was needed. During the same period, fans were excited by the addition of buff, bronzed Lex Luger — who'd come up from Florida — to Ric Flair's faction, the Four Horsemen, and a Dusty creation called War Games — a match consisting of two five-man teams battling in two rings positioned side to side, surrounded by a cage.

Yet, just as McMahon hoped, the interest was counterbalanced by Crockett overextending the company. "Jimmy didn't want Vince to get the UWF, but I was concerned about the debt," said David Crockett. "We did not do our due diligence, considering Watts's production costs that were not paid or how much money it would be to pick up his television stations. We had to run shows in all the new markets we picked up. Plus, Bill Watts had an office building in Dallas."

While David remained at JCP headquarters in Charlotte, Jimmy and Dusty relocated to Texas, moving into the facility previously occupied by the UWF. "Bill Watts signed a lease on that and Jimmy took it over. It was a major error. We didn't need another office. But Dusty had a new wife and wanted to live in Texas.

"So now, instead of flying from Charlotte to Atlanta every Saturday for television, people were flying from Dallas, which was a lot more expensive."

In addition, since the oil crisis had not abated in the cities where Watts promoted, many of JCP's shows in the former Mid-South territory fared poorly.

But, even in the oil states, professional wrestling could still draw money. While Crockett was sending his stars to New Orleans, Little Rock and Oklahoma City, Vince McMahon was hitting those very same markets. For families on a fixed income, it didn't make sense to attend both companies' shows. And with *WrestleMania III* captivating the public's interest, an increasing number of followers had already made the choice about which brand they'd rather watch.

CHAPTER 21

Pro wrestling had long been considered part of Toronto's legitimate sports community. In 1984, for instance, "Whipper" Billy Watson, the NWA World Heavyweight Champion for eight months in 1956, was bestowed the prestigious Order of Canada, a distinction for outstanding merit or service. (Stu Hart would receive the same honor in 2001.) Even when the original Sheik, Ed Farhat, was brawling in mud with Tiger Jeet Singh at Maple Leaf Gardens, Toronto fans could indulge their love of the sport of kings relatively free from the shame frequently cast on followers in the United States.

In August 1986, the WWF presented *The Big Event* at Exhibition Stadium, then home of the baseball's Toronto Blue Jays and the CFL's Toronto Argonauts, headlined by Hulk Hogan defending the gold against Paul "Mr. Wonderful" Orndorff — who'd turned heel again. There was no shortage of other entertainment options that month; during a two-week period overlapping with *The Big Event*, Van Halen, Elton John, Huey Lewis and the News and Judas Priest all performed in Toronto. But the WWF claimed 74,000 fans still attended what was essentially a massive house show.

Almost certainly, the number was exaggerated. Local media maintained that 65,000 were in the stadium, while Dave Meltzer of the *Wrestling Observer Newsletter* listed the number as 64,100. Either way, it was impressive.

In years to come, some reasonably assumed that the purpose of *The Big Event* was to serve as a dress rehearsal for *WrestleMania III*. According to executives who were working for the company at the time, this was not the intention. Regardless, Vince McMahon took note of the crowd — along with the front-page media coverage, reported with barely a roll of the eyes — and likely imagined the possibilities of what he could attract with a little more hype.

WWF publicist Mike Weber was uncertain of the date but clearly recalled being summoned to a meeting with about ten others not long after *WrestleMania 2*. "They laid out the whole plan for *WrestleMania III*, how we were going to get there. Hogan and André were going to be the main event."

On WWF television, the pair had been depicted as brothers who'd never contemplate lifting a violent hand to the other. But that was about to change.

Vince waited until the start of 1987 for André to begin his slow turn on Hogan, manipulated, fans were told, by devious manager Bobby "The Brain" Heenan.

"Back then, when you only were doing an hour of television at a time and you didn't have another pay-per-view every month, you could start building an angle between Wrestler A and Wrestler B a few months before," explained vice president of television production Nelson Sweglar. "You didn't see all the stars wrestle on TV every week, so you could keep the audience hungry."

Fans were reminded that, back in 1984, when Hogan toppled the Iron Sheik for the crown, André had been the first to offer congratulations. But while Orndorff, Piper, King Kong Bundy and Greg "The Hammer" Valentine had all received title shots, the Giant was relegated to the friend zone.

The first hint of conflict occurred when Hogan was rewarded with a trophy for his three-year streak as WWF World Heavyweight Champion. André was presented with a trophy as well, for what viewers were told was a 15-year winning streak. As he contemplated both prizes and realized that Hogan's was larger, a dejected André lumbered off the set.

Was André just being moody? Or was there some legitimacy to his resentment? Although the challenger would play the heel at *WrestleMania III*, it was easy for fans — who'd been passed over for jobs or by romantic partners — to relate to the Eighth Wonder of the World. That nuance made the plot more complex than a rudimentary wrestling angle.

Noted Weber, "This was the ultimate, storyline-driven event if there ever was one."

When viewers next tuned in, there was Bobby Heenan standing with André on "Piper's Pit," facing Hulk Hogan.

"Fans totally bought the story that Bobby Heenan had convinced André to go for the belt," said Jerry Brisco. "And Heenan really understood the whole angle. He carried the damn thing. Every time there was a camera or a microphone in front of him, he just sold it. He was at the top of his career and everything he did was heat-driven."

Upon taking in the sight of André alongside the hated manager, Hogan stared at the ground in hurt and disbelief. Seemingly amused by seeing his former ally squirm, André stuck a large finger below Hogan's chin and forced his head up. "Look at me when I'm trying to talk to you. I'm here for one reason — to challenge you to a world championship match at *WrestleMania*."

Hogan agonizingly raised his hands to his head. "André, please, no, stop. We're friends. We're friends, André. Please."

A smug Heenan interjected. "You can't believe it?" he taunted. "Maybe you can believe *this*?"

At that, André lurched forward, grabbing Hogan by his shirt and tearing it, along with the Hulkster's crucifix.

As the Giant stormed away, Hogan beseeched him to return. "What are you doing, man? You can't leave like this, man. What are you doing, André?"

Piper, who'd become a babyface by now, sympathetically touched Hogan's chest and observed, "You're bleeding."

Of course, Hulkamania was not a movement founded on passive resistance. If you were going to pull off Hogan's cross and draw blood, there had to be retribution.

On a subsequent "Piper's Pit," Hot Rod asked the champion the question on everyone's mind: "Yes or no? Are you or are you not going to fight him at *WrestleMania III* for the World Heavyweight Championship? Yes or no?"

With eyes bulging, Hogan answered the only way he could: *"Yeeeess!"*

The crowd leaped from their seats, throwing their arms above their heads, dancing back and forth with excitement and joy.

The WWF followed up on the exuberance by bombarding TV viewers with a phrase that would categorize *WrestleMania III*: "Bigger! Better! Badder!" — delivered in a throaty pitch by McMahon.

"I'll tell you who I think coined that," said Basil Devito. "It pains me because he's a guy who was only in WWE for a cup of coffee. It was Phil Harmon."

Harmon, a sports television executive, had come to the company from Madison Square Garden, where he'd helped produce cable television broadcasts from the fabled arena.

"We were in a meeting. People are blurting out ideas. Harmon was the one who said, 'Well, it's going to be bigger. If it's going to be bigger, it's going to be better. It always has to be better. And to make it more fun, let's say bigger, better, badder.' And there we were. We were done. That was it."

With no Internet available to cross-reference history, the WWF was able to invent whichever narrative worked best. So fans were led to believe that Hogan and André had never fought before — even though a portion of the viewership had personally witnessed the matches.

Their first memorable clash occurred in 1978 in Dothan, Alabama, for Southeastern Championship Wrestling. During an arm-wrestling match, heel Terry "The Hulk" Boulder used a loaded elbow pad to bloody André, then joined manager Billy Spears — a man so detested that he lost an eye after a fan swung a belt buckle into his face — in smashing the table over the Giant.

Over the years, Hogan and André faced each other in one-on-one encounters more than 30 times. If tag team matches are calculated into the equation, the number exceeds 65.

"When there was all that buildup to *WrestleMania III*, I thought, 'I already had those guys against each other at the Superdome,'" said Cowboy Bill Watts, referring to a 1980 double countout that occurred on the same show as the Junkyard Dog's memorable steel-cage, dog-collar match against Freebird Michael Hayes. "And they were just a feature match, not the main event."

A week later in the WWF, André defeated Hogan at Shea Stadium in Queens, the home of baseball's New York Mets, on a super show dubbed *Showdown at Shea*.

André also bested Hogan at LA's Olympic Auditorium for promoter Mike LeBell in December, on New Year's Day at the Omni Coliseum for Georgia Championship Wrestling and in March at Maple Leaf Gardens.

In August 1982, at an event run by André's Varoussac promotion, the Giant and the Hulkster had their second confrontation at Montreal's Paul Sauvé Arena, with the fan favorite winning via disqualification.

Hogan would later tell Greg Oliver's *Slam Wrestling* website that, at that point of his career, André was "faster, very healthy and very aggressive."

A month before André congratulated Hogan on his WWF World Heavyweight Championship win at Madison Square Garden, the pair were on opposite sides in Kagoshima, Japan, when André and Otto Wanz went to a double countout with Hogan and Antonio Inoki. In May 1984, they'd wrestle to another double countout in Fukuoka when André teamed with Adrian Adonis against Hogan and the Masked Superstar.

Yet, the marketing for *WrestleMania III* was so effective that even Jacques Rougeau claimed that he forgot about the prior clashes. "I thought it was the first time they met. My mentality was like any fan. 'Do or die. Someone's going to be the king and someone has to fall.'"

Noted his brother, Raymond "We were all caught up in it. If Vince McMahon was going to erase the past, he made us ignore it, too."

Much of this had to do with the characters Hogan and André were now playing in the WWF. "Hogan was the hero," said Bruce Prichard. "André was the antagonistic, mean, nasty giant who had Bobby Heenan in his corner. You may have seen Hogan vs. André. But you never saw Hogan against *this* André."

Fans in Japan had, but that was not who McMahon was targeting. Nor was he particularly focused on followers with long wrestling memories. "You have a brand new audience," Prichard said, "whose first experience with sports entertainment is 1984 and 1985. All they know about is WWE."

And McMahon encouraged those watchers to view his product like a movie. "If you watch *Top Gun*, you're not going to say, 'Hey, that's not a real jet fight. I saw that actor somewhere else,'" said Raymond Rougeau. "No, you get into the movie. Well, the people got into the movie of *WrestleMania III*. No one's asking, 'Is it real? Is it fixed? Have they wrestled before?' Who cares? Enjoy the ride. Be part of it."

The contract signing was shot in a conference room at WWF headquarters, with Devito, Sweglar and even Vince McMahon's chauffeur playing witness. "My recollection is someone said, 'Hey, we need some jackets and ties over here,'" said Devito. "And we all went where we were supposed to go."

Sweglar remembered there being "a degree of informality" during these types of shoots. "You could just grab a warm body and say, 'You're now on camera.'"

WWF figurehead president Jack Tunney presided over the ceremony, mildly breaking kayfabe by referring to André by his actual surname. "Will you please sign on the dotted line, Mr. Roussimoff?"

Before André complied, Heenan piped in, demanding a new championship belt after his protégé's victory. "This one," he said, gesturing at Hogan, "was made and designed for this human being, and I use that term very loosely. I want one made that will fit a man, fit a giant of a man."

Hogan glared at the manager, growing increasingly upset. "I thought it was you, man. It's both of you. You're both sick."

Turning his attention to André, the titlist continued, "When you tore the shirt, man, when you tore the cross, you tore the heart and soul out of all the little Hulksters, man. It wasn't just me."

André smugly contemplated the denunciation, then divulged a secret: although he'd been a mentor to Hogan, the Giant had withheld a great deal of information. "*WrestleMania III* will be your last lesson."

When André lapsed into French, the patriotic Hogan banged the table. "Speak to me in English when you talk to me. As far as I'm concerned, it's not signed in ink. It's signed in blood."

Replied André, "If you want me to speak in English, I will speak in the ring at *WrestleMania*."

As Hogan rattled with fury, André indicated that, now that the contracts were signed, his business with Hogan was done for the day. "Au revoir."

Trite as the exchange seemed, it more than served its purpose. In playgrounds and playrooms everywhere, children excitedly argued over whether Hogan could beat the Giant.

Having spent time traveling and visiting the homes of both competitors, Steve Taylor was chosen to take the iconic photo of Hogan and André standing nose to nose. "It was a tough picture to take. I mean, first of all, everyone was so busy that they had a hard time coordinating the schedules. And then, to have those guys go nose to nose and just stare at each other for so many shots, it was a challenge."

Along with the photo and the "Bigger! Better! Badder!" mantra, the WWF took to describing the impending struggle as the Irresistible Force vs. the Immovable Object.

Although the company was not specific about to whom each label applied, a sizeable portion of the viewership took the "Immovable Object" as a statement about the failure of each of André's prior foes to body-slam the large Frenchman.

As with the claim that the rivals had never wrestled before, this was yet another McMahon-generated fiction.

In fact, Hogan himself had slammed André at *Showdown at Shea*, then repeated the feat the next month at a TV taping in Hamburg, Pennsylvania.

Among the others who could make the same boast: Inoki, Wanz, Strong Kobayashi, Riki Choshu, Harley Race, Stan Hansen, Kamala the Ugandan Giant, Butcher Vachon and Mexican superstar El Canek. Additionally, the Wild Samoans, Ken Patera and Bobby Duncum and Inoki and Tatsumi Fujinami had body-slammed André simultaneously.

Fans were similarly told that André was coming into *WrestleMania III* with a 15-year undefeated streak.

Prior to 1972, André, then billed as Jean Ferré, had sustained two losses to Kendo Nagasaki (Brit Peter Thornley doing a samurai gimmick, as opposed to Kazuo Sakurada, who played the character in North America) in the UK, where he also suffered at least two defeats in handicap matches. In 1971, Adnan Al-Kaissie — who'd later play evil General Adnan in the WWF during the first Persian Gulf War — capitalized on his reported ties to schoolmate Saddam Hussein to begin promoting in Iraq, where he beat André — then called Monster Roussimoff — twice via pinfall.

The Giant's first loss on US soil, in 1972 in Detroit to Baron von Raschke, occurred within the 15-year timeline. From there, André would lose cleanly to Karl Gotch, Kobayashi and Killer Kowalski, among others. The original Sheik would program a 1974 win over André via ref stoppage, although this was far from a clean triumph since the Detroit promoter was partial to bloodying foes with weapons and throwing fire. In 1977, Vincent James McMahon — who booked André's dates in the various territories — was infuriated when Bill Apter's wrestling magazine reported that Jerry "The King" Lawler had beaten André in Louisville. The allegation was particularly galling because, from the time that the older McMahon stepped into Andre's life, the Giant was never felled via pinfall or submission in the WWWF.

And the reality was that, even in Louisville, Lawler had first belted the Giant with a chair to squeeze out a win via countout.

The next year, heel Ronnie Garvin boasted that he could beat rival Roy Lee Welch in Knoxville — along with any partner Welch decided to bring along. Welch picked André, but Garvin fought extra dirty and procured the final pinfall victory over the Giant before *WrestleMania III*.

André was rarely this amiable, but he and Garvin had become close in Montreal, and the Giant wanted to put over Rugged Ronnie as an infallible heel.

In 1984, Mexican media maintained that Universal Wrestling Association (UWA) World Heavyweight Champion El Canek had decisively defeated André in a two-out-of-three fall match in Naucalpan. But the third fall was erroneously listed as a pinfall win, even though André was actually disqualified for tearing up the titlist's mask.

Yet, in 1986, André did lose cleanly to Inoki on a New Japan show in Nagoya, the only apparent submission loss of the Giant's career.

But why let the truth get in the way of a good story? In an age when pro wrestling was still treated with amusement by the media, reporters were eager to buy whatever McMahon sold them. Hence, Neal Rubin of the *Detroit Free Press* felt no ethical conflict in forecasting, "André the Giant can't lose. He's invincible."

The article included a quote from Gerald Morton, an English professor at Alabama's Auburn University, who predicted some type of disqualification.

"One wrestler told me that the reason the Giant has never wrestled for the championship is because who would believe he'd ever be beaten to lose it?" Morton, who'd written a book on the One True Sport for a small publisher affiliated with Bowling Green State University, stated with authority. "They have to keep the Giant's unquestioned superiority for later when he's a good guy."

Morton never specified which wrestler told him this or whether the subject knew that André had challenged for the championship in both the NWA and AWA. Either way, the fact-checkers at the *Detroit Free Press* apparently had more important matters to attend to that day. And one can confidently surmise that, up until this moment, no one ever scrutinized the quote enough to ponder its veracity.

CHAPTER 22

Well, maybe Dave Meltzer did.

Officially, wrestlers and promoters were supposed to disdain *Wrestling Observer Newsletter* founder Meltzer and what they referred to as his "dirt sheet." To be certain, the *Observer* did uncover a lot of dirt, but that was only because both the performers and their bosses surreptitiously contacted the writer to vent about real and perceived injustices, reveal tales about backstage dramas and planned storylines and espouse theories about why a certain angle fell flat.

At times, Meltzer seemed to know more about the business than the participants themselves, and he filled his weekly bulletin with not just gossip but match results from all over the world, attendance and financial figures, biographical profiles and historical data.

No "wrestling journalist" had ever done this before; the purpose of the wrestling magazines had always been perpetuating kayfabe. And while no one would dare pull out a copy of the *Observer* in the dressing room, the information exchanged there often emanated from Meltzer's hand.

Obsessing over small facts was apparently a Meltzer family trait. Dave said that his father, Herb, was teaching engineering at Columbia University at age 21, helped develop computer language in the private sector and did some clandestine work for the US government. "When we went to see the movie *Hidden Figures*," about a group of female African

American mathematicians who contributed to the American space program, "he walked out of the theater and said, 'Yeah, I worked with her and I worked with her.' But he couldn't talk about what he did."

Not unlike the members of the wrestling fraternity.

The younger Meltzer and his brother, Scott — a Watson Scholar with degrees in computer science and applied mathematics who left a career at IBM to write comedy, escape straitjackets and juggle knives atop a six-foot unicycle — spent their early years in New York. But when Dave was nine, the family relocated to San Jose.

"I have a brief memory of seeing Lou Albano on TV in New York, but I didn't become a wrestling fan until I moved to California. In fifth or sixth grade, all the kids my age were imitating Pampero Firpo all over the place."

It was Firpo — an Argentinian of Armenian extraction — who coined the "*ooooh yyyyeah*" later appropriated by Randy Savage.

San Jose was part of Roy Shire's San Francisco territory and, at the first show he ever attended, Meltzer saw the Rock's grandfather, Peter Maivia, and Ray Stevens drop the local tag team championship to Pat Patterson and Superstar Billy Graham.

Even then, Dave's goal was sports writing. He pored over *Sporting News* and *Sports Illustrated*, studied baseball stats and, from age five, typed out his own baseball articles. "My friends had the wrestling magazines and I'd read them, but they didn't have what I wanted because I was really into match results from different places."

Some of the publications included fan club listings, though, and Meltzer signed up for the ones with the highest recommendations, hoping to learn about encounters not covered by *Inside Wrestling* or *Wrestling Revue*.

Whenever he attended the cards in San Jose, he noticed a group of older males talking about the gates drawn at arenas around the circuit. Although his knowledge was limited, Meltzer eavesdropped, his mind fixating on the numbers being cited: a $26,000 house in Eureka, $45,000 at the Cow Palace in San Francisco. "They would say the wrestlers were paid a percentage of the house, and I tried thinking about how much a certain star might have made. From watching all the TVs, my friends and I knew which angles worked and how a house would draw. So that became the thing, following the ups and downs."

Roller derby was another obsession — because it was also worked and involved orchestrated chaos. The derby had boomed in the Bay Area in the 1960s, then started playing to half-filled arenas and, ultimately, went out of business. "Same thing for baseball. If a team was drawing really badly, they moved cities. So it helped me understand what I was seeing with wrestling. When crowds went down, you'd get a lower level of talent. Everyone was losing interest, and then another promotion would come to town with a better product. I was trying to figure out what made wrestling click."

He was frustrated by the fact that information traveled to fans so slowly. "I think Bruno Sammartino wrestled twice at the Cow Palace when I was a kid. But because of the magazines, he was larger than life. And then, when he lost the championship to Ivan Koloff, we didn't find out from the magazines for about two months."

Fortunately, Meltzer's family liked to travel, which allowed him to discover information about occurrences in territories away from the Bay Area. During visits to his grandparents in Miami Beach, Dave, along with his father and brother, attended cards at Convention Hall. "We had relatives in Los Angeles so, a couple of times a year, we'd go down there and get tickets to the Friday shows at the Olympic. And I recall going on a couple of trips to Hawaii and seeing wrestling and the roller games," an offshoot of roller derby.

To add to his knowledge, he subscribed to the programs from arenas like the Kiel Auditorium in St. Louis and Madison Square Garden.

Starting at age 12, he was gathering whatever data he could and putting out a newsletter, first dubbed *California Wrestling Report* and then *International Wrestling Gazette*. Although he'd discontinue the endeavor before finishing high school, some of the contacts he established continued after the creation of the *Observer*.

For a period, he shifted to other interests, focusing on college and his goal of covering mainstream sports. Then, in 1979, the Georgia Championship

Wrestling (GCW) show on TBS pulled him back, and he began subscribing to newsletters. His purchase of a VCR allowed him to pursue a social life while recording the wrestling programs he missed. But now that he had the technology as well as access to a network of fans who shared his passion via the newsletters, the transition to tape trading was seamless. Before long, he was following the Japanese scene as ardently as the action in North America and even took photos for *Weekly Gong*, a publication specializing in puroresu — the Japanese term for pro wrestling — at Cow Palace shows promoted by both Shire and rival Verne Gagne.

By 1983 — the year after Vince McMahon purchased the WWF from his father — much of Meltzer's day was occupied with screening tapes of the various Japanese promotions, along with those from Mid-Atlantic, Florida, Calgary, Portland and other territories, as well as exchanging letters and phone calls with fans and even some wrestling industry employees about the many changes occurring in the business. "And that's what spawned the *Observer*."

An online version would be launched in 1996.

"When you think about it, it was only a small amount of people who were following us," Meltzer said. "But it was the only thing they had within the business. There was nothing else like it."

Bruiser Brody, a weathered brawler with an outlaw mentality, became the first wrestler to regularly open up to Meltzer. While training for pro wrestling with Fritz von Erich, Brody had worked as a sports reporter and understood what Dave was trying to accomplish. "Be a sports reporter," the wrestler urged. "Don't be like these other guys. This business doesn't have sports reporters. It needs one."

Despite his defensiveness about the secrets of the industry, Cowboy Bill Watts would engage Meltzer in detailed discussions, describing the conditions responsible for a concept to work or fail. "If a house was down, he'd say something like the heel wasn't aggressive enough on TV the Saturday before, which may or may not have been true. But that's how much he shared and that's how deep these conversations would go."

Houston promoter Paul Boesch brought Meltzer to gatherings of the Cauliflower Alley Club, an organization then serving both retired wrestlers and boxers. "At the time, it was a closed thing," Meltzer said. "It wasn't like it is today. And he introduced me to all these people who played important roles in wrestling history." These included "Nature Boy" Buddy Rogers, Billy Darnell, whose history of neck injuries led to a second career as a chiropractor, Leo Garibaldi, whose booking stops included Atlanta, Los Angeles and Australia, and Clara Mortensen, a women's champion in the 1930s.

"It was the best way to learn history," Meltzer said. "I couldn't really learn it from the magazines. And most of the wrestling historians hadn't come around yet. But Boesch told me, 'History didn't start when you started watching. If you're going to be a good writer at this, you have to know our history.'"

In addition to writing about the headliners of the past, Meltzer offered opinions of what he liked and didn't like about the present in-ring product, developing a star-rating system whose merits were debated by both wrestlers and fans.

When Terry Funk was in the WWF, Meltzer wrote that the former NWA champ was winning matches too often by using the branding iron he brought to the ring. "About a week later, Terry Funk told me, someone came over to him backstage and said, 'You're winning with the branding iron too much. It's getting old.' He thought that was really funny. He goes, 'You're the most powerful guy in the business if you made Terry Funk have to change.'"

During a conversation with McMahon, Meltzer was told that the relationship would always be adversarial. "He said, 'We can't get along because you're spoiling Santa Claus.'"

But the fact that Vince was not above getting on the phone with the guy he'd described as a scourge on the business was a statement about the influence the fan from northern California now wielded. And with the planning of *WrestleMania III* underway, McMahon ensured that his confederates continued passing on the information that he wanted the *Observer*'s select readership to know.

•

Unlike the previous *WrestleMania*s, the third would be the first distinguished by a Roman numeral, subliminally elevating the annual event to the plane of such elite sports competitions as the Super Bowl and Summer Olympics.

While the purpose of *WrestleMania 2* had been to showcase the WWF's national presence, McMahon was resolute about drawing a record gate for *WrestleMania III* and decided that he wanted the show in an NFL stadium. Given the possibility of inclement weather, he resolved to stage the spectacular in a domed building. Of the various options, he zoned in on Detroit due to its proximity to other Midwestern hubs, as well as the Toronto area, where *The Big Event* had underscored the loyalty of the company's Canadian followers — eventually choosing the Pontiac Silverdome, some 30 miles outside of downtown.

Moments after settling on this choice, he phoned executive Ed Cohen at around 2 a.m., instructing him to fly to Detroit in the morning to make arrangements. When Cohen arrived, he learned that the stadium had a convention booked on March 29, 1987. Cohen handed over a $50,000 check and the plans abruptly changed.

Basil Devito was running the WWF booth at the National Association of Television Program Executives (NATPE) convention in New Orleans when McMahon gave him the news. Hulk Hogan was also there in his "travel uniform," red tank top, tights and do-rag with a yellow weight-lifting belt matching his boots, a red-and-yellow duffle bag in one hand. Since most of the attendees wanted a photo of the Hulkster — at that point, people at that level still claimed they were only doing it "for my kid" — Devito trailed Vince and the champion onto the convention floor, talking business as they walked.

"Listen," McMahon said, "*WrestleMania* is going to be at the Pontiac Silverdome."

Devito was familiar with the building and knew that, by curtaining off sections, the seating could be realigned to accommodate a smaller number of spectators. "What's the configuration?" he asked his boss.

"We're going to go all the way. We need to find out the number for the biggest indoor crowd. We have to get more people in there." He peeked over at Devito and raised his eyebrows. "What do you think?"

"Honestly, I'm scared to death."

Up until this point, Hogan's attention had been on charming the execs with a pointed finger, thumbs-up or smile. But now, sensing Devito's hesitancy, the titlist spun around and widened his large eyes. "You're forgetting who's in the main event, brother."

Once the convention ended, Devito boarded an airplane for Detroit to start working on *WrestleMania III.*

Although the city of Pontiac surged with auto assembly plants in the years after World War II, its fortunes changed quickly after workers began using the vehicles they made to commute to work from their new homes in the suburbs. Soon, jobs began to dry up as well. In 1965, local architect C. Don Davidson despaired that the city "looks as if someone has dropped a bomb on it." But upon learning that the NFL's Detroit Lions were looking to build a stadium — they'd been inhabiting the same venue as baseball's Detroit Tigers — he began lobbying influential associates to build the facility in Pontiac. In 1973, he presented a plan for a domed football stadium that could also house a basketball team, offices and a corporate center.

Two years later, Pontiac Metropolitan Stadium opened with seating for 80,311 on 199 acres of land — the largest NFL stadium at the time. Its most outstanding feature: a fiberglass-paneled, fabric roof dilated by air pressure. Although the fabric was technically white, the roof was frequently described as silver, leading to the venue's rebranding as the Silverdome. In 1978, the NBA's Detroit Pistons became a tenant, along with the Lions.

For a while, the Silverdome truly was a source of local pride. In 1982, the stadium hosted the first Super Bowl played in a cold weather city, as fans took refuge from the 15-degree temperatures outside. But as with pro wrestling, the wider world viewed the stadium with an air of condescension, associating Pontiac with the poverty and decay connected to the industrial region. Then there were the problems that came from building a stadium with an air-filled roof. In 1985, an accumulation of heavy, wet snow depressed the fabric roof panels low enough to touch the catwalk inside the building. To the astonishment of witnesses, the loss of air pressure forced the Silverdome to slowly deflate.

"It looked like someone threw hand grenades in there," Lions quarter-back Gary Danielson, who'd been practicing in the building at the time, told the Associated Press. "Then, it started coming down all at once and we ran like hell."

But now, that roof had been replaced and, temporarily at least, *WrestleMania III* would give the Pontiac Silverdome the public relations jolt it needed.

Upon learning of the WWF's intention to run the Silverdome, Dave Meltzer was certain that André and Hogan could break the US attendance record set when "Nature Boy" Buddy Rogers dethroned Pat O'Connor for the NWA World Heavyweight Championship in front of an announced 38,622 at Chicago's Comiskey Park in 1961. "I never expected them to sell out," he said.

Even after 40,000 tickets had been sold in February, Meltzer told *Observer* readers that he did not think the number would hit 50,000. Similarly, he believed that the $19.95 pay-per-view charge would dissuade viewers from purchasing the event.

In Houston, Bruce Prichard anticipated the same type of crowd that had watched Kerry von Erich beat Ric Flair at Texas Stadium. "I thought, 'They're going to hold it in a stadium and draw 25 or 30,000 people and it'll be great.' Ninety thousand wasn't even in the conversation."

Jacques Rougeau anticipated no more than 60,000. "The buildup to André vs. Hogan and the marketing had been so good. But I didn't think wrestling could draw any more than that."

Regardless of the cynicism, the company was doing all it could to attract fans to the Silverdome. "The majority of tickets were nine dollars," said Mike Weber, the company's head of public relations. "Even in 1987, that was a pretty good price. We wanted to make it affordable so people would show up."

In addition, the WWF made sure that local fans could not order the event on pay-per-view. "We essentially blacked out the state of Michigan," Devito said, "cable system by cable system. If you wanted to see *WrestleMania III*, you had to come to the Silverdome."

In fact, the nearest closed-circuit locations were Lorain, Ohio, about 170 miles away, London, Ontario, about 205 miles away, South Bend, Indiana, about 220 miles away and Kitchener, Ontario, about 300 miles away.

But even fans in those cities were being urged to make the drive to Pontiac. "They weren't just marketing in Detroit," Meltzer said. "They marketed in Toronto. They marketed in Columbus, Ohio — any big city with a lot of wrestling fans that were, let's say, five or six hours away. They were counting on people coming in."

Even with the appeal of the main event, McMahon was trying to add to the lineup. After one site survey at the Pontiac Silverdome, Vince and television executive Dick Ebersol rented a plane and flew to Mexico, where Arnold Schwarzenegger, then the entertainment industry's top action star, was making a movie with Jesse "The Body" Ventura. "They talked to Jesse and he said, 'You guys should come down,'" recalled vice president of business affairs Dick Glover. "It was very spontaneous because, if I remember correctly, Vince and Dick didn't have a change of clothes. They stopped at the University of Michigan and bought some sweats. Then, they got on the plane to meet Arnold. But the deal could not be reached."

CHAPTER 23

Tickets for the March 29 show officially went on sale on February 7. For the first two days, fans could only order by phone — "Good luck with that," joked the *Detroit Free Press* — before the Silverdome box office and ticket outlets opened. As part of McMahon's effort to fill the stadium, announcers reminded viewers in every one of the promotion's markets that, if they were willing to travel, they could go to *WrestleMania*, too.

"The commercials were non-stop," remembered Rafael Morffi, a catcher and third baseman on the Archbishop Molloy High School baseball team in Queens. "And I said, 'You know what? I'm going.

"'I don't know who I'm going to go with. I don't know how I'm going to get there. But I'm going.'"

Morffi was accustomed to getting tickets to big events in New York. He'd been at Game Six of the 1986 World Series at Shea Stadium when, with the score tied, Boston Red Sox first baseman Bill Buckner lost a slow roller off the bat of New York Met Mookie Wilson, changing the fortunes of both teams. "My dad had gotten me a ticket and even though I was a Yankee fan, after the Mets won, I said 'I have to be there for [the deciding] Game Seven.' The Mets were rained out the next day, but, in the meantime, I found someone — I won't say who — who worked for Harry M. Stevens," the food concessionaire at Shea Stadium. "All the vendors wore a special button and my cousin and I each got one and lined up outside the gate at 4 o'clock in the afternoon. And then we went inside and watched the Mets win."

He'd also acquired a ticket to *WrestleMania 1* from a friend who had a family member connected to Madison Square Garden. "That's how it worked. You'd know someone who knew someone who knew someone."

Morffi had grown up in Queens's Sunnyside neighborhood, literally down the block from Sunnyside Gardens, where Jim Crockett Sr. and Antonino Rocca attempted to run opposition to Vincent James McMahon. Among his childhood friends was Christopher Klucsarits, who'd later wrestle as Chris Kanyon and Mortis, appearing in both WCW and the WWF. "We were all fanatics," Morffi recalled.

He'd been too young to attend the clash between heel Hulk Hogan and André at *Showdown at Shea* in 1980, but at age nine, recognized its appeal. "Hulk Hogan, even at that stage of his career, jumped off the screen, and the fact that he was wrestling André in Shea Stadium meant that he was rising among the ranks in the wrestling business."

In the buildup to *WrestleMania III*, Morffi had attended the taping of "Piper's Pit" in the New Jersey Meadowlands in which André tore the crucifix off Hogan. "They taped three weeks of television so I saw the stories evolve in front of me. Some folks would say that was a detriment — seeing everything at once. But I thought it was fascinating, being 15 going on 16 and learning how things were produced and laid out. I'm not afraid to admit I watched the soaps growing up and sometimes still do, especially *General Hospital.* I appreciated that slow burn, how everything was episodic and would culminate in a big moment."

Once he made the decision to go to *WrestleMania III*, he explained his intentions to his mother and made a deal with her: he'd provide the money for his tickets — since he needed companions, he'd have to purchase more than one — and she'd write a check that he could send to the post office box the WWF continuously mentioned on television. Despite his age, she believed that he was capable of finding the right people to accompany him to Detroit.

Ten days later, the tickets arrived at Morffi's home. "I was shocked when they came in the mail. And I remember they were in a great section — 127. Now, there was no way I couldn't go."

The only detriment was his baseball coach, Luke Perreira. The year before, Morffi's junior varsity squad had finished 32-0 and Perreira had decided to elevate the teen to the number three batting spot. Although the New York Catholic High School Athletic Association season had yet to begin, the team was preparing by playing against public schools and teams from the suburbs. And there was a non-league game scheduled for the same weekend as *WrestleMania III*.

"At first, he thought I was joking. He just couldn't understand why I was going to go to Detroit to watch wrestling. And I said, 'No, I'm going.' And he thought I was setting a bad example. 'There's no way you can go.' I told him I'd be at practice on Friday, then I'd see him on Monday."

Perreira told Morffi that he'd be benched when he returned from his trip.

Up until this point, when someone in the growing WWF organization needed tickets to an event — often for a friend, who, like the NATPE conventioneers, maintained that the request was only "for my kid" — the staffer would casually leave some type of pass at will call. But with the attention that *WrestleMania III* was generating, ticket entreaties came from every direction. "If you worked there, you now had to sign up to request tickets," public relations head Mike Weber said. "Basil created a new system because the company was becoming too big to operate the old way."

Even access to some of the closed-circuit locations was difficult to obtain. In Toronto, 12,000 were sold on the first day of sales. In other places, fans were told that only standing-room spots were available.

As the momentum accelerated, Jim Crockett Jr. attempted to cash in on the increased interest in pro wrestling by running a live show in Toronto, headlined by Ric Flair defending the NWA title against Nikita Koloff. The WWF already had a card booked that day less than 90 minutes away in

Hamilton, Ontario. Out of nowhere it seemed, Jack Tunney declared that the WWF needed to present a card in Toronto, as well, and locked in both cities before Crockett had the opportunity to file the proper paperwork with the athletic commission. It was only when Angelo Mosca, who was now helping the NWA co-promote in Ontario, complained to the press that the WWF concluded that the Hamilton show would be sufficient.

In World Class, the Von Erichs attempted to spark excitement in the faltering promotion by putting the Texas title on the future Ultimate Warrior, the former bodybuilder then billed as the Dingo Warrior. The *Wrestling Observer* reported that his championship win over ex-WWF jobber Bob Bradley was received so poorly that fans were leaving the building before the finish. Wrote Meltzer, "Dingomania isn't running wild here."

Interestingly, the AWA — while nowhere near the level it had been prior to Hogan's departure — could still hold its own at times, drawing 4,500 in its home base of Minneapolis on a night the WWF was running the same city.

Still, throughout North America, most followers were looking to the WWF, anticipating how the company might garnish the *WrestleMania III* card. Rumors circulated about conversations with Sylvester Stallone — completely unsubstantiated — and an alleged plan to pit McMahon — publicly portrayed as the company's babyface announcer — against heel commentator Jesse "The Body" Ventura.

Vince would not officially don the tights until 11 years later when, at age 52, he battled "Stone Cold" Steve Austin at the height of the company's "Attitude Era" on *Monday Night Raw* on the USA Network.

In 1987, though, no one in the WWF cared to muse over the possibility of Vince wrestling, particularly when the organization was preoccupied with the technology being in place for all those fans in the Silverdome to have a clear view of the proceedings.

Since the first *WrestleMania*, the company's production values had vastly improved. When Ed Helinski was hired to run the WWF's magazine in 1983, television was still taped in small buildings in Allentown and Hamburg, Pennsylvania. "Then we went to a mid-sized arena in Poughkeepsie and did

TV there for a while," Helinski said. "And then we said, 'Let's do TV at a regular arena and charge admission and make as much money as we can.' From a business standpoint, it made all the sense in the world."

The bigger buildings meant larger TV crews and superior equipment. Similarly, the company's engineering capabilities were far better coordinated than the year before when Nelson Sweglar had scrambled to manage the *WrestleMania 2* feeds from three separate locations. "We'd gotten the bugs out," he said. "It's a learning curve. We'd started in smaller venues, and now, we were doing multiples of that."

Yet, the WWF had never done a broadcast from a facility as large as the Silverdome, and no one wanted word getting back to McMahon that the spectators were disappointed. During a visit to the Silverdome, Basil Devito was among a group who accompanied the boss to the top tier and deliberately sat in the worst seats.

The topic that day was inserting four 25-by-20-foot TV screens for the fans to see everything. Since the roof was translucent and air-supported, nothing could be attached to it. Engineers would need to be hired to guarantee that the screens could be safely hung. "That was no small engineering feat," Devito said.

During the conversation, Sweglar pointed out that the show was scheduled to start at 4 p.m., which allowed for the possibility of the sun piercing the fabric until nightfall and obscuring the images on the screens. "We're going round and round," Devito said. "We consider maybe putting a big tarp over the Silverdome. Or do we move the event back? And somewhere along the line, Vince asks the question, which was a reasonable question, 'What time will we be able to see the screens all the way?' The answer was that it depended on whether it was a sunny or a cloudy day. 'Even with the translucent roof, if it's rainy, it'll be fine pretty quickly after 4 p.m.' And it was like a judge bringing down a gavel. Vince says, 'Then, it'll rain. We'll be fine. Move on. Nothing's changed.'"

As it turned out, it was cloudy on the afternoon of *WrestleMania III* with a trace of rain.

"A lot of stadiums still had black-and-white screens then," Devito said. "So we had to advertise that our screens would be in color."

Those employees, more concerned with the wrestling end of the business, worried about whether the top contender could acceptably compete in the main event. In the early 1970s, while wrestling in Japan, André was diagnosed with acromegaly, a rare condition that causes the pituitary gland to produce too much growth hormone, causing swollen hands and feet, enlarged facial features and a deepened voice, among other abnormalities. On two occasions, doctors offered to halt the progression by removing a benign tumor inside André's pituitary gland. Both times, he refused, insisting that the surgery would alter the person he'd become.

Now, he was suffering from those decisions, experiencing constant pain along with headaches and fatigue. Although he tried to dull some of the symptoms with alcohol, he was weakening and, over the past year, had barely appeared in the ring.

One of the reasons a heel André had taken to wearing a singlet was to hide his back brace — along with the extra weight he'd gained while inactive. According to Hogan, he worried about hurting André further by slamming him.

"I had my doubts about whether we could pull off the match," conceded Jerry Brisco. "André's health was fading fast and everybody was kind of holding their breath."

He wasn't the only wrestler whose condition troubled the company. WWF World Tag Team co-titlist Tom "Dynamite Kid" Billington of the British Bulldogs had suffered a horrendous back injury in a bout against Don Muraco and Bob Orton Jr. in late 1986. As a result, other babyfaces began standing in for Dynamite in title defenses. While he recovered from surgery, he was visited by his brother-in-law, Bret Hart, who delivered instructions from McMahon to turn over the championship belt. Dynamite refused and eventually checked himself out of the hospital against the doctor's orders.

At a meeting with McMahon, Dynamite listened quietly as the promoter laid out his plan to have the Bulldogs drop the straps to the Iron Sheik and Nikolai Volkoff. Again, the request was denied. Billington would only agree to lose the titles to family members Hart and Jim "The

Anvil" Neidhart — the men with whom the Bulldogs had been having their best matches prior to the injury.

Before that could occur, though, he had to get through *WrestleMania III* since fans expected an appearance by the tag team champions. Without modern protocols in place, no doctor intervened to bar Dynamite's participation. Instead, a plan was conceived to hide him in a six-man tag match. With so much attention on the other performers, Billington could avoid executing his signature flying moves while the audience was kayfabed about the actual circumstances.

Rowdy Roddy Piper, in the meantime, was considering leaving the WWF to pursue acting. He wanted to go out on a high note but almost did not receive the opportunity. Thirteen days before *WrestleMania III*, he slipped on a water puddle while chatting with Harley Race in the locker room at the Los Angeles Memorial Sports Arena. As Piper reached out to grasp onto a solid object, he inserted a wet finger into an empty light socket in the dressing room mirror. The electrical shock sent him hurtling backwards. When he was helped to his feet, he was nauseous and disoriented.

"He got electrocuted," said Weber, "and he was really messed up there. He was not his own self. No one knew if he could make it to *WrestleMania* or not."

He'd eventually sue the arena, settling out of court the next year.

"After that day, something was off with him," Weber continued. "I couldn't put my finger on it — I'm not a doctor — but he always told me that he felt like the electricity was still in his body. It was like the incident changed his body chemistry or something like that."

CHAPTER 24

On a technical level, the clash between Randy "Macho Man" Savage and Ricky "The Dragon" Steamboat would overshadow anything from the previous *Mania*s. But like Hogan and André, it also contained an emotional component that had been building for months.

In February 1986, Savage had captured the WWF Intercontinental Championship from Tito Santana. As an athlete who paid attention to every small detail of his presentation, Savage viewed Steamboat as a kindred spirit and the ideal challenger. The assessment was not only based on Steamboat's immense skill but his attention to in-ring minutiae, along with the ability to connect with followers on a primeval level. Good looks and conditioning added to his allure. Steamboat was so well-liked that no promoter — not Verne Gagne, Eddie Graham nor Jimmy Crockett — had ever taken the risk of depicting him as a heel.

And in this case, Vince McMahon was aligned with them.

"Randy considered Steamboat the greatest babyface going in the 1980s," Savage's brother, "The Genius" Lanny Poffo, told me for *Inside the Ropes Magazine*. "He was so great at being a baby, I doubt the fans would have accepted him as anything else."

To build interest in their rivalry, Savage wanted to do something so vicious to Steamboat that the fans — many of whom would have still been classified as believers — would be howling for vengeance. So in a match broadcast in November 1986, the Macho Man draped his opponent's throat over the ringside barricade, scaled the ropes, clenched his fingers together over his head and came down on the hero with a double ax handle. With his hands clutching his neck, Steamboat fell back against the apron while Savage pulled him by the hair between the ropes. Then the titlist left the ring and grabbed the timekeeper's bell. As the spectators rose and looked on in horror, Savage climbed the strands again and brought the object down on the Dragon's throat.

"Randy came up with the idea and was the only guy who could do it ... because he was so coordinated," Poffo said. "He understood that the bell was heavy and it was tied to a piece of plywood." Despite what the public witnessed, he'd managed to avoid the type of contact that could have legitimately harmed Steamboat.

Regardless, viewers were told that the Dragon had suffered a crushed larynx. He was taken off the road, as medical updates were periodically provided. With four months to go before *WrestleMania III*, it seemed like he'd never possibly recuperate in time. In fact, viewers were informed, doctors were not even sure if he could regain his ability to speak.

The WWF let the grim news set in for more than a month. Naturally, the plan was to have Steamboat return and challenge for the Intercontinental Championship. But Vince waited for the proper moment to reveal a recovered Steamboat, bringing him back not on the weekly syndicated program but the first *Saturday Night's Main Event* special in 1987.

The series began appearing periodically in 1985, occupying the slot usually occupied by *Saturday Night Live* on NBC. After observing the high ratings MTV had received with *The Brawl to End It All* and *The War to Settle the Score*, Dick Ebersol — *Saturday Night Live*'s executive producer at the time — helped McMahon produce the specials and expose the company to an even wider audience.

That Ebersol, an outsider in the industry, was able to bring a crew backstage to work with the talent was a testament in itself. "Vince was brilliant about recognizing the right kinds of friends to have," observed WWF vice president of business affairs Dick Glover. "With a lot of television executives, it wouldn't have worked because they would not have recognized the unique nature of the WWE internal community, including the wrestlers. Dick got it. He respected what we did, and the wrestlers respected him because of it. And that's a big reason why *Saturday Night's Main Event* was a success."

On the January 3, 1987, installment, Savage was wrestling George "The Animal" Steele. Steele was nearly 50 years old and would have been ready to return to his old job as a Michigan high school teacher and football coach had McMahon not decided that he had a vital role to play in the sports entertainment era. With his bald head and hairy body, Steele portrayed a half-beast who bit open the turnbuckles as the stuffing stuck to his sweaty torso, and he stunned fans by flashing his green tongue (the change of color was the result of sucking a large amount of Clorets, a verdant-colored breath mint). As part of his plotline with Savage, Steele had become obsessed with the Macho Man's manager, Elizabeth.

Steele and Savage had tangled at *WrestleMania 2* and been working some variation of the angle ever since, to the Macho Man's consternation. "I remember he told me, 'I wasted all my time learning how to wrestle, so I could wrestle George Steele and not be able to,'" Poffo said.

Although Steele was incredibly strong, being able to hold a foe aloft by the neck without hurting him, Savage did not view him as an equal in the ring. Recalled Poffo, "George wanted to have a good match and Randy wanted to have a great match. You know, George was great at what he did. The guy had a hell of a gimmick . . . But Randy's idea of wrestling was to prove athleticism to the fans, not only the entertainment . . . George Steele was a great athlete, but he was past his peak."

Now, Savage was about to begin a program with his ideal rival. As he and Steele collided on *Saturday Night's Main Event*, Savage was apparently stunned by the sudden appearance of Steamboat standing outside the ring.

With Savage's attention diverted, Steele whisked Elizabeth away from ringside and carried her backstage.

On commentary, Jesse "The Body" Ventura accused the Animal of "kidnapping." Replied babyface McMahon with a melodramatic flourish, "At least, she's in the arms of someone who *cares* about her."

Vince would later characterize the incident as Steele taking the manager into "protective custody."

When Savage attempted to pursue the pair, Steamboat stood in the aisle, blocking the way. What made matters even worse for the Macho Man was Steele returning without Elizabeth. Crazed, Randy promptly whacked the Animal with the ring bell. As with everything Savage did, the move was purposeful, disabling his rival while reminding viewers of the issue with Steamboat. Now, the Intercontinental champ tried to scale up the attack on Steele, but the Dragon intervened and chased the hated villain to the dressing room.

That night, the two repaired to their hotel to begin plotting their match at *WrestleMania III*.

Regardless of how Hogan and André played out, the WWF brain trust was confident that the quality of the Savage and Steamboat bout would leave watchers euphoric. "It was meant to be the buffer match, just in case Hogan and André went south," said Jerry Brisco. "You always had to have the fail-safe match that could be the saver of the show."

Savage would settle for nothing less than an encounter that would linger in fan memories for generations. To ensure this, he and Steamboat repeatedly rehearsed the match move for move. "They rented a little auditorium in Florida and I went over and watched," Brisco said. "They both asked me if I had any thoughts. And then Savage wanted to go over everything again."

The rivals also prepared in the six-man tag matches the WWF arranged at house shows to allow the *WrestleMania III* participants to go over some routines in the ring together. Since Roddy Piper was scheduled to wrestle Adrian Adonis and Harley Race would be clashing with the Junkyard Dog, the tag matches pitted Savage, Adonis and Race against the Dragon, Hot Rod and JYD.

With each encounter, Randy added a new embellishment to the blueprint.

Although he had never been diagnosed, Savage was almost certainly afflicted with obsessive-compulsive disorder (OCD) and could not let go of a concept once it penetrated his mind, repeatedly tweaking the words to his promos during long car rides and even supervising the way Elizabeth escorted him to the ring. He "makes her walk up the steps and teaches her to go through the ropes probably 150 to 200 times so she wouldn't show too much leg and she could do it very lady-like," Steele told ESPN.com about a scene he witnessed shortly after Elizabeth became her husband's manager. "I felt sorry for her. It was brutal."

But Savage made no excuses for his pedantry, telling the website that his success had largely been predicated on scouting opponents "to see who would blend with my style of work and if they didn't, how I could change my style to make the match as good as it possibly could be . . . It's kind of like catching in baseball and calling the game."

And just as the Macho Man was fixated on the Steamboat clash, McMahon was equally consumed with breaking the attendance record at the Silverdome. To guarantee that every fan within driving distance committed to the event, the WWF arranged for the final *Saturday Night's Main Event* before *Mania* to be taped at the Joe Louis Arena in Detroit.

"Attention, animal lovers," television columnist Mike Duffy declared in the February 20 edition of the *Detroit Free Press*. "The World Wrestling Federation's cuckoo human zoo is coming to town again . . . And this time, a crew from NBC's *Saturday Night's Main Event* will be there to soak up all the craziness and tape it for a March 14 national telecast. That makes sense. Detroit — a hardcore hockey town, a devoted baseball city and one diehard rock 'n' roll community — is also in love with pro wrestling."

This was not a recent phenomenon. Starting in 1971, the original Sheik and Dick the Bruiser engaged in a promotional feud, going head-to-head the same night and drawing decent crowds to Cobo Hall and the Detroit Olympia, respectively, before — like the Rougeaus and Vachons in Montreal — burning the fans out on too much wrestling. But that was part of the distant past, while *WrestleMania III* represented the present and the future.

It was WWF public relations head Mike Weber's responsibility to flood the Detroit media with stories about the upcoming event. "We had good relationships with the two main papers and I worked with every TV station there. But it mostly was radio, having wrestlers call into the radio stations or visit in person. Of course, there was no social media then, so I spent a lot of time in Detroit just working with the media."

By the time of the show, more than 10,000 press kits would be distributed, along with 100 press box credentials, far in excess of any previous pro wrestling event anywhere in the world.

During one of Weber's visits, he was on a pay phone in the Silverdome when he happened to see McMahon nemesis Ted Turner walking through the lobby.

"I'm sure he was there on other business, and it had nothing to do with wrestling. It was just one of those little weird things that happens."

Weber never inquired about what Turner was doing that day — even though the public relations specialist would later work for the mogul after he purchased WCW.

The *Saturday Night's Main Event* that aired on March 14 set a ratings record that held for years, and it pulled fans further into the storylines behind *WrestleMania III*'s marquee matches.

Once again, the show featured a bout between Savage and Steele. To prevent the mishap that occurred in the prior encounter on NBC, the Macho Man insisted that Elizabeth sit on a lifeguard chair at ringside to limit the Animal's access. As in the previous episode, Steamboat became involved in the action, distracting and flustering Randy — who managed to win via countout after Steele helped Elizabeth off the chair, and Savage lifted it up to throttle his foe.

Hogan and André would use a battle royal to tease the *WrestleMania III* main event. To convey a sense of menace, the Giant utilized a headbutt to bust open fellow participant Poffo — a babyface at the time not acknowledged as the Macho Man's brother — who was promptly stretchered out. Hogan was then whipped into André by Paul Orndorff and Hercules Hernandez, prompting a staredown and exchange of punches.

But Orndorff and the tag team of Demolition also jumped into the fight, ganging up on the Hulkster and setting the champ up for André to come up from behind and eliminate him with another clanging headbutt.

As several referees forced an angry Hogan back to the showers, a mob of wrestlers went after André, dumping him onto the floor. Contemplating the circumstances, Mean Gene Okerlund told the audience that it required eight competitors to eliminate André and only one scary giant to get rid of Hogan.

But what would transpire when they met at *WrestleMania III*? The most satisfying way to find out, viewers were reminded yet another time, would be watching their one-on-one bout live at the Silverdome.

CHAPTER 25

T he company's television and photography crews began loading into the Silverdome on March 26, three days before *WrestleMania III*. "I was one of the first people there," said photographer Steve Taylor, "and I remember walking into the empty stadium and thinking, 'Wow, this is where they're going to put the ring, and the rest'" — all the empty space normally part of the football field — "'is going to be filled with fans.'"

The WWF had yet to incorporate a stage or Titan Tron — the giant video wall at the top of the entrance ramp — into its set, allowing for even more room for seating. "We were going back and forth from the dressing room to the ring area, saying, 'Oh my gosh, this is really a long walk.'"

Neither Taylor nor fellow photographer Tom Buchanan had ever worked in an inflatable dome before. "You're in an airlock," Taylor said. "It was held up by air pressure, and the air was being pushed in and out whenever you opened or closed a door. So you had to open one door, a truck would come in, then you'd close the door and open up another one just to make sure you were keeping the air in the building. It was quite an experience."

Because the photographers' responsibilities now included lighting, both Taylor and Buchanan went onto the Silverdome roof to check the rigging points. Recalled Buchanan, "It felt like a giant trampoline with this heavy white material with steel cables running through it for structural support. But the whole thing was inflated from down below. With so much air seeping out, we understood that the rig setting would lower as the day went on."

The roof was lined with small hatches, which could be released to look down into the stadium. "When you'd open those up, the air would rush out," Taylor said. "It felt like a big bouncy house, and we were bouncing around from cushion to cushion. And there was a place there on one of the vents where we signed our names."

Buchanan, a recreational skydiver, enjoyed the high altitude, pushing down the cover of one of the roof hatches and sticking his head through into the Silverdome itself. "The air is rushing out so it feels like a giant fan. When your head is all the way in, you're not attached to anything. It was like we were just hanging there."

At TV tapings, the lighting trusses were set up on the ground, then mechanically raised toward the ceiling. At the Silverdome, the lighting was arranged on much larger trusses before being lifted skyward. Settings were arranged in anticipation of nightfall. "When the show started it would be daylight, so the lights wouldn't be all that necessary," Buchanan pointed out, "but when the sunlight went away, they'd be crucial."

To accommodate to the large audience, the normally three-foot-high ring was elevated by an 18-inch platform. "We marketing guys never thought about that," said public relations head Mike Weber. "But obviously, the operations guys realized that, with the size of the stadium, there'd be so many more people on the floor than at a regular show. I don't think anything like that had ever been done before, so you really have to give those guys credit for understanding how to improve the fan experience."

Some 2,500 workers had been hired to work the concession stands at the event, anticipating sales of 76,000 hot sandwiches, 25,000 orders of popcorn, 13,000 plates of nachos, 7,000 slices of pizza, 3,000 gallons of soft drinks and 15,000 gallons of beer.

Yet, when Ed Helinski was stocking the merchandise stands, he was reminded to be conservative so that there wasn't a glut of inventory left over. "I don't think everyone understood the magnitude of having Hulk Hogan and André the Giant in the main event. So I said, 'We need to get more.'

"The way I saw it, everything was going to sell — Hogan stuff, Macho Man stuff, Ricky Steamboat stuff, British Bulldogs stuff, Killer Bees stuff. I even had them send over some Jimmy 'Superfly' Snuka merchandise. He hadn't been in the company in two years, but we had his stuff in stock and maybe someone would want to buy his t-shirt. You didn't want to leave any dollars on the table so you took your shot to see what would work."

While most in the company were overwhelmed by the large stadium, McMahon appeared to have a clear vision. "It's like the director of a movie who could see things other people don't," noted vice president of business affairs Dick Glover. "He knows how it's going to turn out. The one person I could compare him to would be Steve Jobs. Everybody else is telling you you're crazy, but you know what's in your head and what has to happen to get it done."

The only person who seemed capable of reading the boss's inner thoughts, Glover said, was the vice president of television production, Nelson Sweglar. "I used to chuckle because Vince would be saying, 'We want this. We want that.' And Nelson would say, 'Oh, geez,' but knew what he meant. And he'd go, 'Well, I guess we have to build a lighting grid for that.'"

With a limited amount of time allotted for the event on pay-per-view, it was essential to understand how long each portion of *WrestleMania III* would take. The Piper-Adonis match was scheduled to culminate with Brutus Beefcake rushing the ring and introducing a new dimension of his persona, transforming into "The Barber" — at the expense of "Adorable" Adrian. "Everything had to be timed out," Weber said, "including how long it would take to shoot somebody getting his head shaved. I guess someone said, 'Let's get a ring crew guy.' Because I remember a day or two before *Mania*, coming out of the back and seeing Beefcake shaving this guy's head. I don't know if they paid him extra or somebody told him to be a team player."

The night before the show, Hogan said that McMahon expressed his concern about André's compromised abilities, urging the champion to make sure that when he knocked the Giant down, the contender always had the ropes nearby to pull himself back up.

But even with so much contingent on a successful main event, Vince was apparently thinking past *WrestleMania III*. Over the past several months, he'd been communicating with Bruce Prichard, who'd soon join the list of personnel leaving Bill Watts's UWF for Stamford. Less than 24 hours before the spectacular, the future Brother Love received a phone call. "It was Vince saying, 'I just want to make sure you know we have this little show tomorrow near Detroit. Some pay-per-view. If you get a chance to see it, I'd really love to get your feedback.'

"The entire conversation was no longer than two minutes. But later on, when I was helping Vince put together other *WrestleMania*s, it was astonishing to me that he took those two minutes out of all the other crazy shit that was going on to call me. But that's the way Vince was. He wasn't just looking at *WrestleMania III*. He was already looking at *WrestleMania X*."

CHAPTER 26

Bob Collins had arrived in Albuquerque, New Mexico, the final week of March to get ready for the Ice Capades.

The organization's senior promotions director expected a good showing, even though there were some challenges with the arena. "The building didn't have ice, but we had portable ice equipment and could make our own. It just took several days."

When he arrived at the Tingley Coliseum, though, he discovered that another event had been booked, shutting down the ice-making process.

"*WrestleMania III* was being shown on closed-circuit, so we couldn't have access to the venue. We had to postpone the Ice Capades for a day or two, and I really didn't understand that. I remember thinking to myself, 'Who's going to come and fill up the Tingley Coliseum just to watch wrestling on a big screen?'"

By the time the WWF hired him nine months later, he had a better grasp of the enormity connected to Vincent Kennedy McMahon's version of the One True Sport.

In the Detroit area, everyone already seemed to comprehend the immensity of *WrestleMania*. The *Detroit News* and *Detroit Free Press* were devoting the kind of attention to the event that the region's sports teams received during the playoffs. The *Free Press* even ventured so far as to predict a winner: "One of two things will happen. (1) A double disqualification. (2) André will appear to win, but Hulk will catch him in a small package for a three count. Hulk will still be the champion, but Heenan proclaims André the champ and both will wear championship belts, leading up to a great rematch."

Steve Taylor knew better. "André had done everything before and had his place, his history." Now, Taylor believed, the Giant would elevate the Hulkster to the same level by losing cleanly in the Silverdome. "André wanted to do this for Hogan. Hulk winning in front of that record crowd was going to put him in a different sort of superstar category."

While most local observers were caught up in the speculation, *Free Press* columnist Jim Fitzgerald decided to play heel. "Anyone with half a brain knows professional wrestling is phonier than a country trail air-conditioned by General Electric. But there you are — more than 92,000 wrestling nuts stomping and cheering and actually taking that nonsense seriously.

"'There really is no accounting for taste,' my wife said."

Interestingly, the people at the highest levels of the WWF were unconcerned about this type of mockery. The past few years had proven that exposing the business would no longer contribute to its demise. In fact, McMahon — with the assistance of writers like Dave Meltzer — was engineering a new kind of wrestling follower: a person who embraced the pastime's worked nature and took pleasure in dissecting plot points and character development.

The morning of the event, Dick Glover took a walk around the Silverdome. After months of planning, the day was finally here.

"I found myself just looking at the stadium and thinking about the size. When it was empty of fans, it felt even bigger."

The Rougeau Brothers were also surveying the stadium, walking first to the ring and then to the very top. "We were so far, far up, you could barely see the ring," Jacques said. "It was like having a little dice in your hands."

Raymond tried to imagine himself as a fan. "I was looking around at all the seats, and tried to think about what it would be like when the place was full. And I just sat there, amazed."

"History is made" in the words of announcer Gorilla Monsoon, as *WrestleMania III* attracts the largest North American audience at the time for a wrestling event. The announced attendance of 93,173 is debated to this day.

Because of his immense size, André the Giant, seen here holding his long arms over fellow wrestlers (from left) Chief Jay Strongbow, Mike Pappas and Victor Rivera, was labeled the "Eighth Wonder of the World."

Before the takeover.
Vincent James McMahon
(right) and Toronto
promoter Frank Tunney.
Despite a business
relationship with Jim
Crockett Jr., Tunney
ran Toronto as an open
city, where every major
promotion was represented.
But Vincent Kennedy
McMahon would change
all that.

After launching the
American Wrestling
Association (AWA) in
1960, former U.S. Olympic
alternate Verne Gagne held
the group's championship
on and off for 20 years.
But when the WWF
started expanding, Vince
McMahon went after
Gagne hard, luring away
many of his marquee names.

In many ways, multiple National Wrestling Association (NWA) titlist Harley Race embodied the pre-sports entertainment era. Still, at *WrestleMania III*, Vince McMahon found a place for him on the card — as the newly branded "King" of the squared circle.

Jack and Jerry Brisco exulting with the North American Tag Team titles in Puerto Rico in 1981. The duo would stun the industry by selling McMahon their points in the high-profile Georgia promotion and help him procure the group's valuable TV slot on TBS.

Flamboyant and cunning, Jim Barnett (left), shown here with Pro Wrestling USA live events promoter Gary Juster, arguably knew more industry secrets than anyone and became a critical asset to McMahon. He'd later boast of receiving the largest *WrestleMania III* bonus in the WWF.

The future Iron Sheik, Khosrow Vaziri, and wife, Caryl, on their wedding day, flanked by Verne Gagne (left) and AWA co-founder Wally Karbo. Because of the Sheik's warm feelings toward the Gagne family, he briefly considered accepting the Minnesota promoter's proposal to injure Hulk Hogan rather than lose the World Heavyweight Championship to him in 1984.

GEORGE NAPOLITANO

Vince McMahon's decision to make the charismatic Hulk Hogan the focal point of the World Wrestling Federation was a break with tradition, offending promoters and veterans who believed that champions should be regarded as serious athletes rather than showmen.

"The Yellow Rose of Texas" David von Erich traps "Nature Boy" Ric Flair in the abdominal stretch in 1983. Von Erich's shocking death a year later would trigger a spiral that impacted his family and their popular World Class Championship Wrestling (WCCW) promotion.

The Junkyard Dog was a lynchpin of Cowboy Bill Watts's Mid-South Wrestling territory, a league featuring both believable personalities and compelling storylines. In 1984, he departed for the WWF without giving notice, a move described by one Mid-South insider as "crippling."

During a backstage conversation, manager Jimmy "The Mouth of the South" Hart realized that the piercing noise his ever-present megaphone made would prompt the British Bulldogs' mascot, Matilda, to lunge at the object. As a result, Hart began provoking the dog in the ring, adding yet another element to the WWF spectacle.

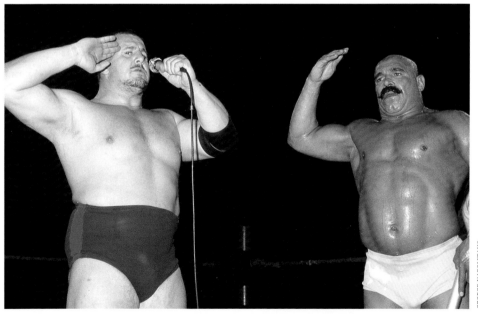

To capitalize on the flag-waving patriotism of Reagan-era America, the Iron Sheik and tag team partner Nikolai Volkoff portrayed foreign menaces. Before their matches, Volkoff would infuriate audiences by demanding that they stand and respect his singing of the Soviet national anthem.

WWF photographer Tom Buchanan, a skydiver in his spare time, fearlessly bounces on the Pontiac Silverdome's inflatable, fiberglass fabric roof prior to *WrestleMania III*.

Detroit's "Queen of Soul" Aretha Franklin sends shivers through the Silverdome crowd with her rendition of "America the Beautiful" at the start of *WrestleMania III*. The inclusion of the first female artist inducted into the Rock & Roll Hall of Fame greatly enhanced the show's reputation as a can't-miss event.

Birth of The Barber. After being ditched by his "Dream Team" running buddies earlier in the show, Brutus Beefcake assists "Rowdy" Roddy Piper by shaving the head of his rival, "Adorable" Adrian Adonis.

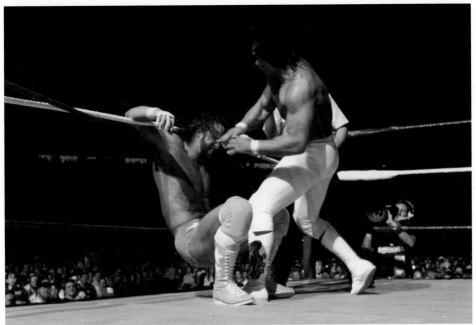

Concerned that André the Giant's physical limitations could inhibit the quality of the main event, WWF officials knew that they could rely on Randy "Macho Man" Savage and Ricky "The Dragon" Steamboat to put on a spectacular match at *WrestleMania III*. At the time, many considered the encounter the best they'd ever witnessed.

With a small American flag protruding from his 2x4, "Hacksaw" Jim Duggan was a recent addition from Mid-South. At *WrestleMania III*, Duggan cut a promo about walking tall for the USA before intervening in the match pitting Volkoff and the Iron Sheik against the Killer Bees.

WWE

When future WWE executive Bruce Prichard left Mid-South to become dastardly televangelist Brother Love for McMahon, he brought along Ted DiBiase, a second-generation great rebranded as the "Million Dollar Man."

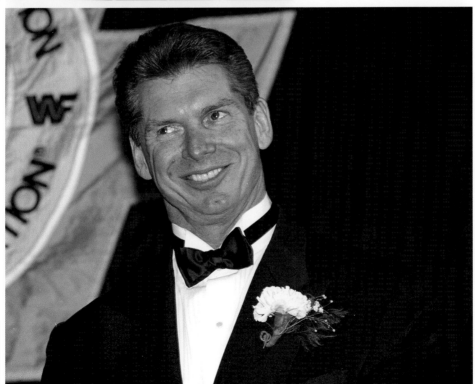

Ten years after *WrestleMania III*, Vincent Kennedy McMahon was in the middle of another wrestling war but still gloating over the way he'd changed the business.

New York superfans Vladimir Abouzeide (with glasses) and Charlie Adorno en-route to becoming beloved members of the WWF community. From Adorno's personal photo album (below): one of the "Federettes" smiles in front of Little Tokyo and Lord Littlebrook. Announcer and future Minnesota Governor Jesse "The Body" Ventura. Bobby "The Brain" Heenan and his protege, Hercules. André the Giant and Hulk Hogan face off. Cowboy Bob Orton and the Magnificent Muraco. Rowdy Roddy Piper. The Honky Tonk Man. Brutus Beefcake helps Piper celebrate his victory.

The Hulkster in the spotlight. Hulk Hogan in his miniature ring cart, holding up his WWF World Heavyweight Championship and the role he played in altering the pro wrestling landscape.

Outside, fans were gathering in the parking lot and starting to line up in front of the stadium entrance. New York superfans Charlie Adorno from Brooklyn and Vladimir Abouzeide from Washington Heights in upper Manhattan were among the first there. The experience was unlike any they'd had before.

"It was the first time I ever flew on an airplane," Adorno noted.

Charlie had been a fan since he saw his first WWF broadcast at eight years old in 1975. He attended a card in Madison Square Garden a year later. By the time of *WrestleMania III*, he'd been to every event at the fabled arena for the past five years.

As other regulars griped about McMahon destroying the institution of wrestling, Charlie and Vladimir were having the time of their lives. "We were making friends, meeting wrestlers, collecting merchandise. When I was a kid, there were no action figures. If you were lucky and went to some show at a high school gym, maybe you'd get a button or an 8x10."

While attending Brooklyn's South Shore High School, Charlie had been able to subsidize his wrestling habit by working in the video store across the street from his home. Vladimir, a muscular, high-energy, Haitian-born fan, was already in his twenties, living with his mother and siblings and earning money as a maintenance worker and doorman at luxury buildings near Central Park.

"I saw him before we became friends," Charlie said. "He was 23 years old, a grown man, when I was 15. But he'd be screaming and jumping up and down. And I thought, 'Wow, this guy really loves it, just like I do.' We exchanged numbers and he became one of my best friends. He still is."

There were lots of other guys in their crew — people every regular at Madison Square Garden knew, either by name or sight. Tom Cusati booked wrestlers on other people's indie shows, paying the performers himself just so he could claim to be a promoter. Sometimes, the rotund, balding aficionado included himself on the cards, accompanying talent to the ring as an invective-spewing manager named Royce Profit. Later on, Cusati would flash a business card listing him as a WWE employee, weaving tales about conducting promo seminars at the organization's Performance Center.

Richie Halbert tended to show up at Madison Square Garden in a white suit and black, open-collar shirt — like John Travolta in *Saturday Night Fever* — a gold chai — the Hebrew symbol for life — hanging around his neck. Although there was no evidence to support this, Richie insisted that he'd wrestled in the past and was known to grouse, "I need to get back on the road."

When the crowd erupted after Hulk Hogan defeated the Iron Sheik for the WWF World Heavyweight Championship, Richie asserted that the victor pointed into the crowd and shouted, "Alright, Richie!"

Before the company began selling replica championship belts, Mike Vartanian would design and carve them out of wood. "Then, he'd go to this place in Sunset Park [Brooklyn], where they would attach the strap and put on the side pieces," Adorno said. "He actually made belts for some of the wrestlers for them to keep at home. I bet some of those guys still have those belts today."

Back then, the WWF would generally run its Madison Square Garden cards on Monday nights. The championship was usually defended in the middle of the show, just before intermission. Prior to the main event, the next month's matches would be announced.

The following morning, fans would wait outside the Madison Square Garden box office for tickets to go on sale. Because Charlie tended to be busy with school, he'd sometimes dispatch his mother to perform the task.

In time, Vladimir and Charlie developed a different routine. After Garden cards, they'd repair to the Ramada Inn on West 48th Street and 8th Avenue, sitting in the hotel bar and waiting for the wrestlers — who always stayed at the hotel and worked out next door at the Mid City Gym — to wander in. "After that," Charlie said, "instead of going home, we would actually go back to Garden and wait overnight for the box office to open."

Shortly before 10 a.m., a Garden employee would come outside and inform the gathered fans that tickets were about to go on sale. Vladimir and Charlie were usually first on line, and they knew the exact sections where they wanted to sit. It was always within the first two rows, and the pair would buy four tickets — to have extras for friends.

During one of their overnight waits, a box office manager approached the pair with a question. "You guys are here every month, aren't you?"

Vladimir and Charlie nodded.

"Alright. If you want to come with me, maybe I can help you out."

The two entered an office and were told that, because of their loyalty, two tickets would be reserved for them every month. "We could just pick them up at our leisure," Charlie said. "They'd have them in an envelope, and we just paid when we got there."

But no special arrangement had been made for *WrestleMania III*, so Vladimir and Charlie ordered their tickets by phoning the number they saw on WWF broadcasts. "It was long distance," Charlie explained, "so you could be charged a lot of money if you stayed on the phone too long. I remember it vividly. I was at my girlfriend's place and used her phone. I called and was on hold for maybe 30 seconds and someone picked up. I was so shocked when they said they had seats across from the main camera, second row center."

Independently, Vladimir had procured seats in the third row. The friends flew separately to Detroit, then met after they touched down. As soon as they were admitted to the Silverdome, the pair repeated what the Rougeaus had done earlier in the day, climbing to the top of the stadium and looking around.

Neither ever could have imagined that a wrestling show could fill a building that large. But as they contemplated the view, Charlie nudged Vladimir and motioned at their seats down near the ring.

"Good thing we're sitting over there. This is *far*."

On a highway near suburban Milford, Michigan, 11-year-old Vince Averill sat in the back of a station wagon with a group of friends, hypothesizing about what might transpire at *WrestleMania III*.

The son of a track and field coach who didn't like wrestling, Vince had to discover the sport of kings on his own, catching the WWF's programs on Saturday mornings or at the homes of friends who had cable TV. "My dad never said, 'Don't watch it,'" he recounted. "He just wasn't interested."

Still, when Vince asked to attend his first live show, at the Joe Louis Arena in 1985, his father consented. "He just didn't go. I went with my mother and some neighbors."

Nonetheless, asking his mother to navigate through Silverdome traffic so they could watch Hogan and André was out of the question. Fortunately, a classmate named Bobby Regal happened to have parents who felt differently. "Bobby's birthday was coming up and I found out he could take three or four kids with him to *WrestleMania*. I was already friendly with Bobby, but now it became my sole mission to make sure I was one of the people who was going. 'You want my Doritos, Bobby? They're yours. Have my pizza, too.' 'You want to play kickball at recess? I'm with you, man. I love kickball.' Bobby was my ticket, and, ultimately, I was selected."

But a few days before the event, Averill's parents had second thoughts. "Another kid wanted to go, and Bobby's father offered the idea of, 'Maybe I'll just give *him* my ticket and drop the kids off.' And the other parents had to have kind of a sitdown and say, 'You're not dropping four or five fifth graders off at the Pontiac Silverdome and leaving.'"

Bobby's father acquiesced. But Averill's parents warned their son to stay in the car if the man didn't exit with the group.

Fortunately, he did.

Although most of his focus was inside the stadium, Nelson Sweglar was aware that a massive crowd was waiting outside and wanted to dispatch a TV crew to interview some of those fans. "I didn't know what we would do with the footage," he said. "Maybe use it for promotional purposes later on. But it seemed like a reasonable thing to me."

When he broached the topic with McMahon, though, the boss wasn't interested. "It just would have been one little crew for a short period of time," Sweglar said. "But, for some reason, Vince didn't get it. Vince McMahon may be this promotional genius, but sometimes there are holes in that."

Tom Buchanan had no such restrictions. In her role overseeing the *WWF Magazine*, Linda McMahon specifically requested that Buchanan photograph those same fans to fully chronicle the historic day. "I ran through the parking lot, taking pictures of people at their hibachis or just hanging out, cheering. They were rowdy but in a good kind of way. It was a family feeling. Everyone was having a good time. A lot of them didn't have tickets."

Ed Helinski was in the parking lot, too, but for a different purpose — purging the property of vendors hawking bootleg merchandise. "The parking lot was enormous, so these guys could set up shop at any given place. But once the show was getting close, the crowds began to disperse and they stuck out. It was more important to get rid of these guys before the show than after the show. Once the fans got into the building, we wanted them spending as much money as possible."

When the negotiations for Aretha Franklin to participate in *WrestleMania III* were complete, Dick Glover oversaw the paperwork and became the contact point for her representatives. Although he was confident in this role, he admitted that his experience dealing with high-level entertainers was limited and had a discussion about his uncertainty with Dick Ebersol before Franklin arrived at the Silverdome.

"Listen," Ebersol advised, "get her in, get her where she needs to go. Don't be overwhelmed. And as excited as you are, don't ask for her autograph."

The words put Glover at ease, although he still worried about circumstances he could not influence. "I had heard that Aretha was notoriously late for everything. So I was thinking, 'Oh my god. What if she's late? I can't control that.'"

This was particularly likely given the high volume of traffic for *WrestleMania III*. Pontiac Police Captain Michael Miles estimated that, even with people carpooling to the event, there were approximately 12,000 fewer parking spaces than the projected number of spectators. To prevent a calamity from occurring, Silverdome and Pontiac officials were routing traffic to the center of town, where free shuttle buses would ferry fans to the stadium.

Regardless of this plan, traffic on the M-59 highway was backed up for more than five miles. Among those gridlocked were Aretha Franklin and her entourage.

Glover would have to calm his nerves and wait. Unless you were Hulk Hogan or André the Giant, no one was going to be granted a special escort to *WrestleMania III*, including Detroit's beloved Queen of Soul.

CHAPTER 27

E xactly how many people were inside the Silverdome remains a source of debate, since McMahon had mandated that he didn't want to see empty seats, and television crews had been instructed to make the vast audience a focal point of the broadcast.

Up until now, the Silverdome attendance record had been set in 1977 when Led Zeppelin played in front of an announced 76,229. At the time, it was a landmark gate for an indoor show anywhere, shading the 75,062 that The Who had purportedly drawn to the same facility in 1975. But McMahon wasn't going to settle for these types of numbers — not with a papal Mass expected to attract more than 85,000 worshippers to the Silverdome later in the year.

While Pontiac Police Captain Michael Miles intended to prepare for the Pope's visit by studying the flow patterns through different sections of the stadium during *WrestleMania III*, officially, the Archdiocese of Detroit was paying little attention. "The crowd for wrestling will probably be slightly different from a congregation," the Reverend William Eaton, site planning coordinator for the Mass, told the *Detroit Free Press*. "At least, I hope they will."

But McMahon — who'd present a match pitting him and his son, Shane, against Shawn Michaels and "God" in 2006 (Vince went over, of course, following interference from a faction coincidentally branded the Spirit Squad)

— apparently viewed the pontiff as no different than Jimmy Crockett, Verne Gagne or Fritz von Erich. Even against the Vatican, the WWF had to win and, like professional wrestling itself, the attendance would be predetermined.

Mike Weber said that, on the day of the show, the late Zane Bresloff, a live events promoter who'd established his ties to the WWF by securing arenas previously exclusive to the AWA, gave him the oft-quoted 93,173 figure to disseminate in the press box. According to one anecdote, Bresloff and Basil Devito had conjured up the number together before one of them wrote it on a cocktail napkin.

"Zane told me it was Basil," said *Wrestling Observer Newsletter* founder Dave Meltzer. "I definitely talked to Zane about that number many times. He said Basil came up with a number because it had to be a bigger number than anyone could draw indoors for anything."

Devito did not recall whether or not he scribbled the number on a cocktail napkin. "But I can tell you a couple of things. I did absolutely understand whatever the prior indoor attendance record was. The papal mass was going to break the record and we had to beat it. And I counted every ticket sold. I also counted every human body in that building, every security guard, every single vendor. Everybody was counted. Let's remember, back in the day, there was no email. Once the number was decided, we would have written it down somewhere and said, 'This is it. We don't want to hear another word.' So as far as I'm concerned, I'm going to my grave saying the attendance was 93,173."

Internally, the WWF staff would joke that there were two sets of numbers for every event — the actual one and the "Titanized" one, a takeoff on the company's corporate name, Titan Sports. But Weber argued that made the organization no more carny than other sports and music promotions.

"I used to work in Supercross," a motorcycle racing series, "and we used to keep ledgers. 'Okay, here's the real number, and here's the number we announce. Here's the number we tell the sponsors.' Everyone does it."

But how many people were really in the stadium? According to former Pro Wrestling USA live events promoter Gary Juster, Jim Barnett — who had a hand in everything — cited 78,000 when the two worked together in WCW a decade later.

And indeed, that may have been the paid attendance — or close to it.

During a period when he had a particularly good relationship with the company, Meltzer said that he was shown ticket accounting paperwork listing 78,500 customers.

Yet, as Devito pointed out, there were a lot more than ticket buyers in the building. This included not just personnel assigned to work the show but tailgaters who didn't have tickets. "I'm not sure if it was Linda or Basil or somebody," said Tom Buchanan, "but they made the call to let people in, whether they had tickets or not. I saw that happening on the concourse level, people just coming into the stadium through open doors."

Whether those uncounted enthusiasts, combined with the Silverdome staff, WWF employees, friends and family of the talent and outside vendors were enough to add up to 93,173 can be speculated about until the Apocalypse.

"It looked great on television," noted Jim Ross. "They shot it brilliantly. I've heard 78,000, 85,000, 90,000, whatever you want to believe. But what does it matter? It looked like a full house and a lot of people were supporting wrestling."

Since Vince Averill and his friends were relatively slight compared to the adults in the Silverdome, the gusts of wind they encountered whenever a door opened or closed felt powerful. "As a little guy, it was like I was trying to walk against the air," he described the journey through the concourse. "I had never been to anything that size or scope and was just looking at those lines of folks, all coming into the building."

The kids were safely in their seats when Vince McMahon appeared in the ring in a black tuxedo and red bow tie, his dark hair swept back and blow-dried. The 41-year-old entrepreneur stared out at the hordes on the upper levels, all small shapes collectively twitching with expectation. As ring announcer Howard Finkel stood dutifully behind him, the boss brought the microphone to his lips and, with a look that conveyed both smugness and satisfaction, created an iconic moment with this husky declaration:

"Welcome to WrestleMania III!"

The crowd responded with an ecstatic yell. Rafael Morffi's ears rang and, for the next few hours, the teenager would forget the repercussions he faced from his baseball coach back in Queens.

After he'd procured his tickets, Morffi had asked around the neighborhood until he found some older companions who met his mother's approval. Together, the group had flown out to Detroit the day before and stayed at a hotel. At least one of the guys had a driver's license and rented a car to bring the contingent to the Silverdome.

"It was a celebration," he said. "Everyone was happy, just excited to be there. It was extraordinary. It was wonderful."

By the time Aretha Franklin arrived at the Silverdome, there were already fans in the building and no time for a sound check.

Dick Glover caught up with the legendary singer as she walked with her entourage through the bowels of the stadium. "I think she and her people had the same reaction everyone did when they walked in. First, you're in the backstage area, and it feels pretty much the same as the backstage area at any other arena. This was very different. You opened that curtain, and you looked at Aretha's baby grand in the middle of everything. It wasn't positioned on a stage far from the ring. It was on a platform right *next* to the ring. And you looked at that with the crowd building up and the only feeling you could have was *Holy shit.*"

Jumping Jim Brunzell was trying to deal with his own nerves by leaving the men's locker room and getting some air when he turned a corner and spotted the Queen of Soul. "Here was Miss Franklin sort of standing there. And she was by herself and just sort of humming. And I grinned and nodded and let her have her peace.

"I'm such a big music fan, I would have loved to have gone up and told her how much I admired her and asked for an autograph. But I didn't dare."

As Glover studied Aretha and her entourage, he thought the singer looked tired and wasn't sure if she was anxious or had been out very late the night before. "But when it came time for her to go out, boy, was there energy! Whatever else was on her mind just melted away."

McMahon, who idolized Franklin as a performer, made sure that he was still in the ring to make the introduction. "And now," he told the crowd, "to sing 'America the Beautiful,' the Queen of Soul" — his voice rose to a raucous crescendo as he swept his arm forward — "Miss *Aretha Franklin!*"

And there she was, already seated at the baby grand, in a dignified beige dress and white collar, the little girl who'd grown into one of the world's finest singers by watching her minister father, C.L. Franklin (known in gospel circles as "the man with the million-dollar voice"), command an audience from the altar at Detroit's New Bethel Baptist Church. The moment her fingers hit the keys, a shiver swept through the immense crowd as everybody was hit with the realization that the *WrestleMania III* experience came with a bonus no spectator had anticipated: bearing witness to the exalted talents of the local hero who, earlier that year, had become the first woman inducted into the nascent Rock & Roll Hall of Fame.

In the second row, Charlie Adorno was awestruck. "I can't believe I'm in this," he said to himself.

"America, America," Aretha sang at the conclusion of the song. "God shed his grace on thee. And crown thy good. With brotherhood . . ."

She paused and let her backup singers finish: "From sea to shining sea."

The diva rose to take in the cheers raining on her from every direction, raising her arms and figuratively embracing this audience that, for a few moments, was so enraptured that the wrestling almost became secondary.

And then, it was over. Aretha and her piano were taken to the back. The ring bell sounded, and the unmistakably resonant voice of Howard Finkel wafted through the air.

"Ladies and gentlemen, this is a tag team contest." Don Muraco and the Can-Am Connection — Minnesotan Tom Zenk and Quebec City's Rick Martel — were ferried down the aisle in carts designed like miniature wrestling rings.

The mobile assistance was a necessity, conceptualized on a site survey shortly after somebody in authority attempted to walk from the dressing room to the location of the ring. "You're talking about 50 or 60 yards," noted Nelson Sweglar. "That's a long hike. The trick was how to make it work."

Already, Silverdome employees were using four-wheel drive vehicles called "scissor cars" to travel around the building. It was just a matter of crafting those vehicles into something more suitable for *WrestleMania*. Not only did the ring carts have a wrestling theme, but the talent was elevated for fans to view from every vantage point.

"Vince always said, 'You want to make sure you get the entrance right,'" recounted Glover. "'And you want to make sure you get the exit right. Everything else will probably take care of itself if you're lucky.'"

As an extra touch, the combatants would be greeted at ringside by the "Federettes," shapely attendants in short purple outfits lined with sequins and complemented by long, almost medieval white collars. Once the carts came to a halt, one of the Federettes unfastened the faux ring ropes and helped each wrestler out of the vehicle.

With Jesse "The Body" Ventura and Gorilla Monsoon doing the play-by-play for closed-circuit and pay-per-view viewers, the action could officially begin.

But first, Finkel needed to finish the introductions and announce the heel team. Taking the temperature of the crowd, all the seasoned Muraco had to do was raise his arms to receive a torrent of jeers.

All four men were considered exceptional workers. Muraco had been a trainer for Verne Gagne and consistent main-eventer. Despite his gimmick bashing people with a cast for Rowdy Roddy Piper, Orton was a second-generation star whose proficiency with the superplex had inspired others to incorporate the maneuver into their respective repertoires. On the babyface side, Zenk, a former bodybuilder, had been trained by ex-Olympian Brad Rheingans, while Martel was an ex-AWA World Heavyweight Champion. Although marketed as pretty boys in matching white trunks, the Can-Am Connection was well-tested as a tandem, engaging in a memorable clash with Terry Funk and Dory Funk Jr. in All Japan before becoming regulars in the WWF.

The quartet had been selected because of each wrestler's ability to have a short, fast-paced match to keep up the audience's energy. To better acquaint the opponents with each other, the teams had been booked together on house shows, smoothing any imperfections that might have come up.

Like everyone else on the cards, none of the combatants had ever been associated with anything as big or involved as *WrestleMania III*. But Orton had played a role in other historic supershows, including *WrestleMania 1* and the first *Starrcade* in 1983 — and knew the myth about the WWF being the first promotion to pull the pastime up from the proverbial smoky arena was exaggerated. So, as best he could, he put the large crowd out of his mind and focused on the in-ring product.

"I thought more about my match than I did anything else, and let other people worry about the non-wrestling stuff," he recalled. "I just wanted to have one of the best matches of the night and go home."

Although no one would characterize the opener as a classic, the talent did everything expected of them, showcasing their skills while the audience contemplated the immensity of the crowd, then ending the clash with an entertaining finish — Zenk hitting the mat on his hands and knees and tripping Muraco while Martel blasted him with a high cross-body block followed by a three count.

This was contrasted by the second match, featuring a battle of strongmen: Hercules Hernandez and Billy Jack Haynes — both displaying bodies that would violate the WWE wellness policy of later decades — locking up to determine which grappler had the superior full nelson.

No one expected technical wrestling in this encounter, hence nobody was disappointed. As the babyface Haynes had Hercules in a full nelson, the villain pulled his foe toward the ropes until both men toppled to ringside. There, Haynes locked on the full nelson again, but since the brawlers were on the arena floor, referee Dave Hebner ruled the bout a double countout.

At that point, the most exciting part of the match began. In an effort to break the hold, Hercules's manager, Bobby "The Brain" Heenan, smashed Billy Jack from behind. Haynes spun around and went after the advisor, allowing Hercules to wrap a chain around his fist, bloody his rival and punish him with the full nelson, all while the referee hollered for order.

Clearly, the feud was only beginning, reinforcing another budding *WrestleMania* tradition. Because pro wrestling was a year-round business, the extravaganza would now serve as the start and end of the WWF season, tying up old rivalries while launching fresh ones.

CHAPTER 28

From the moment the show started, Steve Taylor never once left ringside. "I couldn't miss anything. So I went to the bathroom beforehand. I knew I wasn't getting a chance later on."

By contrast, Tom Buchanan's station included the entire Silverdome. "As long as there was natural light, I could go anywhere I wanted, shooting crowd shots."

That's when he experienced a phenomenon he hadn't encountered before. "As I moved up toward the top, I could feel a wave of energy and sound moving with me."

Buchanan had a very specific photograph in mind. "I tried to find the highest point I could go and took that iconic shot of the crowd from the absolute top deck. There were two versions of that." In both cases, he was positioned behind the fans. "One was shot with probably a 50-millimeter lens or maybe a 35. And the other one was with probably a kilometer lens or full frame fish-eye. The first just shows the crowd. The second shows the people actually being engaged, reacting to what they were seeing in the ring. I think the first shot is the better picture but, from a storytelling standpoint, people really liked the second shot better."

The one pure gimmick match of the show occurred when 6'7" Hillbilly Jim teamed with "midget" wrestlers Little Beaver and the Haiti Kid against King Kong Bundy, billed at more than 450 pounds, and diminutive partners

Lord Littlebrook and Little Tokyo. Until Mexican lucha libre began featuring athletically gifted "mini *estrellas*" in the 1990s, little people were generally booked to add comedy to a card, as was evident when bearded, brawny Hillbilly Jim — who came to the ring shirtless and in overalls — and his partners began square dancing prior to the start of the match.

To add to the absurdity, Bob Uecker, a baseball announcer known for his self-deprecating humor about his lackluster career on the diamond, was brought in as a commentator. Noting the mohawk favored by Little Beaver — who, despite his French-Canadian ancestry, was marketed as an Indigenous warrior — Uecker was quick to point out that he'd dated a woman with a similar haircut 25 years earlier.

"Punk was in 25 years ago?" questioned Jesse "The Body" Ventura.

"I think so. She kept calling me a punk and I believed her."

Ventura said that he was looking forward to watching Bundy "put the big kibosh" on one of his smaller rivals, prompting Uecker to refer to the future Minnesota governor as a "sadist."

Although the rules stipulated that only people of similar size could wrestle each other, the little people amused the audience by tormenting Bundy, whose shaved head and eyebrows lent to his overall menacing appearance. At one point, Beaver dropkicked King Kong from the rear, but the larger competitor no sold. Then, after Hillbilly Jim clotheslined and dropped an elbow on his rival, Beaver and the Haiti Kid attempted to cover the big man for the three count. Bundy raised a shoulder, flinging them away in the process.

He later said that, in the course of the frivolousness, Beaver slapped him hard with a moccasin, stinging his skin. According to one tale, King Kong was angry enough to punish his smaller opponent between the ropes. Indeed, even in retirement, Bundy played up this possibility — although he may well have been trying to enhance his legend as a brute.

Regardless, Bundy lifted Beaver and body-slammed him — earning a disqualification since the villain's aggression was supposed to be confined to Hillbilly Jim.

At this stage, King Kong signaled that he planned to elbow drop his prone rival. This should have been a cue for all the little people to band together and prevent the ambush, Bundy said. But their timing was wrong, he maintained, so, faced with no other choice, he lowered the elbow, rattling the ring and seemingly squashing Little Beaver.

The little people on both sides of the skirmish now pooled their energies to berate Bundy and tend to their fallen colleague, leaving fans with the enduring image of the irate, lonely colossus riding back on the ring cart alone.

Little Beaver was legitimately hurt. He was 53 and had been wrestling since age 15. Because of the mishap, *WrestleMania III* became his final — and perhaps his largest — payday as a wrestler before retiring.

However, he did appear on a WWF show that summer in Boston, once again as a second to Hillbilly Jim. In that instance, the Kentuckian was battling the massive One Man Gang, and Beaver spent a good deal of the encounter harassing heel manager Slick. He also smacked the Gang in the back of the head with a broom.

Once the bout ended — Hillbilly Jim won via countout — Slick provoked his charge into mashing Beaver into the canvas with a "747 splash" as fans cascaded the ring with garbage.

As a counterpoint to all this foolishness, the next *WrestleMania III* bout featured one of the greatest wrestlers who, as the saying goes, ever laced up a pair of boots.

Among pro wrestling purists, few were better in the ring than Harley Race, a man who traversed the planet, drinking, smoking and occasionally fighting after hours, then showing up the next day everywhere from grange halls to soccer stadiums to defend the NWA World Heavyweight Championship. During his numerous reigns, he always left the squared circle bathed in sweat, having somehow held on to his title and, through his performance, elevated his adversary to a new stratosphere.

By the time of *WrestleMania III*, Race had officially been the NWA champion on seven separate occasions, a number that would be revised when the committee deciding such things opted to add his final win in 1984. It occurred during a tour of the Asia-Austro region when Ric Flair opted to drop the belt to his friend in New Zealand and then win it back three days later in Singapore.

Flair and Race were taking kayfabe to a place where it had never been, working not just the fans but the promoters who made the crucial decisions on title switches. According to Flair, no one in the United States was supposed to find out. But almost immediately, the wrong people did.

Perhaps it had to do with the fact that Houston promoter Paul Boesch happened to be a guest at the Singapore show.

Because of Vince's fixation with pretending no rival to the WWF ever existed, the company was not allowed to acknowledge any of this history. Still, even McMahon respected the legend's accomplishments and programmed him to win the company's second annual *King of the Ring* tournament in 1986. As a result, he could be referred to as the "King" — a label no one begrudged — and come to the ring with a crown, cape and scepter.

At *WrestleMania III*, he was seconded by manager Bobby "The Brain" Heenan and "Queen Consort," the Fabulous Moolah, and matched against the Junkyard Dog in a contest that, in keeping with the royal theme, would require the loser to bow down to the victor.

Jim Ross watched the match on closed-circuit in Oklahoma. Despite his loyalty to Bill Watts, J.R. again felt gratified that JYD was being showcased in such an ostentatious setting. "You're happy for these guys," he said. "They're going to make a big payday hopefully. You never wish ill will on people who'd been your teammates at one time. It was a little source of pride that our guys had made it to the [WWF] roster."

Race was nearly 44, his main events primarily in the past. But as a fan, Bob Smith, a sports reporter in Catskill, New York, who'd later work for *Pro Wrestling Illustrated*, believed that the former NWA kingpin belonged in front of the Silverdome crowd. "Everybody who worked for Vince had to have a gimmick back then," Smith said. "So if Harley had to have one, I was okay with them throwing a crown on him. He could still be Harley Race once the bell rang."

As always, Harley took his task seriously, taking wild bumps, including a diving headbutt from the top turnbuckle that missed. As the rivals tangled on the ring apron, JYD leaned his foe over the ropes and punched down on his chest. Rather than simply selling the blow, Race did a 360 into the ring.

The finish came when Heenan distracted the Dog, enabling Harley to score the win after a belly-to-belly suplex. This meant that JYD now had to bow to his rival. Reattaching his robe, Race seated himself in a chair in the middle of the ring, flanked by Moolah and Heenan. In deference to the stipulation, the Dog did not so much kneel as quickly curtsy — twice. But once that formality was out of the way, and Race and his posse were celebrating the win, JYD grabbed the chair and used it to strike his opponent. Grabbing his antagonist's cape, the babyface swept it over his shoulders and rode back on the ring cart with a new sense of majesty.

The kids in the audience were thrilled that, despite the results, the lovable Dog had managed to get the upper hand. Those who admired Race for his contributions to pro wrestling felt differently.

"I'd always been a huge Harley mark," said Smith. "Everyone was watching the WWF, so I was glad he was in a place where more people could see him. I just wanted them to put him over and they did."

CHAPTER 29

Before Race, Heenan and Moolah were back in the dressing room, Jacques and Raymond Rougeau were already on their ring cart, waiting to make the entrance for their match against the Dream Team of Greg "The Hammer" Valentine and Brutus Beefcake. "They wanted to keep the show tight," Jacques recalled. "Everyone knew it was going to take so long to get to the ring, so they wanted you ready even when the other match was still going on."

The son of superstar Johnny Valentine — who once boasted, "I can't make them believe that wrestling is real, but I can make them believe I'm real" — Greg had been taking bumps since he was just short of 19, making his debut against Angelo Mosca for Stu Hart in Calgary. Before the sports entertainment age, he'd taken part in countless super shows, including something called the "Super Bowl of Wrestling" for an organization called the National Wrestling Federation (NWF) at Cleveland's Municipal Stadium in 1972.

Started by Buffalo, New York–based promoter Pedro Martinez as an alternative to the NWA's influence in 1970, the NWF ran shows in such cities as Rochester, Syracuse, Utica, Akron and even Pittsburgh, where Bruno Sammartino attempted to float a regional promotion after his first run as WWWF Heavyweight Champion ended in 1971. Because Johnny Valentine was also part of the league, his son was billed as Johnny Fargo, the gimmick brother of Don Fargo — who'd initially taken the name when he portrayed Memphis legend Jackie Fargo's sibling.

Like a circus, the Super Bowl of Wrestling featured matches conducted simultaneously in three separate rings, challenging the attention of the live audience. The Fargos came into the event as the NWF Tag Team Champions, while in the main event, Johnny Valentine challenged Johnny Powers for his NWF North American belt.

Being depicted as a separate personality "gave me some space to learn without being compared to him," Valentine said.

Once the senior Valentine was paralyzed in the 1975 airplane crash that nearly ended the career of Ric Flair, Greg fully embraced his heritage, becoming every bit the credible headliner that his father had been. He'd been the defending WWF Intercontinental Champion at *WrestleMania 1*, and a year later, he and Beefcake came into *WrestleMania 2* as the WWF Tag Team titlists. Even though they dropped the prize to the British Bulldogs at the event, the fact that the Englishmen were accompanied by rocker Ozzy Osbourne raised the prominence of all four participants.

Valentine was convinced that the Dream Team and the Bulldogs could still generate interest and was disappointed to be matched against the Rougeaus at *WrestleMania III*. "The rivalry with the Rougeaus didn't mean anything because we had no history with them. The Dream Team vs. the Bulldogs would have been better, but I guess we were just lucky to be on the card.

"It was a decent payday."

More importantly, he understood that *WrestleMania III* would be regarded as historically more significant than any of the large shows he'd appeared on for other promotions. "Vince had this vision that nobody could take away. We sold out the Silverdome and, pretty soon, we'd be going to Europe. I was glad to be a part of that."

In the dressing room before the match, Jacques was so nervous that he had difficulty tying his boots. "My foot was jumping up and down so much that I couldn't even get the laces in the holes. My throat was dry. The stress was absolutely the most I ever had in my life."

Once the opponents met to discuss the details of the match, "I just stayed isolated with my brother," Raymond said. "I wasn't interested in talking to other people. Our main concern was, 'We have a job to do. Let's deliver a job.' I worried about little things, like tripping over the bottom rope and falling when I walked into the ring. Everyone would remember that. So I needed to stay focused."

It would be Brutus Beefcake's last night as the cocky Chippendales dancer he'd been playing since 1984 and, later on the card, his first as the likable "Barber." But to make the transition, the Dream Team would have to break up.

All four men knew how to have an engaging match; from teaming with the multifaceted Valentine, Beefcake had become more versatile than some gave him credit for. "I had so much respect for an opponent like Greg Valentine," Jacques said. "It didn't matter if you won or lost, he'd always make you look good. He'd hit you with those chops and, man, the blood would come out of the veins on your chest. But he never really hurt you. He knew how to work and everything he did in the ring was convincing."

In this particular contest, the goal was to build to Brutus's babyface turn, and everybody worked toward it in unison. It finally occurred after Raymond clamped a sleeper onto Valentine. Seemingly in an effort to break the hold, Beefcake came off the second rope with an ax handle attempt. At the final moment, the older Rougeau brother slipped out of the way and Valentine was hit instead. This allowed the siblings to punish the Hammer, with Raymond holding him up while Jacques dove onto him from the top rope.

But as Raymond attempted a pinfall, Beefcake managed to distract the referee, allowing Dino Bravo — who'd bleached his hair blond and accompanied the Dream Team to the ring — to sail off the second rope in his ring jacket, deliver an elbow and push a dazed Valentine on top of his foe.

The official turned around just in time to register the count.

Apparently stunned by the outcome, Valentine, Bravo and their manager, Johnny Valiant, ditched Brutus, leaving him behind in the ring and headed to the dressing room together. Subsequently, Valentine and Bravo would be marketed as the "New Dream Team."

Decades later, Jacques had forgotten that the purpose of the match was facilitating Beefcake's babyface shift. "That moment was so epic in time that I don't remember a lot about what we did in the ring. I remember the event."

But Raymond, who took the loss, recalled being eager to play a role in an important angle. "You can't take anything personally. It's the business. Sometimes, you're the one getting all the attention. Other times, the other ones get more attention. We still got our exposure at *WrestleMania III* and became part of history."

In fact, if he had any trepidation going into the match, it involved something the fans didn't see. "When Dino came into WWE, we didn't want to work with him," Raymond admitted, "because of the differences we had with him in Montreal. And then at one point before *WrestleMania III*, I can't remember how the discussion went, but Vince said, 'I don't want to force you to do anything. But I have an idea for the finish, with Dino coming and costing you the match,' and then, he told us how he was going to be splitting up Beefcake and Valentine, and Dino and Greg would be the New Dream Team.

"So my brother and I talked and we said, 'Let's put our emotions aside and be professional about it. What happened in Montreal is in the past.'"

Jacques realized that clinging to old gripes would make them no different than the promoters who refused to acknowledge that the industry, for better or worse, had moved far from where it had previously been. "Look at the point we'd all reached now? Whatever we did in Montreal was nothing compared to *WrestleMania III*. When we really thought about it, it didn't matter anymore."

In the weeks after *Mania*, when the New Dream Team and Rougeaus began wrestling each other around the circuit, Raymond noted that both duos worked smoothly together. "We had a good time. And eventually, I became really good friends with Dino. On European tours, we'd have supper and go walking around the cities we were visiting. And when the first *Batman* movie came out [in 1989], Dino and I went to the theater in Denver, Colorado, and saw it together."

Valentine was less content with the fallout from *WrestleMania III*. He and Beefcake had been a unit for more than two years and grown to understand each other's styles. Now that Brutus was veering in another direction, Valentine believed that a rivalry between the two would be the proper way to end their narrative.

"I requested that we work against each other," Valentine said, "and the company did not want to do it."

While Beefcake would be given a new character, Valentine was disappointed about remaining in the Dream Team with a partner he characterized as temperamental. "I felt like they stuck Dino on me. He had a bad temper and I hated that. And in the ring, I sometimes felt like his timing didn't work. I remember the two of us had a match [in September 1987] against the Killer Bees in Madison Square Garden and they asked us to put them over. And I was thinking, 'Well, if we're the *New* Dream Team, why are we the ones doing the job?' And I flew home and quit."

The next day, after a lengthy conversation with McMahon, the Hammer was persuaded to come back. In years to come, he'd assume a higher profile in the WWF, going to the quarterfinals at the *WrestleMania IV* championship tournament, engaging in a hard-hitting feud with "Rugged" Ronnie Garvin and forming an entertaining tag team with the Honky Tonk Man.

Yet, he continued to feel frustrated about his place on the *WrestleMania III* card — in stark contrast to Jacques Rougeau, who believed that the WWF positioned his team exactly where they belonged. "We had the people on their feet for the entire match. Everything was leading to Hogan and André. Our job was to keep the people hooked and we did."

CHAPTER 30

O f every bout on the card, before the sun disappeared, the memories of the clash between "Rowdy" Roddy Piper and "Adorable" Adrian Adonis would endure the longest.

Adonis had initially been marketed as a leather-wearing tough guy from New York, but after developing a drug problem in the WWF, his weight ballooned. Unhappy with Adrian's new look, McMahon is said to have punished the performer by recasting him as "Adorable" Adrian, an obese, effeminate competitor in a dress, sunhat and grotesque makeup. Oddly, the fans were fascinated by the gimmick and, after Piper took a hiatus in 1986, Adonis was given an interview segment called "The Flower Shop" to replace "Piper's Pit."

After jeering Piper for so long, the audience had developed a warped connection with him, and his absence was profoundly felt. As a result, when he returned, he received a thunderous babyface reaction. To enhance his new persona, he lambasted the very notion of "The Flower Shop," playing to the biases of the time by using language rife with homophobia.

"That's okay, sweetheart, we don't want you tripping on your pantyhose," he taunted Adonis during one confrontation.

For his righteousness, Piper received a beatdown from old confederate Bob Orton and the Magnificent Muraco — who'd apparently become allies of the LGBTQ community — along with Adonis himself, while the Adorable One's manager Jimmy Hart cheered on the assault.

To further assail Hot Rod's cis-male sensibility, the trio smeared his face with lipstick.

Rather than using the incident to commune with his feminine side, a bandaged-up Piper returned with a baseball bat and decimated the "Flower Shop" set.

As tensions built between Piper and Adonis, the Mouth of the South was never reluctant about becoming physically involved in angles, jumping on Roddy's back on one occasion. Another time, the manager used his ever-present megaphone to smash Hot Rod from the rear.

"I was like a little bee that comes around," Hart said. "You hit the bee, right? You knock it down in the sand. And all of the sudden, the bee comes back. *Son of a gun!* Now, you take your foot and put it on that bee and grind it into the ground. And all of the sudden, you go, '*Damn,* he's back again. What do I have to do to get rid of him?'"

Ironically, after condemning Mr. T as a Hollywood actor who dared to intrude on the wrestling business, Piper now hoped to do the same in reverse, earning a slot in director John Carpenter's upcoming sci-fi/horror flick *They Live.*

The difference was that once *WrestleMania 1* ended, Mr. T returned to the set of *The A-Team.* By contrast, regardless of the outcome of *WrestleMania III*, Piper was committed to retiring from pro wrestling.

Adonis told the fans that either way, he intended to shave Piper bald, emphasizing the point by bringing a pair of oversized hedge clippers to the encounter.

From the instant the bell rang, this was an unbridled melee. As Piper whipped Adonis with a belt, Hart hopped onto the ring apron and was promptly grabbed by the Rowdy Scot. But the distraction was what Adrian needed to gain possession of the belt and flail on Piper.

"Before we went out, Roddy said to me, 'Jimmy, I want to do a couple of things with you,'" Hart remembered. "I said, 'Whatever you want.'"

As the combatants brawled, Piper managed to flip his foe over the top rope, then tried dragging him back into the ring. Hart wrapped his arms around Adonis to make the task difficult, and Roddy pulled both into the ring. There, Piper banged his antagonists' heads together and Irish-whipped the manager into Adonis. The collision seemingly forced the duo to spill over the ring strands back onto the stadium floor.

When they returned to the squared circle, Hart scaled the turnbuckles and tried leaping onto Hot Rod. Before the Mouth of the South could even launch himself, Piper grabbed him from below and hurled him into Adonis.

"I always wanted to take big bumps for these guys," Hart said, "and make it look bigger than life. I didn't want Piper to just hit me. I wanted him to knock me into the middle of next week."

Eventually, Adonis gained the advantage after Hart grabbed Piper's ankles, and Adrian was able to beat down his rival and bounce him off the timekeeper's table. Inside the ring, the Adorable One began to pepper Roddy with punches, but the wobbly babyface refused to succumb and dared his enemy to hit him some more. Adonis not only complied, but Hart assisted by squirting Piper with Adrian's "atomizer," or oversized perfume canister.

Apparently blinded, Piper was susceptible to Adonis grabbing him from behind and applying a sleeper variation. As Roddy seemed to wilt, Hart snatched the hedge clippers, fans were led to believe, to begin the haircutting during regulation time. Fighting to stay conscious, Piper backed his opponent into the turnbuckles, but Adonis maintained his grasp.

Having just been abandoned in the last match, Beefcake appeared to be in the market for new cronies. He quickly gained one by rocketing down the aisle, rushing into the ring and stirring Hot Rod awake.

Revived and bent on retribution, Piper focused on the Mouth of the South and belted him out of the ring.

"Piper cracked my jaw," Hart said. "Lawler had broken it in Memphis, so I understood how it felt. But this was the biggest night of our lives and it really didn't hurt so much with all the adrenaline."

Later, Piper would ask Hart whether the blow was too hard.

"I would have never said yes," the manager recounted, "and I wouldn't have said no. I just said, 'Don't worry.' I was a little sore for a while. But we were too busy for me to go to the doctor and get it wired. I just ate mashed potatoes when we went to restaurants until it healed up.

"I look at it this way. These guys are in the ring every night, busting their bodies up. You think I'm going to complain?"

In the ring, the competitors now worked on finishing up their story. Positioning himself behind Adorable Adrian, Piper applied his own sleeper, and Adonis faded. The referee tried raising the heel's arm — once, twice, then three times. Each time, it flopped back to a flaccid position.

Piper was victorious, and Beefcake was now officially Brutus the Barber, snatching the hedge clippers and trimming Adrian's locks, then shaving part of his head.

To taunt Adonis further, Piper held a mirror up so the vanquished gladiator could contemplate his new look. Livid, Adonis lurched at his tormentor, but Piper slid away and a defeated Adrian returned to the dressing room.

Announcer Howard Finkel proclaimed that Roddy Piper was officially retired. The audience rose, their ovation quaking the Silverdome, as the victor planted a kiss on the top of Finkel's bald pate and a guy in a flannel shirt hopped the barricade to join the celebration, only to be tackled by security and hauled away in handcuffs.

Minutes later, Jimmy Hart was in the ring again — with a different set of protégés and another outfit.

Performing multiple times on the same night had been a custom for Hart since his days in the Memphis territory. "The only difference between working in Louisville, Kentucky, and working at the Silverdome was I made my jackets a little more special. I never wanted to put myself over anybody else so, whoever I was managing, I had a special jacket made for them. Because, believe it or not, there's a lot of jealousy going on in the wrestling business. If I had a jacket for Adrian Adonis and I didn't have one for the Hart Foundation, it might look like I'm playing favorites."

Jimmy had been with Bret "Hit Man" Hart and Jim "The Anvil" Neidhart since they debuted in 1985. But what would make their *WrestleMania III* clash with the British Bulldogs and Tito Santana stand out was the Hart Foundation's tag team partner on this particular evening, recently excommunicated referee "Dangerous" Danny Davis.

For more than a year, Davis had been portraying a corrupt official. The reason Santana had a gripe with him could be traced to February 1986, when the Arriba Kid defended his WWF Intercontinental Championship against Randy "Macho Man" Savage. As Randy stood on the ring apron and Santana attempted to suplex him back into the ring, the contender removed a foreign object from his trunks and clunked the titlist with it. Davis insisted that he never saw anything improper and registered the pinfall when Savage fell on top of his rival, resulting in a title switch.

Davis had also been the arbiter when the British Bulldogs, Dynamite Kid and Davey Boy Smith, lost their WWF World Tag Team Championship to the Hart Foundation in January 1987. In that instance, a legitimately injured Dynamite Kid was thumped in the head by Jimmy Hart's megaphone and fell to ringside to sell the blow. As Davis "tended" to the fallen grappler on the arena floor, the Hit Man and Anvil double-teamed Smith between the ropes — while fans screamed for the referee to turn around. When he finally did, Smith had fallen to his rivals' finisher, the Hart Attack, and Davis slipped into the ring to fast count the fall.

Once again, the official's actions resulted in another title change.

On the WWF's syndicated broadcasts, Davis acted befuddled at times, scrambling around the ring with the back of his shirt falling out of his khakis, leading announcers Vince McMahon and Jesse Ventura to argue about the motives behind his officiating. While McMahon accused Davis of being biased, Ventura labeled him "the law-and-order referee."

Eventually, WWF figurehead president Jack Tunney weighed in, concluding that Davis had lost his objectivity and suspending him for "life plus ten years." Jimmy Hart soon proclaimed that, in preparing for this contingency, Davis had procured a wrestler's license and was a member of the Mouth of the South's stable.

What fans didn't know was that *WrestleMania III* was not Davis's actual debut as a wrestler. In fact, he sometimes appeared on the WWF's syndicated show on a weekly basis, doing jobs for headliners under a mask as Mr. X.

Despite his experience, he felt fortunate to be paired with well-rounded athletes like Hart and Neidhart. "They helped me as much as they could," Davis told Hannibal TV in 2020. "They didn't have to, but they . . . took me under their wing and kind of walked me through some of the rough spots" in the match.

He was also fortunate to have Jimmy Hart on his team to create his own diversions for the fans. Even before any of the wrestlers locked up, Hart had managed to have an altercation with Smith and Dynamite's canine mascot, a bonafide bulldog named Matilda.

"She was incredibly over with the fans," Hart said. "She had action figures. She was on magazine covers, just like everybody else."

When Hart was working in Memphis, he generally relied on a cane as an outside weapon. But when he arrived in the WWF, another personality, Mr. Fuji, was already using the object. Hence, McMahon recommended that Jimmy switch to a megaphone, like the one favored by manager KY Wakamatsu in Japan.

One night in Pittsburgh, Hart was backstage chatting with Bruno Sammartino, who did color commentary and occasionally returned to feud with a leading heel, when the manager pulled a set of batteries out and prepared to insert them into the megaphone.

"Now, put your hands over your ears," Jimmy warned the Living Legend, "because when I put these batteries in, as soon as I put the lid down on it, the batteries are going to touch the condenser. And when it does, a siren's going to go off."

The moment the alert sounded, Matilda raced across the dressing room and leaped at the megaphone. "She jumped up and, boy, she grabbed that megaphone and started pulling on it. And I thought, 'Oh my god, this is great.' And I told the Bulldogs, I said, 'Look, why don't we do this every night in the ring?'

"And that's what we started to do. Before the match, when the ref was giving instructions, I'd push my finger down and set off the siren. And when I did that, Matilda would attack the megaphone, I'd take a bump and all the people would get a kick out of it."

The routine worked just as well at *WrestleMania III*. Once the combatants were in the ring, Hart triggered the warning and Matilda dove at the manager, who fell to a sitting position, holding the megaphone in front of him like a pistol before rolling to the arena floor.

Clearly, the charged atmosphere was too much for the beleaguered animal to handle and Jesse Ventura, of all people, was charged with retrieving Matilda and cruising back with her to the dressing room on the ring cart, soothing the agitated mascot in his arms.

Attention shifted to Davis. From the crowd's perspective, after cheating Santana and the Bulldogs out of championships, the former ref deserved to be punished. And since he'd taken virtually every major move as Mr. X, he could endure whatever his opponents intended to do to him at *WrestleMania*.

So after Santana hit Davis with a flying forearm, Davey Boy executed a kneeling piledriver, vertical suplex and powerslam. But once again, Jimmy Hart's megaphone would play a prominent role in the match. As the babyfaces were prospering, the devious newcomer utilized the weapon to crack Smith over the head and steal the win.

It was not the finish fans necessarily envisioned, but it certainly gave them something to talk about.

Night was starting to fall, and many extraordinary *WrestleMania III* moments were about to be created. But, first, the WWF had one more transitional match to get through.

At just 5'7", Koko B. Ware made up for his lack of size with an entertaining gimmick, entering arenas with a blue and yellow macaw named Frankie and flapping his arms and dancing before the bell sounded. He also understood ring psychology and, during his early years in the Memphis territory, Ware had counseled Hulk Hogan not to oversell for small foes in order to be taken seriously as a big man.

That knowledge qualified Koko to engage in a believable bout with "The Natural" Butch Reed, a three-time Mid-South North American Champion who resembled a copper version of the Hulkster — a Black man with bleached blond hair and a bodybuilder's physique.

Reed had first aligned with his manager, the self-professed "Doctor of Style" Slick — an ordained Baptist minister who, playing to the tropes of the era, portrayed a version of a smooth-talking pimp — in the Central States territory while teaming with the advisor's father, "The Freight Train" Rufus R. Jones. In 1986, Reed and Slick left promoter Bob Geigel behind and departed for the WWF as a tandem.

The match played to the strengths of each performer, with Koko attacking Reed from the air and the Natural using his power to try to pound down his opponent. It concluded after Reed grabbed onto his foe as Ware tried a cross-body block and rolled onto the canvas, holding Koko's tights for the three count.

The most memorable part of the encounter occurred after the finish when Slick smacked Ware with a cane — yet another reason why Jimmy Hart used a megaphone — and Santana came back from the showers, storming the ring to assist Koko and tear away the manager's clothes as he fled.

Since Slick was scheduled to work again later on, he didn't bother changing his wardrobe.

As with everyone else on the card so far, the participants had used their skills as athletes and entertainers to keep the audience engaged. Still, whatever they'd accomplished would be eclipsed by the clash that came next.

CHAPTER 31

Randy Savage would not have settled for anything less.

Before *WrestleMania* had ever been conceived and the Macho Man was still a former minor league baseball player named Randy Poffo, he'd been envisioning a match with Ricky "The Dragon" Steamboat.

At the time, the young wrestler would have accepted a preliminary encounter in front of 150 spectators in Owenton, Kentucky. Instead, Savage and Steamboat would set a new in-ring standard at the Pontiac Silverdome.

The war for the Macho Man's WWF Intercontinental Championship was a dramatic departure from the cartoonish cliché of what the WWF was said to have become. To informed observers, the bout was good enough to headline in Japan and perhaps better than the heralded NWA World Heavyweight Championship skirmishes that occurred during the reigns of Lou Thesz, Dory Funk Jr. and Jack Brisco.

"They went with the mindset of, 'We're going to give you a buffet,'" Bruce Prichard said of the WWF's attitude. "So we had King Kong Bundy squashing one of the little people, we had Adrian Adonis getting his head shaved, we had a heel referee, and then, we had Savage and Steamboat."

Recalled Dave Meltzer, "Savage and Steamboat was something that was 10 to 15 years ahead of its time in a lot of ways. For years, people talked about it being the greatest match of all time. I'd probably seen 10 to 20 matches that I thought were as good or even better, but it was definitely up there."

Still, *WrestleMania III* embodied sports entertainment; hence, both Elizabeth and George "The Animal" Steele were in the respective corners, leaving spectators uncertain about whether the bout was going to trend in a gimmicky direction.

It was that uncertainty that made the match less predictable and likely even better than most watchers anticipated.

Savage had been the Intercontinental titlist for close to 14 months and, as a student of the art form, even he was among those advocating for a championship switch. According to his brother, "The Genius" Lanny Poffo, Randy believed that there would be no better forum than *WrestleMania III* to lose to Steamboat.

By the time the two arrived in Michigan, Steamboat all but had their match memorized. "We were using a yellow pad and writing down steps," Steamboat told Brian Campbell for ESPN.com. "And it got into like 100-something steps."

For weeks, the pair had been quizzing each other on the high points of the bout. "I would say, 'Okay, I'm at step number 55 and it's this and this. Now, tell me the rest of the match.' And he would go, 'Step number 56 is this, and number 57 is this.'"

Not leaving any detail to chance, Savage had also demanded that the clash be refereed by Dave Hebner. "He said he picked him because he was the most intense person, throwing his body down and counting" the near-falls, Lanny Poffo told ESPN.com.

Observed Steamboat, "Dave knew when to be there and when to disappear."

During a meeting between the three at the Silverdome, the Macho Man impressed upon the official the need to call the bout like a shoot. "If the man's shoulders are down, you count to three and I don't care if it ruins the finish. Whoever's shoulders are down has the responsibility to get their shoulders up."

Hebner had been unable to sleep the night before, and Savage's demeanor backstage did nothing to soothe him. According to announcer

Mean Gene Okerlund, the Intercontinental kingpin was behaving as though "he was ready to be shot out of a cannon."

Savage told Campbell that the atmosphere in Pontiac "can never be equaled as far as a rush going down to the ring."

Said Steamboat, "I was so stressed out. I guess I burned up a bunch of nervous energy behind the curtain. But what I do remember is, we came through on the cart and . . . I completely forgot all about the stress. I was in awe of all the people in the stadium. And then, I had to gather myself" and remember the various parts of the match.

Steamboat, the perennial babyface, was clad completely in white. But as soon as Savage stepped between the ropes, he practically ignored his opponent. Instead, the Macho Man eyed Steele warily, leaving the ring to march Elizabeth to a spot far from the Animal's clutches.

Steamboat swarmed onto his enemy, awing the audience with high arm drags — Savage believed that Ricky executed the move better than anyone in the business — and snatching Savage by the throat and lifting him in the air. When Randy attempted to throw his foe over the top rope, Steamboat gripped the strand, hung above the arena floor for a moment, then pulled himself up and flipped back into the ring.

He wasn't the first wrestler to excite the crowd by "skinning the cat." But, until the emergence of Shawn Michaels as a superstar, there was nobody in the industry who could do it better.

Interestingly, in addition to his fixation with Elizabeth, Steele's character had become almost paternally protective of the Dragon. After Savage clotheslined his rival out of the ring and chucked him over the commentary table into the front row, the Animal lifted the Dragon out of the crowd and carried him back to the squared circle.

Provoking the crowd's wrath, Savage snapped the challenger's vulnerable throat off the top rope, but, during convalescence, Ricky had apparently grown stronger. When Savage tried covering his foe for a three count, Steamboat pushed the champion skyward. The Macho Man tried a pinning combination again following an atomic drop, then a suplex. On each occasion, Steamboat kicked out, leaving his rival in apparent disbelief.

All told, there were 22 false finishes in the Savage-Steamboat encounter.

After attempting to roll Savage up, Steamboat tried a jackknife pin, then an inside cradle. Following a scoop slam, the Dragon catapulted Savage into the corner. As the Macho Man's head bounced off the ring post, the contender rolled him up for a near-fall. Savage kicked out and Steamboat attempted yet another rollup. Randy let the momentum carry his body and he ended up on top of Ricky and nearly scored the win.

Many of the false finishes were conceived at house shows in the weeks before *Mania*. "We would take bits and pieces," Steamboat explained. "If we got a pop from it, I would say, 'We're going to use that in the pay-per-view.'"

Although fans were accustomed to unresolved finishes in championship matches, the WWF seemed to have made a pact with the audience about this particular collision. By the time the match ended, it was understood that one man would be the undisputed winner. Thus, whenever another false finish occurred, people jumped to their feet, anticipating that this was the moment when the title would change hands.

"All those false finishes were close," Hebner told ESPN.com. "You could see my hand going down and hit the mat . . . This was the big time. You just can't make a mistake . . . But I never thought that I couldn't do it."

Each time one of the combatants managed to raise his shoulder, Hebner theatrically threw up two fingers. Poffo later said that he was surprised that the referee did not dislocate his rotator cuff by moving his shoulder so dramatically.

"There's nothing better than two people in synchronization proving they are athletic," The Genius told me for *Inside the Ropes Magazine*. "You cannot beat two really athletic guys of the same size going after each other with high spots and false finishes. I mean, how much entertainment can you give a fan?"

In his seat, 11-year-old Vince Averill sat mesmerized, trying to commit every move he witnessed to memory. "The things they did inside that ring," he said, "felt like nothing I'd ever seen on Saturday morning TV."

In the dressing room, Jacques Rougeau was among a group of wrestlers stationed in front of a monitor, reacting to the action much the same way. "I was thinking that this had to be one of the best matches of the decade. The boys were freaking out over how good it was."

A few feet away, his rival from earlier in the show, Greg Valentine sat dourly, studying the performers onscreen. "I was jealous. I wanted that kind of a match. Everything was very believable and the way they put the different pieces together was fantastic."

Steamboat would later boast, "André and Hogan sold the show. But Steamboat and Savage stole it."

As night fell, Tom Buchanan had migrated to ringside. With so much to shoot, though, he did not stop to analyze what he saw. "Throughout my entire career in WWE, I never dissected a match while I was shooting it. It was only later when I could look back and understand the story."

But the fans felt no such constraints while the two gladiators continued their battle. In keeping with the plan, Hebner stepped in front of Steamboat as he went gliding across the ring, colliding with the Dragon and taking a hard fall to the canvas. With his characteristic twitchy movements, the Macho Man briefly contemplated the scenario, then appeared to revise his strategy. Scaling the turnbuckles, Savage executed his finisher, the flying elbow, onto the fallen contender. Moving quickly, Randy covered his opponent and hooked his leg, but Hebner was unable to rise to register the count.

Savage desperately struck the referee, trying to jar him awake. Still, Hebner could not be roused. To the astonishment of the spectators, the Macho Man scrambled to ringside and pulled the bell from the time-keeper's hands, apparently determined to once again injure the Dragon's neck. As Savage grasped the object on the ring apron, Steele attempted to prevent the carnage, but the Macho Man kicked him away. Now, climbing the turnbuckles, Savage appeared set to put Steamboat down for good.

Nonetheless, Steele persisted, shoving Randy forward, where the bell fell out of his hands in the ring. There, Steamboat was ready to engage Savage again. The Macho Man tried maintaining his edge with a scoop slam, but Steamboat managed to shift his body and roll up the titlist just as Hebner came to life.

The referee's hand slapped the mat three times, and the Silverdome celebrated the crowning of a new WWF Intercontinental Champion.

"History is made," declared Gorilla Monsoon.

"When Steele shoved Savage into the ring, a second sooner or a second later would have ruined it," Poffo told me. "It was perfect, perfect timing, and you have to give George Steele credit."

Overcome by apparent exhaustion, the new champion was carried to the ring cart by the faithful Animal. Breathing heavily, Steamboat raised the belt above his head as the cart trundled toward the dressing room, while Steele fell to his knees and grabbed his ally's midsection in a childlike embrace.

In his own ring cart, the vanquished former titlist leaned his face into his forearm on the top rope and appeared to weep as Elizabeth placed a gentle hand on his arm. Together, the couple rolled away from the camera, growing smaller and smaller before disappearing into the darkness.

Interestingly, the Intercontinental title would be the only championship that Steamboat would hold in the WWF. After his son was born later that year, he asked to take time off and agreed to drop the strap to the Honky Tonk Man. He would later leave the company and win the NWA World Heavyweight Championship from Ric Flair during a classic trilogy of matches in 1989.

Because he and Flair understood each other between the ropes so well and felt comfortable calling their matches in the ring, Steamboat said that he enjoyed this series even more than the confrontation with the Macho Man in the Silverdome.

Following his bout with Steamboat, Savage was ecstatic backstage. Everything he'd painstakingly planned had come together, and he was convinced that the match was just as significant as the 1961 masterpiece in which Buddy "Nature Boy" Rogers had defeated Pat O'Connor for the NWA crown.

Finally, Savage believed that he'd unearthed his Pat O'Connor.

Sadly, he never found another one, but spent the rest of his career searching for him.

CHAPTER 32

When Jake "The Snake" Roberts clashed with the Honky Tonk Man in the next bout, the protagonist brought along not just his pet python Damien but shock rocker Alice Cooper.

Cooper pointed out that, at times, his own stage act had included a boa constrictor. "Detroit is my hometown," he told the *Detroit News* in 2017, "and that's where they were going to have this thing. It was a perfect fit. And it was our kind of theater anyway, so I fit right in."

The vocalist was so excited about participating in *WrestleMania III* that he claimed not to remember asking about compensation. "I said, 'Let's do it. Come on. This will be the one time we ever do this.'"

As a second-generation wrestler, Roberts knew when he was being worked but seemed to admire Cooper for his effort to act like a carny. "It was business," Jake told the newspaper of the rocker's involvement. "Vince paid him."

Like Roddy Piper, Roberts had been such a gripping heel — speaking in a soft, gravelly voice and tapping into the trauma of his dysfunctional upbringing — that the fans gradually turned him babyface. But when the rivalry with the Honky Tonk Man started, he was still a villain. "I went from being hated to being loved," Roberts told interviewer Kenny McIntosh during a live Q&A for the Inside the Ropes franchise in Manchester, England.

To push them over the threshold, the WWF had the pompadoured, jumpsuit-wearing Honky Tonk Man attack Jake with a guitar. Under other circumstances, the instrument might have been "gimmicked," or cut to break upon impact. In this case, though, Roberts took a blow from a piece of solid wood, sustaining enough damage to eventually require surgery. "He came down on me hard, man," Jake told McIntosh, "and he blew out two discs in my neck. It wasn't supposed to be a head shot. It was supposed to be across the back. But for some reason, he missed my back and hit me in the head." Jake maintained that the pain was so intense that he couldn't remember a time when it wasn't there. Although he resented his opponent for not being more careful — "You're trusting the other guy not to fuckin' kill you," he pointed out — not for a moment did he ever contemplate missing *Mania*. The Honky Tonk Man embraced many of the same attitudes. Both he and Jake had bounced around the southern territories and been conditioned to believe that if you didn't show up for a match — regardless of whether you were harboring a serious, on-the-job injury — you didn't deserve to be paid.

Said Roberts, "My thought was if I stopped, everyone would forget about Jake the Snake."

As Wayne Ferris, the Honky Tonk Man had debuted a decade before *WrestleMania III*, training with Koko B. Ware under promoter Henry Rogers, who ran an informal feeder system in southern Missouri for wrestlers hoping to gain a foothold in Memphis. As a member of the Blond Bombers with Larry Latham, who'd later work as Moondog Spot in the WWF, Ferris engaged in what is believed to be the first concession stand brawl at the Tupelo Coliseum against his legitimate first cousin Jerry "The King" Lawler and Superstar Bill Dundee in 1979.

Reportedly, Ferris was originally supposed to play the role of Brutus Beefcake but became afflicted with hepatitis at the time, and Hulk Hogan instead advocated for his former tag team partner and close friend, Ed Leslie.

Either way, despite whatever other notoriety he achieved in pro wrestling, Ferris would forever be known as an in-ring Elvis impersonator, a role he initially started playing not in the WWF but for Stampede Wrestling in Calgary.

"When I die, no one will say Wayne Ferris died," he told me for *Inside the Ropes Magazine*. "Nobody knows who the hell Wayne Ferris is. They'll say the Honky Man died. I'll always be the Honky Tonk Man."

By the time they boarded their ring carts, Roberts and the Honky Tonk Man realized that they'd be performing after what was arguably the best technical match of the past several years. "Following Steamboat and Savage, for me, wasn't that big of a problem," Roberts told the *Detroit News*. "The only people that have a problem following a great match is a guy that doesn't know what the hell he's doing. Number one, if you're following a great match such as Steamboat/Savage, the last thing you do is go out there and try to kick it off and get to their speed when they left the ring. You don't do that. What you do is settle people back down and get them flat in their seats again and take a deep breath, and then you start to build back. . . . I can't be Ricky Steamboat, I can't be Randy Savage, but I do a damn good Jake the Snake."

Likewise, Jake's companion, Alice Cooper, understood that, despite his general naivete about the One True Sport, the wrestling audience was jazzed to see him on what the WWF would refer to as "The Grandest Stage of Them All." "It was a different kind of theater, but I got it immediately. I figured, 'Okay, now I've got to play this game. I know how to play Alice, so I've just got to be Alice in a different situation.' When I look at these guys, it's pretty much the same thing I do. I play a character, Alice, so I have to . . . act like Alice. These guys do the same thing. They assume their characters. If anybody's close to what I do, it's the wrestlers."

As Roberts and Cooper observed the large, animated crowd, Jake told McIntosh, "I felt like the hair was growing on my arms."

Before they even arrived at the ring, Cooper turned to Roberts and said, "I can't breathe. Too much rush." After the prior bout, few in the audience were scrutinizing the performers' move sets; that's not why this encounter was being presented. Still, the competitors knew how to work a good match to further their narrative. The Honky Tonk Man attempted his Shake, Rattle & Roll neckbreaker, but Roberts avoided it by executing a back body drop. After Honky uncorked a series of punches in the corner, Jake fought back with an inverted atomic drop.

Of course, the intention had always been for Honky's manager Jimmy Hart to interfere and end up in a confrontation with Alice Cooper. It occurred after Roberts signaled that he was going to deliver his finisher, the DDT — catching his opponent in a front facelock and driving his head into the canvas — and pointed at his snake Damien, who Jake generally kept in a large, foreboding sack at ringside. But Hart crawled under the bottom rope, grabbed the babyface's ankle and tripped him. When Roberts turned to confront the meddler, Honky managed to roll up his foe and hold onto the ropes for the three count.

That's when the celebrity guest became involved. "We talked about it in the back beforehand," Hart remembered. "It was either going to work or it wasn't going to work. Jake and Honky and I were all going to just kind of be spontaneous, like we learned how to do in the territories, and told Cooper to just follow along with what we were doing."

As Hart and the singer squared off, Roberts was both impressed and entertained by Alice's enthusiasm. "Cooper got into it," Roberts told the *Detroit News*. "He lost himself in the moment. And it was so funny, man. He ripped his jacket off. The guy might weigh 125 pounds. And it was so funny, when he ripped that jacket off, I was like, 'Oh god, put that back on.' And Honky Tonk is dying, laughing."

Seemingly infuriated by the loss, Jake snatched the Honky Tonk Man's guitar and took a mighty swing at him, busting the object on the ring post while the victor ran down the aisle, back toward the showers. Now caught in the ring without his ally, Hart looked for a way out, but Jake came up behind the manager and placed him in a full nelson.

"He squeezed so hard, I was like, 'Oh my god, take it easy, baby,'" Hart said. "I was kicking and kicking and kicking."

Boldly, Cooper grabbed the bag from the corner and removed Damien, waving the snake at the ref and scaring him away.

Together, Roberts and Cooper attempted to hurl the snake onto the manager. As it went through the air, Hart tried dodging the reptile. "I hated that snake, but I didn't want to hurt an animal, so I put my arms out and took a bump backwards because I didn't want the snake just getting thrown onto a flat surface. And the snake kind of grazed my body and went over my head onto the mat. I didn't even have to keep it on me. We still got a great pop."

The confrontation ended with the Honky Tonk Man returning from the back and rushing the manager away as Cooper and Roberts reveled in the fan adulation.

And then, they were gone, and another chaotic match was about to begin, the final confrontation before the long-anticipated main event.

Although the Islamic Republic of Iran was as hostile toward the Soviet Union as it was to the United States, wrestling fans never would have known by watching the team of the Iron Sheik and Nikolai Volkoff. Apparently united in their hatred of all things American, both men were personally quite loyal to their adopted homeland; Volkoff was actually Croatian, but he'd been playing a hammer-and-sickle-bearing Russian for so long that few were aware of his legitimate ethnicity. Still, there was little room for subtlety in WWF storylines and, before every match, he antagonized the audience by singing a mangled version of the Soviet national anthem.

As the crowd was still booing, the Sheik would grab the microphone and declare, "Iran Number One. Russia Number One. USA," he'd twist his face and pretend to spit.

The pair had been managed by "Classy" Freddie Blassie, but as the white-haired manager aged, he began to cut down on his travel and, the year before *WrestleMania III*, announced that he'd become business partners with Slick. Because of this, it was the Doctor of Style who accompanied the Sheik and Volkoff to Michigan for their encounter with the Killer Bees, B. Brian Blair and Jumping Jim Brunzell.

As an added touch, Slick still was wearing the garments shredded during his earlier confrontation with Koko B. Ware and Tito Santana.

Blair was confident that both teams would amuse the audience. "You can't have three characters like the Sheik, Volkoff and Slick in the ring and not have fun," said Blair. "Even when we were going over our match earlier, Slick was saying things that had everybody laughing."

This despite the fact that Blair and the Sheik had had personal issues in the past. To the Sheik, Blair, the future commissioner of Hillsborough

County — a Florida district that includes Tampa — was a backstage politician who'd ingratiated himself so thoroughly with Hulk Hogan that the champion had reserved a spot in his dressing room for the tag team performer to change. Blair believed that the tension came from a different place.

"We used to always wrestle each other a little bit, kind of halfway shoot. Because we were both amateurs. Yeah, he was a better amateur than I was but, you know, I learned a few things and could hold my own. I forgot how it started but, during one session, he double wristlocked me and somehow I rolled over and held him in a front facelock.

"That wasn't an easy thing to do. He was a strong son of a gun and he had a neck that was hard to facelock. But Nikolai was watching and he started teasing the heck out of him about it. So I guess the Sheik got mad over that and he carried a grudge."

As with Piper and Adonis, the purpose of the match in many ways was to highlight an unscheduled participant. In January, "Hacksaw" Jim Duggan had left Bill Watts's UWF after headlining for the company since 1982. "There's not really a lot you can do if you're the promoter in that situation," noted Jeff Jarrett. "If a guy doesn't want to be on your roster anymore, you can't really force him to stay there. It never works."

Unlike Brutus Beefcake, who waited until the end of the Piper-Adonis confrontation to come out as the Barber, Duggan revealed himself instantly, storming the ring during Volkoff's singing of the Soviet national anthem. As always, Hacksaw came with his signature two-by-four — in this case, topped by a miniature American flag. "You could always find a two-by-four lying around," Duggan said of his gimmick to the *Detroit News*. "Jake had to carry that heavy snake around. I'd just show up and break off a piece of a pallet in the back."

Snatching the microphone, Duggan delivered a sermon about his view of patriotism: "Volkoff, understand one thing. Do not sing that Russian national anthem because this is the land of the free and the home of the brave."

By Duggan's definition, this allowed him to ignore Nikolai's First Amendment rights. Still, the crowd cheered anyway.

Not surprisingly, Volkoff and the Sheik jumped the Bees from behind when the bell rang — Pearl Harboring them, as the saying went — prompting the fans to bombard the ring with trash. As the referee tried calming the situation, Blair and Brunzell managed to propel the heels toward each other. In an effort to allay the momentum, the villains locked arms and do-si-doed, only to be knocked off their feet.

That was the basic tenor of the match, and disorder continued to reign from that point forward. After a series of gut-wrench suplexes, the Sheik trapped Brunzell in the Camel Clutch. Meanwhile, outside the ring, Duggan chased Volkoff with weapon in hand, prompting Jesse Ventura to exclaim, "I think it's terrible that Jack Tunney allows this guy to run around with a two-by-four like that."

To escape Hacksaw's wrath, Volkoff retreated inside the ring. Duggan followed, the plank slung over his shoulder like a rifle. As he marched past Sheik and Brunzell, the bearded hero seemed to grasp that one of the Killer Bees was in trouble and stopped to clonk the Iranian with the lumber.

The referee called for the bell, disqualifying the babyfaces.

Recounted Brunzell, "That was the worst frickin' finish I ever saw in my life."

Blair was equally disenchanted. "The whole thing was stupid. Sheik and Volkoff are cheating. Then Duggan comes in and instead of shifting the match in our favor, the referee disqualifies us and we lose.

"I would have preferred being in a title match that night. I was think-ing, 'Man, we busted our balls in this place,' and then they bring us to *WrestleMania* just so Duggan can take the spotlight in our match.' I mean, god bless Jimmy Duggan. He's a wonderful man and we're friends and I'm always happy when he has good news in his life. But this was not good for the Killer Bees."

And more was to come. Once again, Duggan took the microphone, this time declaring, "There's a new spirit in America and you can hear it now." The fans rose as he led them in a chant of "USA, USA."

To add insult to injury, Blair and Brunzell picked up the mantra as well. Opined Ventura, "I don't know why the Bees are patting this guy on the back. He cost them a chance to win a match."

Decades later, both Blair and Brunzell were adamant that this might have been a good period for the Killer Bees to make a heel turn, as the Rougeau Brothers would in 1988. "It would have given us new life," Blair said. "They'd promised us the belts three times, but obviously, wouldn't put the belts on us as babyfaces. So we could have put on our masks to start screwing over the other fan favorites and won the title that way."

Brunzell asserted that the repackaged Bees "would have gotten some heat and probably made some good money. But I'm convinced that nobody even took the time to think about it. I don't know what was on Vince's mind back then, but it definitely wasn't us."

CHAPTER 33

Just before Hulk Hogan made his entrance, fans watching on pay-per-view saw him on camera, making a bold prediction about the outcome of the upcoming war.

"The intensity of Hulkamania, the way it's turned this whole state upside down, the way the whole world's turned upside down, what are you going to think when the Giant hits the ground, he feels the wrath of Hulkamania and the whole world shakes at my feet?"

And at that, the golden symbol of sports entertainment flexed his tanned pythons, turned sideways, pumped his arms up and down and walked backwards out of frame.

At ringside, even without glancing behind him, Tom Buchanan could feel the anticipation of the audience. "The crowd knew what was coming and the crowd cared. As a news photographer, I knew some events were bigger than others. This wasn't just a wrestling match. Whatever Hogan and André were going to do, the people were completely into it."

From the time they'd spent together in Montreal, Raymond Rougeau had a friendly rapport with André. But in the period leading into *WrestleMania III*, the physically addled Giant had kept "pretty much to himself," Rougeau said. "He was obviously in a lot of pain, and he wanted to deliver the match and pass the torch to Hulk Hogan. He wanted to live up to the hype and do it correctly."

Just prior to the clash, Hogan said that André respectfully invited the champion to sit next to him in the changing room. Although the challenger's tolerance for alcohol was legend, Hogan claimed that André consumed two quarts of Crown Royal, a blended Canadian whisky with an alcohol content of 40 percent. When André asked his rival to partake, the Hulkster said that he agreed, then managed to dump his beverage while his opponent's attention was elsewhere.

Hogan was also adamant in his assertion that André refused to discuss the finish beforehand, and the two headed out to the Gorilla position — the area, named for Gorilla Monsoon, just inside the curtain, where wrestlers receive last-minute instructions — with the titlist uncertain over whether the Giant intended to win or lose.

It seems fanciful to imagine that Vince McMahon would loosen his iron grip enough to trust even these valuable talents to simply call the match in the ring. But Hogan maintained that by the time the strains of "Real American" began, he still didn't know if he was going to leave Michigan with the WWF World Heavyweight Championship.

Now that the sky above the Silverdome had blackened, Steve Taylor noted that crowd shots became problematic. "You could not see the people. We didn't have crowd lighting like they do now. I mean, whatever stadium you're in, you constantly get the feeling that you're in a stadium. That's not how it was for Hulk and André. It was the old-fashioned set up — basically a spotlight on the ring. You could not really see the reactions of the fans. You could hear them, though."

Noted Buchanan, "One of the things about wrestling is you feel that if you yell loud enough and scream at the right times, you can have an influence on the match."

That wasn't the only way that spectators made their presence felt. Flashbulbs popped from everywhere. As a tuxedoed Bob Uecker rolled down the aisle on his ring cart to serve as guest ring announcer, someone tossed what appeared to be a jacket at him.

It was far worse for André and Bobby "The Brain" Heenan, who were showered with garbage. "It was a lot of paper cups, thank goodness," said New York superfan Charlie Adorno. "Bobby was getting whacked in every direction."

Interestingly, Hogan was the only performer on the card who did not utilize a ring cart. Like a recently elected US president greeting the masses in downtown Washington prior to the inauguration, Hogan walked between the barricades, pumping a pointed finger in the air, a bandana inexplicably resting between his teeth.

The Silverdome buzzed as referee Joey Marella began delivering his instructions to the combatants in center ring. Then, the bell rang and Hogan moved toward a stoic André with bulging eyes, head shaking, apparently intent on expressing fury that it all had to come to this.

"It didn't matter whether they'd have a good technical match," said future *Pro Wrestling Illustrated* writer Bob Smith. "André and Hogan staring at each other was an image people never forgot. It was off the charts, a great moment in wrestling history."

Eventually, André appeared to tire of Hogan's sermonizing and shoved the champ. When Hogan shoved back, André tried slugging the Hulkster — only to be blocked and hit with a punch. From there, Hogan seemed to be trying to end the match quickly, scooping up André and going for a body slam. Before the titlist could hoist his opponent any higher, his knees buckled, and the Giant fell on top. The fans looked on in shock as Marella slapped the mat quickly — so quickly, in fact, that his hand struck the canvas a third time even after the titlist managed to curve his shoulder.

André raised a triumphant arm, but Marella signaled to the time-keeper that Hogan was only down for the count of two. To emphasize this further, the referee squatted in front of the Giant and held up two fingers on each hand.

"I have never been in a building that had the same level of emotion and excitement," recalled Dick Glover.

André now unleashed his apparent anger over being denied a victory on his ex-friend. Always aware of the positioning of the camera, Hogan put on a masterclass on selling for the Giant. As one cameraman shot handheld from the mat level, Hogan went up for a slam, then came down directly in front of the lens. To communicate the agony of his predicament, Hogan rose slightly from the canvas, groaned loudly and flopped back down.

In case they couldn't discern this themselves, the erudite Monsoon — who spent a chunk of his early career depicting a man-beast found wading nude by manager Bobby Davis in a Manchurian stream — told the viewing audience that André was targeting "that lower lumbar region, that kidney area that's already been damaged.

Ventura replied, "He almost drove Hogan right through that mat."

At ringside, Buchanan felt assured that, when his photos were developed, the range of options would be endless. "The guys were moving so slow that it was a lot easier to set up pictures. You could get Hogan in focus, you could get André in focus because nothing was happening so quickly that you were ever in danger of missing it."

To those who believed, Hogan's championship appeared to be very much in peril. In a move short on athleticism but high on drama, André stepped onto his foe's back, allegedly bringing his bulk down on the Hulkster's spine, then casually strode back onto the canvas.

"I've never seen Hogan beaten down like this," said Ventura. "I've never seen Hogan crawling on the mat. Obviously, he hurt his back, attempting to go for that body slam."

Grabbing Hogan by the tights, André yanked his foe off the mat, then slung him into the corner.

Even as he did very little between the ropes, André's storytelling was impeccable. When Hogan managed to throw a series of defensive blows, the contender sold them by leaning against the turnbuckles and rubbing his head. During a long bearhug sequence — likely inserted into the bout so the Giant could replenish his energy — André distorted his face, conveying the impression that his powerful arms were grinding down his opponent's bones. As Hogan appeared to weaken, the referee lifted his arm once, then twice. Just before completely fading, the Hulkster thrust a fist into the air and the fans shouted for him to recover.

After watching their hero take a thrashing, spectators were ready for Hogan to become aggressive. Taking the battle outside the ring, Hogan pulled the mats — the same mats whose presence had been derided by the talent the year before because the padding was added to protect the NFL players in the *WrestleMania 2* battle royal — up off the ground. Feigning naivete, Ventura asked Monsoon why the champ was taking that approach.

"To expose that concrete," Gorilla responded in a knowledgeable tone.

Between the strands, André slung Hogan off the ropes and went for a big boot. Evading the maneuver, the Hulkster hit a clothesline that cut down the big man. "That's the first time I think the Giant's ever been knocked off his feet like that," said Ventura with such conviction that it appeared even he believed he was telling the truth.

With the shouts of the Hulkamaniacs invigorating him, Hogan's body pulsed with energy as he reached under André, successfully elevating him from the canvas and crashing him down with a body slam.

In the upper reaches of the stadium, Bobby Regal's birthday party was drawing to a close when Vince Averill felt the building quake as he and his friends rushed through the corridor. "I heard the slam. I heard the reaction to the slam. But I did not see the slam with my own two eyeballs."

It seemed that, as the main event intensified, Bobby's father became worried about post-event traffic and decided to herd the kids out early. "If we would have just sat there for another 30 seconds or a minute, we would have seen it. But we missed the most dramatic moment of *WrestleMania III.*

"What really bothered me was that we didn't even go straight home. When we got closer to Bobby's house, we went to Dairy Queen. I didn't understand. What was the rush? Hogan slammed André the Giant and we left to go to Dairy Queen."

While the boys descended toward the parking lot, André lay sprawled on the ring apron, allowing Hogan to bound off the ropes, hit his signature legdrop, cover the Giant and retain the gold.

His body tremoring to the crowd's rhythm, the Hulkster motioned skyward. "He's thanking the guy upstairs, Jess," said Monsoon, "as he always does."

A disenchanted André sat down on the canvas, seemingly contemplating the ramifications of his defeat. Holding his championship, Hogan spread the belt at his feet, daring André to try to take it.

Instead, André left the ring, pointing menacingly at Hogan before boarding the ring cart with Heenan, then looked back at the champ with contempt, making it clear that, while the main event had ended, the threat remained.

On commentary, Monsoon called the Hulkster "the greatest professional athlete in the world today."

In 1987, that included Michael Jordan, Diego Maradona and Mike Tyson.

Lapsing out of heel mode, Ventura claimed that the André-Hogan clash had been "the greatest match I've ever seen."

But in Yonkers, New York, Cory Pipcinski missed it.

As Hogan and André were coming to the ring, the 14-year-old's cable transmission went out. "I guess the show was running long," he said. "So instead of seeing the match, we get a slate telling us that the replay was coming up next."

This was unacceptable to Cory, who'd grown up in the 20-square-mile city just north of the Bronx and became a fan literally as Vince McMahon was pulling the trigger on his plan to transform the industry.

"I was 10 years old and there was someone in my class who'd come in with wrestling magazines. It made me interested enough to start watching on Saturday mornings."

Within weeks, Pipcinski turned on the television to learn that the previous Monday in Madison Square Garden, Bob Backlund had been dethroned by the Iron Sheik. "I was caught up in the intrigue of the baddest man in the world becoming the champion. How could this happen? Was anyone going to save us? And then, a few weeks after that, Hulk Hogan comes in and wins it for America. In all honesty, I did not have much of a social life, and that's what did it for me."

After putting in his order for *WrestleMania III*, Pipcinski would periodically walk over to the television and simply stare at the graphic indicating that the show was coming up next. "For me, *WrestleMania III* wasn't just a three-hour pay-per-view. It was an all-day thing, waiting for it."

When Hogan and André crashed, Cory raced into the bedroom, where there was another cable TV box that teased viewers by showing a scrambled picture of pay-per-view offerings, with the audio going in and out. "I could just barely hear what was going on. I needed to know the finish of that match."

Still unsatisfied, Pipcinski alerted his mother, who happened to work for Cablevision of Yonkers as the general manager's secretary. "I thought maybe she could do something to help, and we drove down to the Cablevision office."

He immediately saw about 15 other fans out front, yelling and banging on the window.

Cory and his mother went inside, where he noticed the customer service phone bank lit up. "People were really upset, and the chief engineer of the cable system was there. And he just made an executive decision on the spot to turn the replay on for free for everybody."

Although it never became part of local lore, according to Cory, the historical record should reflect that if you happened to be a cable subscriber in Yonkers, New York, on March 29, 1987, *WrestleMania III* — albeit a late-playing version — was available free of charge.

Perhaps the engineer was practicing community relations. Or maybe he, too, was among the legions slain in the spirit of Hulkamania, *brother*.

Hogan argued that, by doing business and taking the loss, André the Giant reinforced all of Vince McMahon's hard work and buttressed the company's success.

"There's a picture of Hulk Hogan on the ring cart being taken away, raising the belt," said Buchanan. "That picture is mine. I shot it with 320 Tungsten film, basic film. It's very grainy. It's not good film and it's a terrible image because the light is terrible. But it's what I had to do, and it tells the story of how *WrestleMania III* ended."

After he began working in the wrestling industry, Bob Smith would rewatch *WrestleMania III* on VHS several times. "There's a scene near the end of the broadcast. It's Gorilla Monsoon and Jesse Ventura from up high, looking down on this massive crowd after Hogan and André. And the look on their faces — it was totally real. It wasn't kayfabe. They were as blown away as the rest of us."

During those viewings, Smith remembered his own experiences, watching the WWF on the rickety chairs in the Washington Avenue Armory in Albany just a few years earlier. "I could not believe that this was the same company that literally sold tickets and gave you change out of a cigar box."

CHAPTER 34

A s fans lingered in the Silverdome, still absorbing the spectacle they'd just witnessed, Tom Buchanan walked into the backstage area and put down his gear. "I remember feeling relief that the show was finally over. My shoulders dropped and I knew I did my job and didn't have to worry about fucking up anymore."

It had been five years since Steve Taylor made the choice to come to work for Vince McMahon, and the event forced him to reflect on that decision. "I was a chief photographer at a daily newspaper with a decent future, and people really couldn't understand why I was giving that up for professional wrestling. But I took a chance, and now I was really glad I did."

Dave Meltzer's *Wrestling Observer Radio* broadcast would later report that Hulk Hogan and André the Giant each received $750,000 for main-eventing *WrestleMania III*, with André gifted an extra $250,000 for doing the job. The information apparently came from Jim Barnett, who'd boast to Canadian journalist and author Greg Oliver about receiving the largest post-*WrestleMania III* bonus of anybody.

Still, at times, Barnett was too much of a yenta — although the term belongs in the carny lexicon, it is actually a Yiddish expression describing a woman who derives all sustenance from listening to and disseminating gossip — to stay out of his own way. Not long after *WrestleMania III*,

McMahon apparently became aware of a clandestine correspondence between his confidant and Jim Crockett Jr. and is said to have summoned Barnett to a face-to-face meeting. Glaring across his desk at his longtime associate — the way only Vince could when he felt betrayed — McMahon told the illustrious dealmaker that he was fired.

According to the story, Barnett immediately went home and tried to kill himself with an overdose of sleeping pills.

As with some prior associates he'd driven out of business, McMahon's differences with Barnett had nothing to do with a loss of affection. Reportedly, the WWF sent flowers to the colorful huckster's hospital room, and Linda McMahon paid a personal visit to his bedside.

Barnett recuperated. To the shock of no one, upon his release, a job at Jim Crockett Promotions was waiting for him.

News of the spectacular made its way to Europe slowly, as did home videos of the event. When British wrestler Darren Matthews — who'd become best known as William Regal — finally grasped what had transpired in the Pontiac Silverdome, he was unsurprised. "It's America," he said. "Everything's bigger in America. So why wouldn't a wrestling promotion be able to sell out a stadium?"

Either way, whoever this Vince McMahon character might be, he was probably too busy in North America to think about competing with promoters like Max Crabtree and Brian Dixon in the United Kingdom. "I expected we'd keep our identity and keep our style unique, just like they did in Mexico," said Liverpool-born Robbie Brookside, who'd later work for World Championship Wrestling (WCW), wrestle Chris Jericho in New Japan and coach at the WWE Performance Center.

According to UK pro wrestling rules, matches were divided into six five-minute rounds (three minutes for title clashes), with a 30-second break in between. There were championships based on weight classifications, and wins were awarded to either the first competitor to win two falls or the wrestler ahead at the conclusion of the contest. A knockout or disqualification automatically ended the match.

In tag team bouts, a wrestler who lost a fall immediately returned to the dressing room, leaving the surviving member of the team to compete under handicap rules.

"In America, fans would often feel like they needed a winner," said Brookside. "Yet, some of the best matches I can remember ended in ties, especially in the final round, when fans see you putting in the commitment and energy before the bell."

As for what was transpiring across the Atlantic, "it had no impact whatsoever on anything I was doing in my world," Regal said.

Rarely did he bother viewing tapes of the matches in the US. "I'm out working every day, driving 2,000 miles a week in England. I've got a wife. By the time I was 20, I had my first son. I've got a home. I've got a life. I don't see a lot of wrestling except for the wrestling I'm on."

When American tapes did arrive, they usually came courtesy of wrestler Steve Fury. "He had a nickname, 'The Pizza Thief,' because he could get his hands on anything," said Brookside. "If you needed a color TV, Steve could get it for you. It might not have a remote control, but Steve would get it."

It was Fury who first showed Regal footage from the Charlotte territory. "I thought it was pretty good," Regal said. "There were a few things I couldn't get my head around, though. One of the only people I ever saw putting on a proper wristlock was Ric Flair. I later found out the reason for that was that he was trained by a British wrestler [Billy Robinson].

"And there was something else I noticed. When someone was standing on the ring apron, his opponent would pull the rope and, like magic, he'd throw himself into the ring."

Brookside was perplexed by the performers hitting each other with closed fists. "In England, we were never allowed to punch, especially on TV. If you had a TV match and you punched someone in front of the referee, it was an instant disqualification."

Although there were distinct British grappling styles from regions like Lancashire, Cumberland and Westmorland, pro wrestling in the UK had the same carny roots as in North America, and the business was generally closed to outsiders. "Unless your dad was a wrestler or you had a serious martial arts or amateur wrestling background, no one was going to train you," Regal said.

"If you were working class, you had to leave school at 16 and that was it. There was no further education. If your father worked in a factory, you were in a factory. My family were bricklayers, and that was the plan for me. But from the time I was four years old, I wasn't having it."

That's because every Saturday at 4 p.m., he would go to his grandparents' home and watch the *World of Sport* pro wrestling program on ITV. In the summers, Regal went to the Blackpool resort area, visiting promoter Bobby Barron's "wrestling booth"— the equivalent of a tent on the carnival midway — at the Pleasure Beach amusement park.

In 1983, at age 15, he'd make the two-hour journey from his village on Friday nights and hang around the wrestling booth until Sunday. Generally, bouts featured wrestlers with various gimmicks taking challenges from the crowd. Sometimes, the challengers were part of the show while, on other occasions, a civilian would attempt to embarrass the feature act by engaging him in a shoot. As a result, every attraction in the wrestling booth regarded himself as a "hooker," a performer who could legitimately torture any foe.

"After just sort of watching what went on for about a month, I got enough courage to go up to Bobby Barron and tell him I wanted to be a wrestler. And he said, 'Okay,' and started putting me in as a challenger from the crowd. And then, a few of the wrestlers began showing me things. And within a couple of months, he'd put me in with other people, doing little matches. And that's how I really started."

Still, Regal finished school and even took his final exams at 16. But by the time the results came back, he was living in Blackpool, working in the wrestling booth and being regularly dispatched by Barron to holiday camps, working-class vacation spots that included family entertainment on the grounds. "We'd do a minimum of two shows a day. Each show was two singles matches, then an hour break, then the same four people in a tag team match."

From the beginning, the veterans told the teen not to worry about wins and losses. "You're in a crooked business," he was advised. "Whether you win or lose, do a good job and people will give you work."

The more he became indoctrinated in the trade, the more people he met, including Marty Jones, who Regal had seen on *World of Sport* defending the World Mid-Heavyweight Championship. Jones, in turn, introduced him to stars like Pete Roberts, Dave Taylor and Johnny Saint, along with Britain's most powerful promoter, Max Crabtree.

Crabtree ran London-based Dale Martin Promotions and, more importantly, was the Jim Crockett Jr. of Joint Promotions, a conglomeration of leagues from around the United Kingdom. It was Joint Promotions that presented the *World of Sport* wrestling shows each Saturday and, under Crabtree's leadership, British wrestling enjoyed a boom period starting in the late '70s.

Much of the resurgence was centered on Max Crabtree's brother, Shirley "Big Daddy" Crabtree, a favorite among children for, among other routines, splashing down on villains with his big belly.

Big Daddy's lengthy run as a headliner had much to do with the way he was positioned, teaming up with young, athletic performers like Regal — then known as Steve Regal — "Gentleman" Chris Adams and the future British Bulldogs, Davey Boy Smith and Dynamite Kid, who did most of the work before tagging out to their popular partner for the finish.

Nearly every one of Big Daddy's teammates considered the task unsatisfying, and, over time, there was a backlash against the Crabtrees. By the mid-1980s, Liverpool-area promoter Brian Dixon's All Star Wrestling group had become an alternative for some performers. "I remember giving Brian a call," Regal said, "and saying I wanted to work for him. And his first words were, 'Are you fuckin' insane? You're already on TV with Big Daddy. Why the fuck would you want to work for me?' And I told him, 'I need to wrestle better wrestlers and you've got the best wrestlers.'"

Regal never regretted the decision. "In the next six months, my wrestling IQ just got better. It was the right move on my part."

It was in All Star that Regal would form a successful tag team with Brookside, who — unlike most of the premier wrestlers of the time — never worked for Joint Promotions. That's because Brookside was a Scouser — the term for a Liverpool native, based on the word "Scouse," or Merseyside region dialect — and Brian Dixon was his home promoter.

The family lived in the shadow of Goodison Park, home of the Everton football club since 1892. But Robbie's interests drifted toward the *World of Sport* wrestling broadcasts on Saturdays. "My dad would come home from work and yell, 'Get that bloody rubbish off,' and he'd put the rugby on. And I'd wait until he got up to go to the toilet. We had one of them big TVs and he could hear me changing the channel in the next room; there were only three channels. And he'd scream, 'Turn it off.'"

But Robbie's grandmother, like many elderly English women of the era, loved wrestling, attending the All Star shows at Liverpool Stadium. "There was one wrestler named Jack Pye and when he'd sit down on the stool between rounds, she'd go down to the front and smack him on the ass."

In 1978, when Robbie was 12, his aunt brought over a flyer about an upcoming show featuring Jon Cortez, "Exotic" Adrian Street and Jackie "Mr. TV" Pallo and received permission from his mother to attend. "Liverpool Stadium was in sort of a secret part of the city center. It was near an old mill by these old, big, cobbled roads. And Liverpool Stadium was a magical place."

Despite the name, the building was actually a 3,700-capacity boxing arena, but the Beatles, David Bowie, Black Sabbath and Led Zeppelin had all played there. "I can remember walking up and looking around like I was in a museum. The posh had the big, velvet, plush seats. I never went there. It was always with the scallywags."

Brookside was so impressed, he decided that he never wanted to leave. By 14, he was already training. "It was my dad's worst nightmare. So he spoke to some of my best mates who used to go to the wrestling with me to put a wrench in the machine. And, unbeknownst to me, one of them went to a wrestler named Carl McGrath and said, 'That kid down there with the blond hair thinks it's all fixed.' That was the worst thing you could say to a wrestler. And McGrath said, 'Tell him to come up to Kirby to the English Electric on Sunday at 3 o'clock.'

"I thought I was being invited to a show. I opened the door and there's these old guys, all warming up and bridging and everything. And Carl McGrath points me out to the rest of the boys and he goes, 'This kid thinks it's all fixed.' So I'm looking behind me and there's nobody there. And then he asked me to get on the mat.

"It felt like my neck and shoulders were ripped out. He tied me in a knot and really hurt me. There was blood coming out of my nose and ear, which I never experienced. But it had the adverse effect of what everyone expected. I went back the following week and then the week after that. And after they saw how much I wanted to be there, they started showing me the amateur stuff."

Like Regal, a young Brookside found his way to Blackpool and wrestled for Bobby Barron at Pleasure Beach. "There were so many characters in Blackpool. All the shops and cafés and amusement arcades were open, and it was vibrant. Blackpool kept me alive when it could have gone so wrong."

In time, he also found himself in Wales, where promoter Orig Williams had a program on the Welsh language station, S4C. In the summers, Williams ran a series of events in the resort area of Rhyl in northern Wales, where families vacationed in caravans near the grounds of an old castle. "It was cotton candy and fish and chips and slot machines for six weeks. Wrestling was on the promenade, and there was a ring in a garage. That's where I met the likes of Crusher Mason and Kung Fu and Chic Cullen. I invested in boots and had two sets of wrestling gear. If I was really hungry, a lady at the fish and chips booth used to give me the scraped-off batter."

As with Regal, Brookside's experiences were putting him in the direct orbit of his idols, in this case, Tony St. Clair and Mark "Rollerball" Rocco. "Jackie Robinson was one of my favorites, as well. He was Billy Robinson's cousin, but very different. Jackie was warm and friendly. And Billy was called 'Billy the Bully' for a reason."

It was all so self-contained that Brookside rarely devoted much thought to what might be occurring in New York or Charlotte or Atlanta. But in 1985, Steve Fury handed him a VHS cassette of *WrestleMania 1*. "It blew me away — the size of it and the celebrities. Real celebrities, like Liberace and Muhammad Ali and Cyndi Lauper. And I just thought, 'What is this?'"

The same year, ITV canceled *World of Sport*. As the name implied, the show had been divided into sections, highlighting a variety of sports. Pro wrestling was too much of an institution to completely exile from the airwaves. However, it would no longer be seen in its popular slot at 4 p.m. on Saturdays.

Among the UK wrestlers, the name of ITV program director Greg Dyke became notorious. "He killed British wrestling," Regal said. "He thought it was too lowbrow. The first thing he did was move it from 4 p.m. to midday. But the viewing figures fell off because the working class still worked half a day on Saturday. So the fellas were still at work and the women were shopping at 12 p.m. And the kids weren't around. At 4 p.m., even if the fellas were at football, the women and the kids were home."

It was the reason a generation of English people would spend the rest of their lives remembering the experience of watching *World of Sport* with their grandmothers on the only TV in the house.

Under the new arrangement, the time slot would be shifted so often that fans could never be sure when wrestling was on. But perhaps even more impactful, the Crabtree family lost their exclusive deal with ITV. Although the network continued showing the Joint Promotions broadcasts, the programs were rotated with Brian Dixon's All Star Wrestling and Vincent Kennedy McMahon's World Wrestling Federation.

No one in the UK saw it, but the WWF's full invasion was just a few years away.

By the time the British wrestlers were passing around their VHS copies of *WrestleMania III*, the plans were already in place.

"Our shows were in town halls and leisure centers," noted Brookside. "WWE was more of a spectacle, more razzmatazz."

As with the NWA, the competitors on the British scene believed that their technical wrestling was better. But that hardly mattered. "Anything that's American, the people in Britain wanted," said Regal. "We grew up watching American TV shows and now we were getting American wrestling. America influences the rest of the world, good or bad."

CHAPTER 35

As promised, Rafael Morffi's baseball coach at Archbishop Molloy High School in Queens benched him when he returned.

"I'm disappointed in you that you went and actually did it," Luke Perreira told the catcher and third baseman.

"It was a non-league game," Morffi defended himself. "I wanted to go to *WrestleMania*. You only live once."

Perreira was not persuaded. "You're a leader on the team. It was the wrong message. I have to bench you so everyone understands."

For the next two weeks, every time Morffi missed a ground ball during practice, the coach would tease him about placing too much of his focus on wrestling.

"It was always in a good-natured way, never malicious," Morffi said. "But he'd say it in front of everyone, and they all had a good laugh."

Interestingly, both baseball and wrestling would follow Morffi into adulthood.

In 1999, Morffi was the assistant director of media relations and marketing for the New York Mets when Stone Cold Steve Austin threw out the first pitch before a game against the New York Yankees. During pre-game warm-ups, Morffi approached future Yankee Hall of Famer Derek Jeter in the visiting dugout to see if he was interested in having a photo opportunity with Austin. Jeter excitedly agreed.

WWF announcer Michael Cole had been at the game, and both he and Austin spread the word that Morffi would be a welcome addition to their company. He was eventually hired as a manager of live events.

When the organization's chief rival, All Elite Wrestling (AEW), was founded in 2019, Morffi became its vice president of live events and touring. He would remain there until the end of 2023 before coming on board as the vice president of sports programming at Brooklyn's Barclays Center.

His tasks include booking major wrestling events in the city where he grew up.

As Michigan residents read about the strong response to *WrestleMania III*, many were disappointed that, because of the blackout on local cable systems, they had been unable to see the show on pay-per-view. On April 12, more than a half dozen Michigan cable companies agreed to remedy the situation by showing a rebroadcast of the extravaganza.

The move was not entirely charitable. The rate for ordering the show was $19.95 — the same fee that had been charged on March 29.

Some 20,000 households took the offer.

In the article I wrote for the next edition of the *WWF Magazine*, I emphasized that orders for VHS copies of *WrestleMania III* were flowing into the office. As if these points could not be overstated any further, I cited the purported attendance of 93,173, the dozen "electrifying and thrilling" contests and the fact that some of the spectators had come "from as far away as California."

The event "broke new ground," I stressed, "showing the entire universe that Hulkamania and the World Wrestling Federation were definitely here to stay."

Up until *WrestleMania III*, those tenets were sometimes in question.

In the months leading up to the show, Jerry Brisco worried about whether, in the long term, the company could sustain interest in the annual event. "*WrestleMania III* just put the stamp of acceptance on us," he said. "We could get the NFL-type crowds. We could get the rock 'n' roll crowds. Major sponsors looked at the show and said, 'This McMahon guy knows what the hell he's doing. We better latch onto him.'

"In the media, in the marketing world, in the promotional world, that WWE banner was burning bright, and it was going to get nothing but bigger and better."

Or more specifically, *bigger, better, badder.*

WrestleMania III created so much media recognition that Mike Weber no longer had to pitch talent appearances to television talk shows. "They just came to me," he said. "Hogan and André was a worldwide deal, and it was a big jumping-off point."

The increased interest resulted in the company expanding its public relations department, with new hires being reminded to repeat a specific mantra. "We talked about selling out the Silverdome for three years. It was one of our calling cards."

In the *Wrestling Observer Newsletter*, Dave Meltzer reported that the paid attendance was 90,873, while an additional 375,000 attended closed-circuit simulcasts.

By this point, Meltzer was talking to McMahon's confidant Pat Patterson and his lieutenant Terry Garvin every week, going over show attendance and gates. "I remember the conversation after *WrestleMania III* because I didn't believe the number," Meltzer said. "I mean, they'd always exaggerate. Garvin told me that there were 2,300 comps. He wouldn't give me the attendance figure, just the comps. That was the only gate I ever asked for where I got that response."

Using the comp calculation as a guidepost, Meltzer subtracted 2,300 from 93,173, concluding that 90,873 had paid to be at *WrestleMania III*.

He held onto that belief for several years until a television special repeated the 93,173 figure and former WWF live events promoter Zane Bresloff phoned the journalist, marveling, "I can't believe people still think that was the number."

"Well, wasn't it?"

That's when Meltzer said that Bresloff informed him that the paid attendance was actually 78,500.

Yet, in 1987, Meltzer tended to trust his inside data since — unbeknownst to his readers — he was now on the WWF payroll, having been recruited for the position by Patterson's longtime romantic partner, Louie Dondero. The job consisted of filling the company in on the Japanese wrestling scene, a challenge for the WWF given the language barrier and absence of electronic communication. "I think they were looking to get into that market and also Japan had a lot of good foreign talent. So they wanted to know who was on what tours. Back then, the only way to find out that information was by word of mouth."

The relationship broke down quickly, and Meltzer eventually regretted his choice. "It wasn't a good mix because, since they were paying me, they expected me to change how I wrote, and I don't think I ever did."

As feared, the official figure for John Paul II's papal mass on September 18, 1987, bypassed the reported number for *WrestleMania III* — 93,682 to 93,173. "We joked that because the Pope's altar was smaller than the ring that they could fit more seats on the floor," said Dick Glover.

Well, not everybody joked. "How do we know that the Pope's number wasn't prefabricated, too, along with the Rolling Stones and everyone else who played there?" questioned Jimmy Hart.

In fact, even among churchgoers, a popular opinion in the Detroit area was that both the WWF *and* the Vatican exaggerated the figures, particularly the Holy See, which — during a period when Catholics in the US were becoming less observant — did not want the message sent that Hulk Hogan was a better drawing card than the Vicar of Christ.

As the years passed, the Silverdome's website alleged that the Pontiff set the Silverdome attendance record, listing the number at 88,000. The implication, of course, was that the WWF drew far lower. Following an email campaign by irate fans, the stadium repeated the company figure of 93,173, relegating the Pope to second place.

In time, WWE would surpass the oft-cited statistic at other events, including *WrestleMania 32*, which was said to have drawn 101,763 to AT&T Stadium outside Dallas for a main event that saw Roman Reigns unseat Triple H for the WWE World Heavyweight crown, and a 2021 clash between WWE *SmackDown* Women's Champion Bianca Belair and Carmella in front of an alleged 200,000 at the Rolling Loud festival in Miami Gardens, Florida. Still, the 93,173 figure — whether a work or shoot — continues to live large in the public consciousness.

While *WrestleMania III* infused a sense of pride in people in metro Detroit, the outlook for the Silverdome remained grim. Four months after the event, the *Detroit Free Press* reported Pontiac Stadium Building Authority chairman William Waterman's assessment that the show helped contribute to only the second profitable year in the stadium's existence:

"A good marketing strategy must be employed to help the stadium weather the departure of the Pistons, who will move to a stadium in Auburn Hills for the 1988–89 National Basketball Association season," Waterman said. "The loss will leave the Silverdome with 100 dates to book."

In 2002, with the opening of Ford Field in downtown Detroit, the NFL's Lions left, too. Without a permanent tenant, the Silverdome sat empty for eight years. Maintenance costs multiplied, and the city of Pontiac did not have the money to pay the bills. At an auction in 2009, Greek-born Canadian developer Andreas Apostolopoulos bid $583,000 to purchase the stadium and took ownership of the venue for approximately one percent of the price of building the dome. Reportedly, Apostolopoulos invested another $6 million in the project and was able to reopen the next year, staging soccer matches, boxing and monster truck shows.

Then, in 2013, an accumulation of snow and strong winds caused a section of the roof to tear — leaving a gash that some believed symbolized southeast Michigan's overall decay. Without a suitable company to repair the aging, air-supported building, and the city already unable to pay for police, emergency services and road maintenance, the Silverdome closed for good.

Whatever remained of value was auctioned off in 2014 and, for several years, the parking lot where wrestling fans gleefully tailgated was used to stockpile recalled Volkswagen vehicles.

Thirty years after *WrestleMania III*, a series of controlled explosions were detonated to collapse the beams supporting the Silverdome's upper deck. But like everything else tied to the venue in recent years, the effort failed, and demolition crews returned the next day to complete the job. Whatever remained was dismantled in sections with hydraulic excavators, with the final portion coming down in March 2018.

By 2021, an Amazon distribution and delivery center stood on the site, the shrine to Vince McMahon's infinite ambition now just one more bastion in Jeff Bezos's expanding realm.

CHAPTER 36

To World Class Championship Wrestling producer Keith Mitchell, the success of *WrestleMania III* strengthened his commitment to remaining in the wrestling business. Rather than look for opportunities in other production venues, "I realized that this could be a permanent career choice."

As the years passed, Mitchell would enhance his reputation as a television professional without ever landing in WWE, working instead for WCW, Total Nonstop Action (TNA), Ring of Honor (ROH) and AEW.

Still, in 1987, it had become apparent that WCCW had become too dysfunctional for him to grow there.

With his brain chemistry apparently altered by his 1985 bout with toxic shock syndrome, Mike von Erich continued to act out in ways that were inconsistent with his prior personality. In February 1987, he was ordered to pay $900 to a Fort Worth man after kicking in his car door. Then, in April, police pulled over Von Erich on Highway 377 after seeing him driving erratically. Inside the vehicle were 78 pills, including painkillers, barbiturates and anxiety medication. Hoping to spare WCCW another embarrassment, he offered an officer a bribe and was placed under arrest.

A family attorney was sent to bail him out. But when his family tried reaching him afterwards, he didn't respond. At his apartment, a note was found: "PLEASE UNDERSTAND I'M A FUCK-UP! I'M SORRY."

Along the side of the page, he'd written, "I love U Kerry, Kevin & your families."

Yet, there was no sign of Mike. His car was soon located at the entrance of a park near Lewisville Lake. Inside, another note read, "Mom and Dad, I'm in a better place. I'll be watching."

Everyone who cared about Mike resigned themselves to what undoubtably occurred. Several hours later, a police dog found the 23-year-old's body in a sleeping bag in a heavily wooded area. The official cause of death was acute Placidyl intoxication.

It was April 12, 1987 — exactly two weeks after *WrestleMania III*. But this time, nobody was faulting Vince McMahon.

"All that tragedy wore the territory down," said Mitchell. "It took a lot of steam out of the territory."

No longer were the brothers perceived as clean-living Christian role models. "The deaths showed them to be fallible human beings," said former WCCW director Dan Bynum. "And that was so incredibly disappointing to fans that it destroyed a lot of support for the promotion."

The annual Parade of Champions card in May was now renamed to honor both David and Mike. Less than 6,000 spectators trickled into Texas Stadium to watch Kevin defend the promotion's World Heavyweight Championship against Nord the Barbarian, a mid-card powerhouse who'd later perform as the Berzerker in the WWF.

"It was approximately what they'd draw at the Sportatorium almost every Friday night when WCCW was hot," noted Dave Meltzer.

At this stage, it was understood that business was never going to rebound. In 1989, Memphis promoter Jerry Jarrett purchased 60 percent of WCCW — the Von Erichs continued to hold on to the rest — and attempted to merge it with his territory, creating a new organization called the United States Wrestling Association (USWA). The two wrestling philosophies did not mesh, and the arrangement fell apart in 1990.

Just prior to uniting with World Class, Jarrett vainly attempted to work out a similar deal with the AWA. In the meantime, after experiencing moderate success with Rick Martel as his kingpin, Gagne now decided to crown 29-year-old Curt Hennig, having him upend Nick Bockwinkel at a special event called *SuperClash II* on May 2, 1987, at the Cow Palace, just outside San Francisco — albeit with the assistance of a roll of quarters provided by Gagne's real-life son-in-law, Larry Zbyszko.

"The original plan was for the finish to be overturned and then Curt was going to take an offer from the WWF," said Dave Meltzer. "I was actually with Louie Dondero and he told me, 'I have a scoop for you. Curt's coming in.' But then, someone else called me and said, 'Verne decided not to reverse the decision and Curt's going to stay.' And Louie said, 'No, no, no, no,' and called Curt right in front of me. And Curt confirmed that he was keeping the title."

As magnetic, athletic and wise to the ways of the business as he might have been, Hennig would not become a superstar until he went to the WWF and was rebranded "Mr. Perfect." Although he held the AWA World Heavyweight Championship for more than a year and rarely had an off night, he was still largely seen as AWA regular Larry "The Ax" Hennig's son.

It would take Vince McMahon to turn him into a pro wrestling luminary.

During the same period, the Midnight Rockers, Shawn Michaels and Marty Jannetty made the decision to defect to the WWF while still holding the AWA World Tag Team Championship, forcing the Minnesota promotion to quickly have them drop the straps to Soviet heels Boris Zhukov and Soldat Ustinov on May 25, 1987.

Five days later, McMahon unveiled the dynamic tandem at a house show in what was once the bosom of the AWA: St. Paul, Minnesota. Against the WWF World Tag Team Champions, the Hart Foundation, the renamed Rockers showed how exciting the future could be in the growing organization — particularly when Shawn was in the ring against the man who would arguably become his greatest rival, Bret "Hit Man" Hart.

But the run only lasted a few weeks before the newcomers were fired. Although a flurry of reasons was cited, the most accurate and all-encompassing one would be the duo's overall immaturity.

No longer in a position to hold a grudge, Gagne welcomed back the troubled pair and even had them win the titles again.

Ultimately, though, talent like Hennig, Jannetty and Michaels were too good for this incarnation of the AWA, and soon all three were reunited in Stamford.

"After *WrestleMania III*, it was all over for mostly everybody," Greg Gagne admitted. "Vince had the talent, and he had the television stations and you couldn't compete with that. I told Verne all the time, 'Why don't you just retire?' But he wasn't a quitter."

During the period when Jerry Jarrett and Gagne were attempting to forge their own axis, the Memphis promotion arranged for their number one babyface — and co-owner — Jerry "The King" Lawler to win the AWA World Heavyweight Championship. Lawler had become a national name through his high visibility in Bill Apter's magazines as well as the feud with Andy Kaufman. When Gagne finally decided to stage his first pay-per-view, *SuperClash III*, in Chicago in 1988, the main event featured a unification match between Lawler and World Class kingpin Kerry von Erich.

Still, just slightly more than 1,000 fans were in the building and — with so much emphasis on both the WWF and NWA — only the most hardcore followers ordered the event. As the representatives of the various promotions bickered backstage, Lawler became the "Unified World Champion" when the match was stopped because Kerry was bleeding.

Video of *SuperClash III* circulated among WWF officials, who noted the competitors who stood out and added them to the list of names they planned to acquire.

In the aftermath, Lawler claimed that he never received his promised portion of the pay-per-view revenue and refused to defend the AWA's own title on the organization's cards, forcing the group to strip him of the championship. Given the funds that he said he was owed, the King held on to the AWA belt out of spite, forcing Gagne to spend the money to make a new one. It would later be displayed in a glass case in Lawler's bar and grill in downtown Memphis.

With options dwindling, Gagne had Zbyszko win the AWA strap following an 18-man battle royal in 1989. As amusing as Zbyszko could be on the mic, he was not regarded as being on the same level as Gagne and Bockwinkel in their respective primes, or even Hennig and Lawler more recently.

Verne stubbornly stayed in business, but whatever fan appeal the company once had was swiftly dissolving.

In Houston, promoter Paul Boesch made the dramatic decision to align himself with McMahon after *WrestleMania III*. In place of the weekly show featuring UWF talent, fans tuning into the Houston promotion's time slot now received WWF syndicated programming featuring former Mid-South mainstays like Jake Roberts, Hacksaw Jim Duggan, Nikolai Volkoff, One Man Gang, Butch Reed and the Junkyard Dog. As in Quebec, local announcers were used, apparently, to translate Vince's product for entrenched audience members.

Although he'd live for two more years, Boesch received a wrestling funeral of sorts on August 28, 1987, when the WWF staged a retirement show for him in Houston. This included a formal ceremony in which the ring was filled with longtime Boesch associates. A telegram was read from US Vice President George Herbert Walker Bush, whose congressional district had covered a chunk of western Houston. Facing the sellout crowd of 12,000, Boesch graciously wished McMahon continued success in the future.

All the dignitaries applauded except for Verne Gagne.

Mindful of the setting, the WWF made certain to include local touches like stationing former Mid-South booker Ernie "The Big Cat" Ladd in the corner of fellow Black stars Tony Atlas and JYD for their match with Kamala the Ugandan Giant and Sika the Wild Samoan, and teaming Mexican icon Mil Máscaras with Tito Santana against Demolition. To further appeal to the Latino audience, the babyfaces were led to the ring by Monterrey-born, Texas legend José "El Gran" Lothario, whose most celebrated accomplishment would turn out to be his training of Shawn Michaels earlier in the decade.

Even "Living Legend" Bruno Sammartino, who would journey far from the WWWF's northeastern base to defend his title on Boesch's shows, made an appearance, beating Hercules Hernandez via countout. The next night in Baltimore, Sammartino wrestled his last match ever, teaming with Hulk Hogan and defeating King Kong Bundy and the One Man Gang.

Like the disassembly of the Houston territory, Bruno's withdrawal from in-ring competition was akin to a beloved neighborhood sweet shop being bulldozed and replaced by an office tower. Perhaps the candy store had outgrown its purpose and failed to keep pace with the changes many associated with progress. But to those who cherished their memories, it was sad nonetheless.

Boesch's association with McMahon only lasted four months before misunderstandings prompted him to switch affiliations to Jimmy Crockett. But during the period when the WWF's version of Houston Wrestling aired in the region, the announce team included the future "Brother Love," Bruce Prichard.

Even before Bill Watts's decision to sell the UWF to Crockett in April 1987, Prichard could see that the company was no longer healthy. "'Frustration' would probably be the best word to describe it. There was always the promise that opportunities were coming to make more money. I remember rumblings that Bill was going to offer guaranteed contracts. But other than the top guys, there really wasn't a lot of money being made — and everyone was driving thousands of miles each week. Duggan leaving made things a lot worse. After JYD left, if there was one guy who Bill was going to fight to protect, it would have been Duggan.

"It was just a time of uneasiness. No one believed anything was going to change."

In October 1986, "Hot Stuff" Eddie Gilbert and his future wife Missy Hyatt had met with McMahon, and Prichard asked his friend to put in a word. For a period, it looked like the couple was going north. Hyatt even taped an interview segment called "Missy's Manor," which never aired. Then Watts offered to make Gilbert the booker alongside Ken Mantell. "He really wanted the opportunity to do that and prove himself," Prichard explained.

Still, once Gilbert made the introduction, Prichard's conversations with McMahon continued and increased in frequency. Just after *WrestleMania III*, the Texan agreed to join the WWF without being issued an official job title. "Vince asked me to sit in with different people in live events and TV and other areas. There were a lot of possibilities."

To ingratiate himself with his new employer, Prichard mentioned that he had a friend from the UWF who was also looking for a job. As a result, McMahon hired "Million Dollar Man" Ted DiBiase, as well.

"I went to my first TV in Worcester, Massachusetts," Prichard recalled. "Vince said, 'Hey, you're going to meet somebody at the airport and you can ride to TV together. I think you'll know him.' I get off the plane and go down to baggage claim. I look up and I see [Watts's stepson] Joel Watts. And what's going through my mind is, 'Should I hide? I don't want him to see me here and tell his father.' And then, Joel walks up to me and says, 'Hey, as soon as we get our bags, we'll rent the car to Worcester.'"

In the WWF, the two found a dressing room with an attitude far different than the one they'd left behind. However, some of the wrestlers were convinced that McMahon would never be able to top what he'd accomplished at *WrestleMania III*. "They were saying he'd blown it all on that one show," Prichard said. "That was the peak. But I started understanding Vince pretty quickly. In 1989, he was talking about having his own network. In 1993, he was thinking about taking the company public and the whole thing would be worth billions. Vince was rarely in the now. He was always looking ten years ahead."

Just as the organization was basking in the post-*WrestleMania* glow, though, an incident occurred that, in the recent past, would have been regarded as a fatal calamity.

In May 1987, the Iron Sheik needed a ride to a show in Asbury Park, New Jersey, and asked his in-ring enemy, flag-waving Hacksaw Jim Duggan, for a ride. Duggan said that they were cruising down the Garden State Parkway on a sunny afternoon when the former WWF World Heavyweight Champion suggested that they purchase some beer. Hacksaw was more of a pot guy than a beer guy, but they made a quick stop and the ride continued, with the pair both imbibing and passing around a series of joints.

They were about 30 minutes from their destination, passing Middletown, New Jersey, when the Sheik noticed that a police car was parked in the woods, its nose pointed out at the highway. When he voiced his concern to his companion, Duggan reassured him that nothing was wrong. While working for Watts, Hacksaw had been living in Louisiana, where drive-through daiquiri huts were common, and, by his estimation, law enforcement took a relaxed approach to drinking and driving.

The rules were apparently different in New Jersey. The pair were pulled over and the officer immediately noticed the smell of marijuana. Again, Duggan was unconcerned, believing that if he handed over his stash, he'd be allowed to proceed. Instead, both wrestlers were pulled out of the car, handcuffed and searched — while people drove by, taking in the sight. As the officer sifted through the Sheik's bag, he spotted an eight ball of cocaine, zipped it up and called for backup.

The pair were hauled to the local police substation, where two more grams of coke were uncovered. Duggan was charged with possession of less than an ounce of marijuana and drinking while driving, the Sheik with felony possession of cocaine. Regardless, both men believed that the cops would work with them, and, to a degree, they did.

The Sheik confided that the two were scheduled to wrestle each other in the main event in Asbury Park, wondering if it would be alright for them to come back another time and address the legal issues. Remarkably, they were issued summonses and driven back to the car.

As soon as they entered the arena, they were approached by George "The Animal" Steele — who was starting to work as a road agent — and fellow backstage employee and former champion Pedro Morales.

"What happened on the Garden State Parkway?" Steele asked the Sheik.

"Why?"

"People saw you."

"Did they see who was with me?"

"No."

The Sheik was relieved. To him, the arrest was secondary. As long as no one knew that the main-event rivals had been traveling together, the business was safe.

Pot smoking was a common diversion for the WWF talent, and the Sheik told Steele and Morales that marijuana was still burning in the ashtray when police stopped the car. What he didn't say was that law enforcement had also confiscated cocaine. Steele appeared relatively unconcerned and said that he knew a local police chief who could possibly fix the matter. Neither wrestler bothered to request that the matter be kept from Vince. The Animal was obviously on their side, and the two changed into their gear and had their usual match, sending the fans home happy.

After checking into their hotel, Duggan phoned his wife. "I got arrested for smoking marijuana and the Iron Sheik had cocaine," he told her. "But I don't think anybody knows about it."

The couple chatted for several minutes longer before Hacksaw hung up and went to sleep.

He was awoken early the next morning by a ringing telephone. Once again, his wife was on the other line. The two words she uttered next sent fear into his heart.

"*Everybody* knows."

The story was national news.

In the Atlanta suburbs, where the Sheik owned a home, his wife, Caryl, glanced at the *Atlanta Journal-Constitution* and was shocked to see coverage of the episode on page one. Mortified, she kept their three daughters home from school for three days.

Duggan phoned the office. Generally, if he called and asked for Vince McMahon, he was placed on hold for 15 to 20 minutes. This time, the boss was patched through immediately.

"Jim, what have you done to us?"

Both stars were instantly fired. At the next TV taping, McMahon stood in front of the entire roster and declared that neither would ever work for the company again. Maybe pro wrestling *was* sports entertainment, but when it came to bitter adversaries driving and drugging and getting arrested together, the boss was still old school.

But Vince modified his position. Within months, the pair was working house shows against each other again before Duggan was switched to a program against Harley Race. The Iron Sheik left the WWF in October but, by the next year, he was back on television.

In the end, the public didn't care. In fact, that confirmation that the battles between the ropes were not born of hatred but an elevated sense of showmanship seemed to stimulate the new breed of fans.

It wasn't good for business. But it wasn't entirely bad, either.

CHAPTER 37

McMahon's foray into Europe occurred much quicker than most observers anticipated.

"Vince was always looking for worldwide recognition," explained Jumping Jim Brunzell, "and the success of *WrestleMania III* just perpetuated the thought that we were an international company."

Some seven months after the event, the WWF crew boarded an airplane to Paris for a show at Bercy Arena on October 23, 1987. As in North America, McMahon made certain that his stars would receive maximum exposure during their short visit and arranged to have the card broadcast on Canal+, a premium channel with more than one million subscribers.

Although André was only making periodic appearances at this stage of his career, he was brought over for the show not as a wrestler but as a referee in a Harley Race–Junkyard Dog reprise from *WrestleMania III*. As expected, the Frenchman received an ovation when he came to the ring but quickly established himself as a heel, displaying a clear bias by holding open the ropes for fellow Bobby Heenan protégé Race and helping him off with his robe. By contrast, he took an authoritarian approach with JYD, questioning his tactics and outright refusing to count his pinfalls. Eventually, the Giant awarded the contest to Race via disqualification.

In a match featuring three other French speakers, Jacques and Raymond Rougeau tangled with former Montreal promoter Dino Bravo and Greg "The Hammer" Valentine.

The owner of one of the city's most exclusive nightclubs was in the front row and, after Raymond beat Valentine with a sunset flip, the brothers were invited to her venue.

When they arrived, they were introduced to actor Michael Douglas and Sade, the Nigerian-British singer who'd later be honored as an Officer of the Order of the British Empire. "I remember we were all sitting in a booth, just talking, and after about a half hour, Michael Douglas asked me if we could take a picture," Raymond said. "The photo ran in *Paris Match* and Michael Douglas made sure he had my information and sent it to me. The whole experience taught me that the WWF was different than everywhere else. Dusty Rhodes and Ric Flair weren't getting into these kinds of situations working for Jim Crockett. They were having cool experiences, but it wasn't at the same level."

Still, Crockett was trying very hard to get there.

In the week after *WrestleMania III*, he reportedly was planning to run the Silverdome, but wiser minds apparently prevailed on him to abort what certainly would have been an embarrassing showing.

Then, on September 25, 1987, "Hands of Stone" Ronnie Garvin defeated Flair for the NWA World Heavyweight Championship. In terms of working a hard-hitting, believable match, and taking and administering Flair's style of knife-edged chops, Garvin was in a special class. Yet, neither Rhodes nor Crockett viewed him as a long-term titlist and the plan was for Flair to win back the gold at *Starrcade*.

And this *Starrcade* would be different than those that came before. Dubbed *Chi-Town Heat*, the Thanksgiving show took place not in its traditional Greensboro location but at the UIC Pavilion on the University of Illinois–Chicago campus. It would also be JCP's first pay-per-view event.

Both decisions turned out to be abominations.

"Basically, the company was farting on the fans in Greensboro," said David Crockett.

Announcer Jim Ross, who was now part of the JCP team, had been a fan of *Starrcade* from the beginning and believed that, in its four short years, it had become an institution at the Greensboro Coliseum. "You don't walk away from something like that to a place that is not your home base. But Crockett and Dusty felt, 'We have to grow. We have to get big.' And Chicago was obviously bigger than Greensboro. But the people in Greensboro felt like they were no longer appreciated."

Yet, even though the event happened to be emanating from Chicago to Windy City residents, the UIC Pavilion was not a major building, said Crockett. "The look was not there. The system and the times for loading in were not great. I know I didn't sleep the entire day before because we were moving in and we spent all night programming lights. I think it snowed the next day, too. And so I was worried about the uplink. Luckily, we had a C-band uplink, which can burn through snow."

Although about 100 closed-circuit locations carried *Starrcade*, the pay-per-view audience would be limited — due to a number of maneuvers perpetrated by Vincent Kennedy McMahon.

"Pat Patterson was the architect of so much during this period," recalled B. Brian Blair. "He was a tremendous psychologist when it came to laying out a match and understanding what the fans wanted to see. And so he came up with the concept of the *Survivor Series*."

Instead of a rudimentary tag team or six-man match, the *Survivor Series* would consist of two teams of five to ten performers facing each other in an elimination contest. After each competitor was removed from the encounter, the teammates would continue, until one side was completely eradicated.

"It was a tremendous idea," Blair said. "Rather than having all the guys in the ring, tripping over each other, you had crowd control since there were only supposed to be two people in the ring at a time. You could work so many angles off of it. There was room for everybody to shine. It was different."

In the fall of 1987, plans were put in place to stage the first *Survivor Series* at the Richfield Coliseum outside Cleveland. It would take place on Thanksgiving — the very same night as *Starrcade*. "We did not anticipate that happening," said David Crockett. "But Vince knew what he was doing and created a new event just to hurt us."

Similarly, it was no accident that this particular show involved teams comprised of multiple athletes. Essentially, the *Survivor Series* was an amped-up version of the NWA's *War Games*, fueled by the WWF's star power. In fact, the two bouts were so similar that, in 2022 — 21 years after McMahon purchased WCW's assets, including what the organization had inherited from JCP — WWE combined *Survivor Series: War Games* into a single match.

At first, Jimmy Crockett hoped to turn a negative into a positive. If the *Survivor Series* was going to air after dark, JCP was willing to run *Starrcade* in the afternoon, allowing viewers to spend their holiday watching both shows. "The cable people I talked to thought they were going to have a windfall," Meltzer said. "They'd broadcast the two big ones on the same day and encourage people to buy both shows."

That's when McMahon delivered an ultimatum: any cable company that aired the NWA event was putting itself at risk of losing access to future WWF pay-per-views, including *WrestleMania*. "This is right after *WrestleMania III*, which I think had been the biggest pay-per-view event up to that point of time," said Meltzer. "If you were making decisions at a cable company, you did not want to miss out on *WrestleMania*.

"There were a couple of companies in the Carolinas that probably felt they'd do better running the Crockett show and maybe they did. And then there was a cable company in San Jose — my home city — that decided they'd made a promise to Crockett. The person there told me, 'We're going to lose money, but we gave our word.' This might have been the only guy in the frickin' world who cared about something like that. Everyone else also gave their word, and they just went with more money."

As a result of the executive's apparent principles, Meltzer was forced to drive to a friend's house 45 minutes away to watch the WWF show.

"We couldn't see the *Survivor Series* here because we had the one company where the guy gave his word, and his word was good."

On those systems where *Starrcade* was available, the event — highlighted by Flair regaining the NWA World Heavyweight Championship following a bloodbath in a cage with Garvin — was reportedly ordered in 20,000 homes. Given the obstacles McMahon deliberately set up, it was a respectable number but nowhere close to the more than 300,000 buys the *Survivor Series* is said to have garnered.

"I was hating Vince quite a lot," said David Crockett. "Quite a lot. It was, 'Yeah, you son of a bitch.' But, if the roles were reversed, I would have done it to him."

Steve Taylor would not fully understand his boss's philosophical motivations until the company purchased WCW. "I was part of a group that flew down to WCW headquarters to go to their warehouse to see what we wanted to load up on trucks and bring to Stamford. I was talking to Vince about it and said, 'Wow. Suddenly, all these people were just put out of business.' And he goes, 'Hey. It could have been them coming to our headquarters and then you'd be out of a job. Don't feel bad. We won.'"

CHAPTER 38

Just before Christmas in 1987, the WWF presented its second annual Slammy Awards ceremony at Caesars Atlantic City. The pro wrestling spoof on the Oscars was deliberately campy, with members of the Heenan stable receiving a Bobby "The Brain" Heenan Scholarship Award, "Million Dollar Man" Ted DiBiase using his purported funds to have himself designated Humanitarian of the Year, and George "The Animal" Steele edging out Koko B. Ware's bird, Jake Roberts's snake and the British Bulldogs' canine to receive a Best Performance by an Animal honor.

But the most memorable portion of the event occurred when Vince McMahon performed a song and dance, warning all business competitors that they'd never stand a chance.

With high-haired showgirls sashaying across the stage in glistening outfits, Hulk Hogan strummed a bass guitar behind a rhythm section that included the Killer Bees and a shirtless JYD. Nearby, a lost-looking George Steele shook a tambourine. On the opposite end of the platform, Roberts, Brutus Beefcake and Randy "Macho Man" Savage, who'd recently been born again as a babyface, played faux trumpets.

As the music reached a crescendo, McMahon burst out in a black jumpsuit over a white, open-collar shirt. Shaking their bodies, the dancers moved alongside and circled the owner, striking provocative poses. In yet another act of intrepid fearlessness, McMahon then held the mic to his lips and sang:

> *When I was just a boy, everybody told me,*
> *What I should do and who I should be*
> *I've got some advice I finally have to say,*
> *"Stand back."*

The women sang along, "*Stand back.*"

"*Stand back,*" Vince replied in his baritone.

When the song lapsed into an instrumental, McMahon and the dancers lined up, glancing sideways at the audience while the mogul wiggled his mighty hips.

Had social media existed at the time, the posts from Bob Geigel, Buddy Fuller and Ole Anderson might have turned out to be as timeless as the routine itself.

Vince pledged,

> *Never slowing down,*
> *And I'm never gonna stop,*
> *On the way, you're gonna see a lot of men drop* [pointing to
> the ground].
> *Baby, watch 'em drop.*
> *Baby, ba–bbbbby.*

He ended the song by sinking to his knees, flanked by the seemingly adoring showgirls.

As ostentatious as the act may have been, it was also well-earned. Over the past 12 months, McMahon had changed wrestling like no one before. Even casual followers no longer viewed *WrestleMania* as a curiosity. What occurred at the Silverdome had convinced people that this was a pilgrimage all should experience at least once in their lives.

"When you're sitting at home and the camera pans over that large crowd, it makes you go, 'Oh god, I want to be there, too,'" said Jimmy Hart.

"People remember *WrestleMania 1* for all the bells and whistles," noted Jerry Brisco. "People don't really remember *WrestleMania 2*. But *WrestleMania III* — it just set the scene for all the other *WrestleMania*s."

By *WrestleMania IV*, the WWF's new vice president of live events promotion, Bob Collins, was finding ways to transform the spectacular from a one-time affair to an extended fan experience, organizing a "Bacon, Bagels and Biceps" breakfast with guest talent, a special dinner the night before *Mania* and a 5K run and children's race on the boardwalk in Atlantic City, New Jersey — where future US President, and WWE Hall of Famer, Donald Trump's hotel and casino, Trump Plaza was sponsoring the show.

Collins's confusion about why the public was watching *WrestleMania III* instead of attending the Ice Capades had opened his eyes to an entertainment form he'd never studied.

Without realizing it, Collins was all but destined to be in the wrestling business, having spent much of his childhood in Sarasota, Florida, where, in 1927, John Ringling moved the winter quarters of his Ringling Bros. and Barnum & Bailey Circus. The decision meant that clowns, trapeze artists, tightrope walkers and lion tamers all relocated nearby, deeply influencing Sarasota culture.

Eventually, Collins became the circus's regional marketing director and even met Pat Patterson when, as one of the San Francisco territory's headliners, the future McMahon deputy rode an elephant as part of a cross-promotional campaign.

Collins would discover that there were many parallels between the circus and wrestling in terms of the barnstorming, sleight of hand, even the use of carny to cut the uninitiated out of the conversation.

In the months after *WrestleMania III*, the WWF reached out to him after receiving a recommendation from the former president of the Ice

Capades. Like Steve Taylor, Basil Devito and Dick Glover before him, Collins was ready to make the leap.

"What startled me more than anything else was that the Ice Capades played in a lot of the same venues," Collins said. "But I really had to work my ass off to sell tickets to the Ice Capades. The WWF would go to the same place and sell the place out. They could just rely on their formula of selling the show on TV because all they had to do was put these great entertainers in front of the camera, and everyone knew how to generate excitement.

"I was also blown away by the size of the crowds, and the number of children in attendance who knew all the characters and the stories behind them. So now, the challenge was just making that audience bigger."

One of Collins's main missions was finding sponsors for *WrestleMania*, and the revelry in Atlantic City was a small window into the WWE Fan Axxess festivals and other adjunct events that would turn the week of the extravaganza into a holiday for devotees. In the short term, the gatherings that preceded *WrestleMania IV* were well-received. But from the perspective of many fans, the Trump Plaza tie-in was problematic.

Since Trump ended up sponsoring both *WrestleMania IV* and *V*, prime seating was reserved for big spenders at his casino, regardless of their level of fandom, leaving superfans like Vladimir Abouzeide and Charlie Adorno feeling pushed aside. "The best tickets we were able to get was in the fifth row," said Adorno. "They wouldn't even sell the first four rows because they would give them to high rollers. It felt like a step down."

When Tom Buchanan observed the crowd at ringside, he could tell by their lukewarm reactions that they didn't share the level of conviction he encountered everywhere else. "It was dreadful. The sound didn't carry. The venue was terrible. But we still had the genetics of *WrestleMania III* in us, and we understood that we could go back to that kind of spectacle again. And we did."

After being upstaged by the creation of the *Survivor Series*, Jim Crockett Jr. appeared to be reeling. But just as he'd wrested away the TBS slot in 1984, McMahon's rival kept flailing at the WWF until he finally connected with a punch that did some noticeable damage.

By design, the incident occurred on the same day as *WrestleMania IV*.

After Crockett scheduled another pay-per-view, *Bunkhouse Stampede* — held in Vince's backyard, the Nassau Veterans Memorial Coliseum in the Long Island suburbs — for January 1988, the WWF managed to cut his buy rate again, simultaneously airing the debut *Royal Rumble* broadcast on the USA cable network. But Crockett finally managed to do the same thing to Vince, reducing *WrestleMania IV* sales by programming the first *Clash of the Champions* special on TBS.

On this one night, Crockett's decisions to secure a spot on TBS and purchase the UWF seemed to pay off. Although a sizeable number of Bill Watts's former wrestlers felt like they were underutilized in JCP, *Clash of the Champions* is remembered for elevating former UWF standout Sting, who fought NWA World Heavyweight Champion Ric Flair to an electrifying 45-minute draw. By the time the show ended, the 29-year-old had graduated from a promising talent to an undisputed superstar.

Much of this had to do with the Nature Boy's ability to, as he was fond of boasting, engage in a classic with a broom. But Sting proved that he had the capacity to hang with him, and Crockett provided both men with a meaningful forum to showcase their skills.

Interestingly, the backlash against JCP for presenting the show did not come from Stamford. "There was pushback from the cable operators," said David Crockett. "They were mad at us for putting on a free special because a lot of people decided to watch it instead of *WrestleMania*. They said we were taking money from them and called Ted [Turner] and threatened to pull [his networks] TBS and CNN off their cable systems. Which Ted probably did not take kindly to."

While Vince would have countered with a threat equally as alarming to the cable companies, Jimmy Crockett did not have that leverage. The debt from the UWF television contracts, expenses paid to tour cities where the promotion didn't draw, unnecessary spending on limousines, private air travel and a Dallas office, and inconclusive finishes to important matches had all conspired to weigh the company down. Before it all crashed, Ted Turner stepped in and purchased majority interest in JCP.

"The only thing Vince had to do was wait around and things would fall apart," Jim Ross observed. "They were going to run out of cash, and they did. And then, Turner got the company for a pretty good deal."

Crockett still had a minority stake as well as a consultant's title, but in the not-too-distant future, Turner executives would be making a disproportionate number of big decisions.

That included identifying the promotion by the name Jim Barnett had imported back from Australia, World Championship Wrestling (WCW).

The stage was set for the Monday Night Wars of the 1990s. But that's a story for another book. And a lot was going to transpire in the interim.

CHAPTER 39

A ndré didn't simply pass the torch to Hulk Hogan.

As his health and mobility continued to disintegrate, the Giant seemed to know that the business would move on without him. But before he went away, there were a few gifts that he wanted to bestow. From his visits to Calgary, André had watched Bret Hart develop from a promising teen with an amateur background to the versatile tag team specialist he had become in the Hart Foundation. Although he was still largely a tag team performer, the Hit Man had shown his potential as a singles standout, and André wanted to give him the opportunity to do it on a large stage.

On April 8, 1989, the WWF was in Milan for an event broadcast live on Tele2. Because of his stature, and the novelty of a pro wrestling special emanating from Italy's fashion capital, the Giant knew that whomever he wrestled that night would receive an outsized amount of attention. So he deliberately requested a one-on-one confrontation with the Hit Man.

As predicted, André dominated and won the match, but he allowed — and encouraged — Hart to display enough to open observers' eyes to the possibility of this second-generation star representing the future.

When André died in 1993, the WWF was as hot in Europe as it had been in North America during the time of the Rock 'n' Wrestling Connection. The trend was largely powered by children and their excitement for youthful, versatile talent like Shawn Michaels, the Undertaker, British Bulldog Davey Boy Smith and Mr. Perfect. But, as the "Excellence of Execution," Bret Hart — who began the first of his five WWF World Heavyweight Championship reigns in 1992 — arguably stood out from all others.

Bret described André's generous decision in Milan as a pivotal moment in his ascent.

Unfortunately, the Hart family's promotion did not fare as well.

Despite presenting absorbing content, Stampede Wrestling suffered from financial challenges and internal clashes — common trials in smaller promotions attempting to stay afloat without the budget or visibility of the WWF or WCW of that era. Although numerous efforts would be made over the next two decades to revive the company, the promotion officially closed at the end of 1989.

The AWA would only stay in the game slightly longer. In its waning days, sales representative Eric Bischoff was brought in to do backstage interviews and eventually take over as host of the television show. Still, the company was virtually broke, and Bischoff auditioned for an announcer's spot in the WWF in 1990. He didn't get the job, but used the knowledge he garnered in the AWA to eventually become the executive producer and senior vice president of WCW, managing to beat the WWF in the ratings for 83 straight weeks, starting in 1996.

With little talent and an ESPN contract still in place, the AWA reportedly planned to put its championship on Sergeant Slaughter, who — because of a highly charged feud with the Iron Sheik in the WWF and his popular action figure — had name recognition. But in 1990, Vince brought Slaughter back, changing his character to a contemptible turncoat to coincide with the buildup to the first Gulf War.

In yet another affront to Verne Gagne, Vince put the belt on Slaughter just as he did with Hulk Hogan.

The ESPN relationship fell apart and, in early 1991, Verne Gagne shuttered the AWA and applied for bankruptcy.

Meanwhile, the WWF continuously tweaked its business model to keep pace with the changing times. "You had this evolution where closed-circuit represented the biggest portion of the major shows," explained Dick Glover, "and then, every year, home pay-per-view became bigger and bigger. And then, as cable became more mature, closed-circuit stopped completely."

As did the territories, for all intents and purposes, leaving McMahon with a wider pool of seasoned wrestling advisors to help him expand his product.

Long before there was a WWE Performance Center, McMahon began using the Memphis territory as a developmental league, allowing young wrestlers like Dwayne "The Rock" Johnson — then called Flex Kavana — to gain experience there. The relationship began in 1993 when the group's top star, Jerry "The King" Lawler, began a rivalry with Bret Hart in the WWF. As part of the arrangement, both Hart and Lawler would also feud in Memphis, but with a twist. "Jerry was still a face on Memphis TV and a heel everywhere else," said Jeff Jarrett, the son of Memphis co-owner Jerry Jarrett and a future WWE Hall of Famer. "And in Memphis, Bret was the heel."

In fact, it was in Memphis where Vince first tried out the evil "Mr. McMahon" character that would become the foil for "Stone Cold" Steve Austin during the WWF's Attitude Era later in the decade.

More significantly, after federal prosecutors indicted Vince McMahon for alleged steroid distribution, Jerry Jarrett was commissioned to run the WWF in the event that the mogul was convicted.

As it turned out, McMahon was acquitted after an 18-day trial in 1994 and the alliance — like so many others in pro wrestling — broke up, with the Jarretts raising the capital to start the Total Nonstop Action (TNA) promotion as a WWE alternative in 2002.

After selling his business to Crockett, Bill Watts watched from the sidelines as Turner Broadcasting took charge, then, in 1992, took a job with WCW himself, holding the position of executive vice president for less than a year.

In 1995, he accepted a three-month gig with the WWF, joining the booking team. "Vince and I were able to work together because we booked the same way," Watts said. "For example, Vince knew who he wanted for his main event at *WrestleMania*. The whole thing was putting the stories in place to get you to *WrestleMania*. You knew what the blow-offs were going to be there, and what you were going to follow it with. You always had something ready so you didn't have that precipitous drop-off afterwards."

Still, Watts said that he noticed an erosion in some of the basic pro wrestling concepts that existed before the WWF's explosion. "I was amazed that when I'd lay out a match for two guys, they needed an hour to sit there and plan out every single high spot. I couldn't believe how the business had changed in just a few years. They couldn't be spontaneous. They couldn't work. All they could do was routines."

Yet, despite that — and everything else that had transpired in the years leading up to *WrestleMania III* — Watts asserted that his relationship with the company remained respectful. He was inducted into the WWE Hall of Fame in 2009. Three years later, WWE acquired the entire Mid-South and UWF archive — with the exception of Paul Boesch's Houston programs on KHTV — eventually airing the broadcasts on the WWE Network.

Verne Gagne was inducted in 2006, the same year his son Greg also took a job with WWE, working as a road agent as well as with aspiring stars in the Ohio Valley Wrestling (OVW) developmental league, a small outfit operating on the border of Kentucky and Indiana.

Just as his father had overseen the coaching of future superstars like Flair, the Iron Sheik, Slaughter and Steamboat, the younger Gagne found himself advising such talent as Cody Rhodes and CM Punk. "I was trying to teach these kids to let their inner personalities come out," Gagne said. "'Let's see who you really are. That's how you're going to get over.' I like to think I helped them."

As McMahon was attempting to appropriate Europe into his own large territory, Joint Promotions in the UK was trending in the direction of World Class Championship Wrestling from Florida and Lutte Internationale in Quebec.

Once ITV began swapping Joint's television shows with programs produced by Brian Dixon's All Star group and the WWF, interest in the established entity dissipated. In 1991, Max Crabtree's promotion, now called Ring Wrestling Stars (RWS), was touring small buildings, still relying on the formula of teaming Big Daddy with a young, athletic partner who did most of the work in the match. But Big Daddy didn't mean as much to a younger generation who'd seen Hulk Hogan, Randy "Macho Man" Savage, the Ultimate Warrior and the Undertaker. Plus, the one-time headliner was in poor health. A stroke in late 1993 forced him out of the business entirely.

Max Crabtree limped along, slotting British Bulldog Davey Boy Smith to the top of cards during a period when he became disaffected with the WWF. But after the differences were repaired in 1994, the Bulldog returned to Stamford. RWS continued to run shows for less than a year before closing for good in February 1995.

Although All Star was off the air by 1988, Dixon was never overly dependent on television and continued promoting his venues, sometimes playing off storylines that fans had seen during the brief period when the show was on ITV. Of these, nothing seemed to generate as much interest as the angle in which exotic Kendo Nagasaki hypnotized a young Robbie Brookside into turning on Steve Regal (William Regal) and other allies. Because All Star no longer had television, fans were forced to go to the arena to experience the next chapter in the saga. The promotion's schedule only brought it to certain locations sporadically, allowing Dixon to keep this angle going literally for years.

But both Brookside and Regal were spending less time in England by this point. Starting in 1988, they were accompanying friends like Pete Roberts, Terry Rudge and Dave Taylor on international tours. In France and Spain, Regal grew accustomed to working the right side of an opponent's body — the way it's done in Mexico — as opposed to the rest of Europe, where applying moves to a foe's left allowed him to use his free, right arm to make a comeback.

Brookside looked forward to summer visits to Germany, where promoters would put up a circus tent for weeks and house the talent in caravans on the grounds. "I loved it, not having to be stuck in the car like sardines. You could walk out of the caravan and be in the locker room in 30 seconds."

Always, he maintained his fondness for All Star and usually worked for Dixon during trips back to the UK. This continued into the early part of the 21st century when some British promoters began discarding the old rules and staging American-style WWF "tribute shows." Rather than featuring established British names, the cards consisted of unknowns cosplaying WWF stars and using gimmicks like "UK Undertaker and the "Big Red Machine" — the nickname used by the Undertaker's gimmick "half-brother" Kane. When Yokozuna — whose obesity issues caused the WWF to release him in 1998 — died in his sleep from pulmonary edema during an All Star tour in 2000, the group alienated much of the industry by continuing to advertise him.

"The tribute shows were a mistake," said Brookside, "especially for a company that always had such good wrestlers. Where I drew the line is when they wanted me to be a fake Edge," the so-called Rated-R Superstar who'd hold 31 championships in WWE. "I'm not that desperate. I'd rather go and stack shelves at Tesco than do that to myself."

CHAPTER 40

T he stigma attached to pro wrestling did not entirely vanish after *WrestleMania III*. But the enormity of the event forced some people to reevaluate their biases. Even if the motive was completely capitalistic, the business and entertainment communities had opened themselves up to the benefits of working with the WWF, and by the early 1990s, the mainstream media was gradually acknowledging Dave Meltzer's journalistic tenacity, enabling him to more fully embrace the trailblazing mission that Bruiser Brody — who'd been stabbed to death in a locker room shower in Bayamón, Puerto Rico, in 1988 — charted for him.

While much of the press initially ignored Meltzer's coverage of steroid abuse in the industry, in time, the *Wrestling Observer Newsletter* founder became a source for news outlets around the world. "They didn't want to touch it at first because it was wrestling and nobody took it seriously," he recalled. "But I wrote about it so much that they had to. And then the WWF started drug testing. I was talking to Vince McMahon about it a lot at the time and believe if I wasn't there, this wouldn't have happened.

"I like to think that, in the long run, maybe this saved some lives. Because it always bothered me that when a wrestler died, people outside the business acted like it was a cartoon character. And it wasn't a cartoon character. It was a human being. Many times, I knew them and their friends and their wives and their kids. And I wanted these kids to have their fathers."

While Meltzer's involvement in the business intensified over the decades, once Tom Buchanan stepped away from the WWF in 2001, he turned his back not only on pro wrestling but photography in general.

"When I left the job, the cameras went away," he said. Instead, he moved to Vermont and became a recreation guide and instructor, specializing in skiing, snowboarding and fly fishing. "I don't even own a camera anymore, just my cell phone."

New York superfans Vladimir Abouzeide and Charlie Adorno became so ever-present at events like *WrestleMania* that the company allowed them to reserve tickets for major shows before everyone else. "They always made sure we had good seats and would come over and talk to us to see that we were comfortable," said Adorno. "Sometimes, they brought a t-shirt or another piece of merchandise. We never asked for anything for free, but they'd do it because they got to know us and just wanted to be nice."

The pair would attend every *WrestleMania* except *WrestleMania 36*, which, due to COVID restrictions, was shot at the WWE Performance Center over a five-day period in front of only essential personnel — with the wrestlers coming and going in shifts to avoid unnecessary interactions. Even then, there was talk of hiring Vladimir and Charlie temporarily simply to keep their streak going. "Unfortunately, it didn't pan out," Adorno said. "The law is the law, and they could only have a certain amount of people in the building at a time."

Once restrictions were lifted, Abouzeide — the subject of a 2023 WWE documentary, *Superfan: The Story of Vladimir* — resumed his attendance, even after being diagnosed with Parkinson's. Since he had difficulty walking at times, he was assisted by Charlie and other friends he'd made in the wrestling community and had become so recognizable that ring announcers tended to point him out at smaller wrestling shows. "When I was a teenager, Vladimir told my mother he'd always look after me," Adorno remembered. "Now, it's my job to look after him."

Although it's been decades since Vince Averill last saw Bobby Regal, whose birthday party at the Pontiac Silverdome had a permanent impact on the Michigan boy's life, the tour manager, musician and comedian still tries to attend most *WrestleMania*s. Even during periods when his interest in the One True Sport waned, Averill remained a steadfast *Observer* reader and returned to the fold each season to ensure that he could follow the storylines leading to the annual event.

"To this day, when I'm talking to someone who doesn't have a clue about wrestling, they call it '*WrestleMania*,'" Averill said, "even if they're talking about a house show. And that's because of Hulk Hogan and André the Giant. That's because *WrestleMania III* is the cornerstone of what the whole business became."

The pandemic prompted WWE to expand *WrestleMania 36* to two nights for viewers largely confined to their homes. But when the company decided to allow spectators back at *WrestleMania 37* in 2021, the decision was made to continue the format, enabling WWE to fill up a stadium on two consecutive days and generate twice the revenue.

Three years later, at *WrestleMania XL* at Lincoln Financial Field in Philadelphia, WWE implemented a new storytelling device, ending Night One with a cliffhanger leading into Night Two. In this particular case, it involved the first night culminating with WWE Universal Champion Roman Reigns and his cousin Dwayne "The Rock" Johnson defeating Dusty Rhodes's son, "The American Nightmare" Cody Rhodes, and Seth Rollins. According to the stipulations established beforehand, Rhodes would challenge for the title on Night Two, but Roman had won the right to set the rules, fortifying the contender's position as an underdog. Hence, his eventual victory was more emotional and more satisfying.

Having learned the art of connecting with the disenfranchised from his father, Cody characterized his title as a symbol of retribution for everyone accustomed to being sold short.

"Once undesirable," the son of a son of a plumber — who had to leave WWE and play a leading role in the launch of AEW before the company welcomed him back — described himself, "now undeniable."

Despite fans smartening up to the business over the decades, 37 years after *WrestleMania III*, a good babyface promo and the slaying of a giant — for Rhodes, that was Reigns, whose 1,316-day reign was the longest since the Hogan years — could always pop the crowd.

Still, what was novel in 1987 has become standard in some ways. The completion of each *WrestleMania* is generally followed by a press conference and release, listing records broken. *WrestleMania XL*, for instance, boasted the highest gate ever for a WWE event the moment that tickets went on sale eight months before the show. On each night, the company said, more than 70,000 people packed the Philadelphia Eagles' stadium, resulting in a cumulative total of more than 145,000 witnesses, while records were set for merchandise, viewership, social media and sponsorships.

Among those sponsors were Snickers and *WWE 2K24*, the 24th installment of the company's video game series, both of which were listed as "presenting partners" of *WrestleMania*. Wheatley Vodka was labeled the event's official vodka. PRIME — a beverage co-owned by English Internet personality, boxer and musician KSI and WWE United States Champion Logan Paul, a social media influencer with more than 23 million YouTube channel subscribers — was the "official hydration drink partner" and the first sponsor whose logo ever appeared in the center of the WWE ring.

There was also a PRIME energy drink "hydration station" at ringside, allowing the Rock — arguably the biggest star in Hollywood — to openly take a gulp of the elixir on Night One before expectorating it into Rollins's face.

Almost a year to the day earlier, the Monday after *WrestleMania 39* began with the confirmation of the rumor that the company had been sold. In fact, WWE was fusing with the Ultimate Fighting Championship (UFC) into one massive combat sports enterprise, TKO, a division of Endeavor Group Holdings Inc., which was founded in April 2009 after the merger of the William Morris Agency and Endeavor Talent Agency. Endeavor would now hold 51 percent of the controlling interest in TKO, compared to the 49 percent held by WWE shareholders.

Combined, both WWE and UFC were projected to reach more than a billion fans in 180 countries and produce more than 350 annual live events.

Initially, Vince McMahon was slated to be TKO's executive chairman. But by the time of *WrestleMania XL*, the man who'd commanded his minions to sell out the Silverdome would be exiled. The news was announced the night before the 2024 *Royal Rumble*, following a lawsuit by a former female employee alleging sexual assault, exploitation and trafficking. The plaintiff's attorney would describe McMahon's behavior as being "in its own class of depravity."

In other words, like his vision to make *WrestleMania III* the model for every supershow that followed, even McMahon's alleged perversions belonged in a category too elaborate for most humans to imagine.

By the following morning, his profile on the WWE website was inaccessible.

During an earnings call later that year, TKO President Mark Shapiro asserted, "We don't talk to him . . . He doesn't work for the company. He doesn't work at the company. He doesn't come into the offices. He's not coming back to the company."

Yet, with or without Dr. Frankenstein, the monster created in his lab still walked the earth, more daunting than ever before,

Just three days before McMahon's resignation, WWE announced that *Monday Night Raw* would be shown in the US on Netflix, starting in January 2025. The ten-year deal would earn the company about $5.2 billion, according to multiple reports. Outside the US, the streaming service would broadcast the company's premium live events (PLEs) — the term "pay-per-view" was discarded by WWE following the advent of streaming — along with the organization's other marquee programs.

As part of another ten-year accord, signed with the government of Saudi Arabia in 2018, WWE began presenting two streaming events from the oil-rich kingdom each year, receiving a reported $50 million per show — or $100 million in addition to the money garnered at *WrestleMania*.

The year before McMahon's permanent departure, WWE generated $1.326 billion in revenue. The market capitalization, or total value of the shares of stock for WWE, along with UFC under TKO Group Holdings, was just under $14 billion.

Regardless, McMahon was now gone, his achievements relegated to history. When *WrestleMania XL* began, instead of Vince on the big stage leading to the entrance ramp, there was his son-in-law Paul "Triple H" Levesque, the company's creative mastermind in recent years and architect of WWE's highly touted developmental system, shouting into a microphone: "Welcome to a new time. Welcome to a new era. Welcome to . . . *WrestleMania!*"

To underscore the point that the organization had severed ties to Vince, the mogul's own daughter — and Triple H's wife — Stephanie McMahon used the event to publicly announce her return to WWE, after resigning as co-CEO in January 2023 when her father was said to have maneuvered his way back to the company following a previous resignation tied to the sexual misconduct allegations.

At the start of Night Two, she greeted the crowd, stressing that, although she'd attended each prior *WrestleMania*, she was probably most proud of this one because "this is the first *WrestleMania* of the Paul Levesque era."

He inherited an operation that, while still carny, carried enough respect that people could take off from work — and even school — to go to *WrestleMania* without automatic ostracization. In the days leading into *WrestleMania XL*, many of those devotees flooded downtown Philly, engaging in other WWE-oriented pursuits, spending money at the company's massive superstore at the Pennsylvania Convention Center, then doling out extra at the adjoining WWE World at WrestleMania exhibit.

Activities included a *WWE 2K24* gaming tournament, podcast recordings, meet-and-greets and autograph sessions, and a central stage hosting roundtable discussions with WWE's top talent. But the most impressive feature was the touring wrestling museum curated by WWE's extraordinary archivist Benjamin Brown.

There were collections of belts the company had accumulated over the years — both internally and from collectors and promotions it supplanted — including the WCW Television Championship (titlists included Steve Austin, Ricky Steamboat, Arn Anderson and Chris Jericho), Rhea Ripley's Women's World Championship, the Million Dollar Championship, a gimmick title held by "Million Dollar Man" Ted DiBiase (who shot vignettes in Vince's home, pretending to be in the DiBiase mansion), his manservant Virgil and Austin when he was billed as "The Ringmaster" prior to the "Stone Cold" days. A robe Austin wore in Philadelphia-based renegade promotion Extreme Championship Wrestling (ECW) in 1995 was also displayed, along with a wealth of other memorabilia.

On another wall was the "Bloodline Family Tree," representing the various branches of the industry's most important Samoan family, indicating that the Rock's grandfather Fanene Pita Anderson — a.k.a. "High Chief" Peter Maivia — formed a brotherly bond "in a blood oath" to Roman Reign's grandfather, Amituana'i Anoa'i.

No longer does WWE have to blatantly fish for outside pop figures to lend the show credibility, although, after *WrestleMania III*, a widening range of music stars, actors and athletes began attending *WrestleMania* as spectators, sometimes simply to heighten their own visibility. The company has its own crop of homegrown celebrities now — The Rock, John Cena and Dave Bautista, who all channeled their squared circle fame into cinematic careers, along with Logan Paul, who, among his many options, elected to join the troupe.

Indeed, *WrestleMania* week has become so big that, of the estimated 200,000 visitors who came to Philly the week of *WrestleMania XL*, some chose not to attend any WWE events at all. That's because of the dozens of ancillary wrestling gatherings taking place nearby: cards staged by "indie" and international promotions, one-man shows featuring mat notables, documentary screenings and comedy nights, among other attractions.

Around the city, fans congregated in bars, exchanging anecdotes, rumors and memories and dissecting the matches they'd just witnessed, bonded by their love for a pastime that had long been derided as illegitimate and lowbrow.

And it was at one of these assemblies, at the Rainbow on Sunset Boulevard in West Hollywood, after *WrestleMania 39* that, after arguing for the third or fourth time that *WrestleMania III* was responsible for the phenomenon we see today, I understood that I had no choice but to write this book.

As Tom Buchanan put it, "*WrestleMania III* told us what was possible."

It also begot conclaves like WrestleCon, which in 2024 was a four-day affair held in various ballrooms at the Sheraton Philadelphia Downtown, where fans could interact with both ascending talent and the legends of the One True Sport, including those who'd appeared on *WrestleMania III*.

"No one expected *WrestleMania* to be as big as it is," observed "Hacksaw" Jim Duggan as he signed 8x10s, old magazines and action figure packaging alongside his wife, Debra. "I started out doing high school gyms and National Guard armories. And now, I'm 70 years old, traveling the world and signing autographs."

When the Honky Tonk Man debuted in the WWF, in the period between *WrestleMania 2* and *WrestleMania III*, the only wrestler doing regular signings was Hulk Hogan. Not anticipating a demand for squared circle iconography after his career wound down, the Tennessean naively tossed out jumpsuits, posters and other merchandise associated with his character. "That was probably $15,000 I threw in the garbage and I still think about it. I guess there were a lot of things I didn't see."

But his *WrestleMania III* adversary Jake "The Snake" Roberts understood that, because he performed during a special era, his services would always be in demand. As the COVID-19 pandemic was slamming the shutters on the rest of the world, Roberts made his managerial debut in AEW. Despite chronic obstructive pulmonary disease and emphysema, his career continued; if he needed an oxygen tube on a particular day, fans were willing to overlook it, like a pulled punch or an overly dramatic bump. And now, in 2024, both Jake and Honky were again working the same venue on *WrestleMania* weekend, greeting followers at WrestleCon, seven miles away from where the titans of what some were labeling pro wrestling's "Renaissance Era" were about to clash at Lincoln Financial Field.

Roberts was accustomed to being paid for his time but agreed to take one question on the condition that it wouldn't disrupt his revenue flow. Asked if any of these opportunities would be possible without *WrestleMania III*, he replied with a one-word answer.

"No," said Jake the Snake, his hand scraping a Sharpie against an old photo, the side of his face curling into the same sly smile seen by all those fans in the Silverdome when he and Alice Cooper hurled Damien at Jimmy "The Mouth of the South" Hart.

ACKNOWLEDGMENTS

Perhaps more than any other project I've ever done, the creation of *Bigger! Better! Badder! WrestleMania III and the Year It All Changed* is a collaboration of representatives from the far-flung sectors of the pro wrestling community,

Although I'm old enough to remember being told that a pro wrestling book couldn't sell because wrestling fans "can't read," that mentality no longer exists — in part, I'd argue, because of the success of *WrestleMania III*. And I could not have told this important story without the assistance of other pro wrestling authors who generously lent both their expertise and support. These include Brian R. Solomon, Greg Oliver, Tim Hornbaker, Kenny Casanova, Pat Laprade and Bertrand Hebert.

Although I'm among those who sometimes roll their eyes at the mention of "wrestling media," there are legitimate journalists out there who cherish the history of the industry and give voice to the talented men and women of the ring. Of those, Mike Johnson of *PWInsider* is among the most respected, and I was grateful to have his help.

Same for my friend Barry Werner, the former publisher at WWE Publications.

As a monthly columnist for *Inside the Ropes Magazine,* I am proud to be part of a group of gifted storytellers preserving the tales of this once-marginalized business and thankful for Kenny McIntosh, founder of the Inside the Ropes media franchise, and managing editor Dante Richardson.

Over the past several years, Dave LaGreca, the creator of the *Busted Open* radio show on Sirius XM, has featured me as a regular guest and brought me in as a member of the family he's formed, including his rotating cast of co-hosts — Tommy Dreamer, Bully Ray, Denise Salcedo, Thunder Rosa, Mickie James, Mark Henry and Nic Nemeth, among others — and a team that includes Paul Erlick, Eddie Borsilli, Kelly Murphy, Marissa Rives and Mike Tomcsyk.

Likewise, podcasting pioneer Conrad Thompson, his site administrator Evan Polisher and their AdFreeShows.com crew went out of their way to ensure that I had the information I needed during my research.

I also have to give credit to the Cauliflower Alley Club, the fraternal organization of active and retired wrestlers, not to mention the many people quoted in this book.

From WWE, I was assisted by public relations specialists Joel Zietcer and Gregory Domino, along with senior manager of talent relations John Cone.

Several representatives of AEW were helpful as well, including Adam Hopkins and John Schneider in public relations.

A special sentence needs to be reserved for Daniel Patton, librarian at the main branch of the Detroit Public Library, who helped me pore through old articles about the lead-up to and aftermath of *WrestleMania III* and seemed to have as much fun as I did.

And then, there are the many people who did a variety of tasks and favors, all contributing to what this book ultimately became, including the late Dennis Brent, Jian and Page Magen, Mark Handwerger, Lori Greenberg, Nils Suling, George Gordon, Randy and Suzy Tyson, Dave Menard and Giovanni Tafuri.

As always, ECW Press executive editor Michael Holmes not only believed in this project from the day I pitched it but was always willing to get on the phone and brainstorm. While most of our conversations revolved around the book, he was also open to discussing wrestling trivia or dissecting a particular angle that either enticed or repelled us. But those conversations will perennially remain kayfabe.

Thank you also to the entire team at ECW Press: co-publisher Jack David, senior editor Jen Knoch, title manager Victoria Cozza, typesetter Jen Gallinger, proofreader Sammy Chin, publicist Claire Pokorchak, sales & rights director Emily Ferko, and cover designer David Gee.

Still, I wouldn't be mentioning any of these people if it wasn't for indie wrestler and actor Monique Dupree, who happened to be standing next to me at the Rainbow in West Hollywood while I pontificated about the significance of *WrestleMania III*. As I continued expounding, she listened patiently, then spurred me to action by simply stating, "You need to write a book about this."

KEITH ELLIOT GREENBERG
NEW YORK CITY
OCTOBER 26, 2024

KEITH ELLIOT GREENBERG is a *New York Times* bestselling author, as well as a monthly columnist for *Inside the Ropes Magazine*. A lifetime New Yorker, he co-authored the autobiographies of "Classy" Freddie Blassie, Ric Flair and "Superstar" Billy Graham, as well as two editions of the *WWE Encyclopedia of Sports Entertainment*. His previous books for ECW Press include *Too Sweet: Inside the Indie Wrestling Revolution*, *Follow the Buzzards: Pro Wrestling in the Age of COVID-19* and *Best Seat in the House: My Life in the Jeff Healey Band*, co-written with Tom Stephen. He regularly appears as a wrestling historian on A&E's WWE documentary series.

Entertainment. Writing. Culture. ─────────

ECW is a proudly independent, Canadian-owned book publisher. We know great writing can improve people's lives, and we're passionate about sharing original, exciting, and insightful writing across genres.

───────────────────── **Thanks for reading along!**

We want our books not just to sustain our imaginations, but to help construct a healthier, more just world, and so we've become a certified B Corporation, meaning we meet a high standard of social and environmental responsibility — and we're going to keep aiming higher. We believe books can drive change, but the way we make them can too.

Certified
Corporation

Being a B Corp means that the act of publishing this book should be a force for good — for the planet, for our communities, and for the people that worked to make this book. For example, everyone who worked on this book was paid at least a living wage. You can learn more at the Ontario Living Wage Network.

This book is also available as a Global Certified Accessible™ (GCA) ebook. ECW Press's ebooks are screen reader friendly and are built to meet the needs of those who are unable to read standard print due to blindness, low vision, dyslexia, or a physical disability.

The interior of this book is printed on Sustana EnviroBook™, which is made from 100% recycled fibres and processed chlorine-free.

FSC
www.fsc.org
MIX
Paper | Supporting
responsible forestry
FSC® C016245

ECW's office is situated on land that was the traditional territory of many nations, including the Wendat, the Anishnaabeg, Haudenosaunee, Chippewa, Métis, and current treaty holders the Mississaugas of the Credit. In the 1880s, the land was developed as part of a growing community around St. Matthew's Anglican and other churches. Starting in the 1950s, our neighbourhood was transformed by immigrants fleeing the Vietnam War and Chinese Canadians dispossessed by the building of Nathan Phillips Square and the subsequent rise in real estate value in other Chinatowns. We are grateful to those who cared for the land before us and are proud to be working amidst this mix of cultures.

ecwpress.com